The Economics of the Mishnah

Chicago Studies in the History of Judaism

EDITED BY

William Scott Green and Calvin Goldscheider

The Economics of
The Mishnah

Jacob Neusner

The University of Chicago Press

Chicago and London

The University of Chicago Press, Chicago 60637
The University of Chicago Press, Ltd., London

© 1990 by The University of Chicago
All rights reserved. Published 1990
Printed in the United States of America

99 98 97 96 95 94 93 92 91 90   54321

Library of Congress Cataloging-in-Publication Data

Neusner, Jacob, 1932–
   The economics of the Mishnah / Jacob Neusner.
      p.   cm. — (Chicago studes in the history of Judaism)
   Includes index.
   ISBN 0-226-57655-8 (alk. paper). — ISBN 0-226-57656-6 (pbk. :
alk. paper)
    1. Economics—Religious aspects—Judaism. 2. Judaism—Doctrines.
3. Mishnah—Criticism, interpretation, etc. I. Title. II. Series.
BM509.E27N47   1990
296.3′8785—dc20   89-5153
                                                CIP

In memory of
Aaron Diamond
1918–1989

Contents

Preface

[Aristotle] will be seen as attacking the problem of man's livelihood with a
radicalism of which no later writer on the subject was capable—none has
ever penetrated deeper into the material organization of man's life. In
effect, he posed, in all its breadth, the question of the place occupied by
the economy in society.

Karl Polanyi [1]

Judaism, a world construction, encompasses all subjects that pertain to the life
of an entire nation and society. Such a program of world construction by its
nature involves three principal intellectual tasks of theoretical thought: politics, economics, and science or learning. A system that proposes to set forth
the main frame and structure of a society will commonly make its statement in
what it says about all three matters, establishing the same fundamental principle or viewpoint or attitude in treating each critical component of its theory
of the social system. That basic harmony and coherence in what is said by a
system about economics, politics, and science will ordinarily characterize a
well-composed theory of world construction.

For the study of economics, this point has been made by Joseph A.
Schumpeter: "In economics as elsewhere, most statements of fundamental
facts acquire importance only by the superstructures they are made to bear and
are commonplace in the absence of such superstructures." [2] The Judaism the
economics of which is under study is the one that rested on the myth of
Moses' receiving the Torah at Sinai in two media, written and oral. The written one corresponded to the Hebrew Bible, or Old Testament. The oral one
was ultimately written down by the sages of Judaism in late antiquity, beginning with the composition of the Mishnah, a utopian system expressed in the
form of a law code and closed in ca. A.D. 200. The Judaism of the dual Torah,
bearing the adjectives normative, talmudic, rabbinic, classical, and the like,
unfolded through the exegesis of the two Torahs, written and oral, Scripture
and Mishnah, through the first seven centuries of the Common Era (=A.D.)
and yielded as its authoritative document the Talmud of Babylonia, or Bavli.

But only the initial and fundamental document of that Judaism, the Mishnah, forms the object of study here. My purpose is to describe the economics of a Judaism in its systemic context, to offer an account of economics in the foundation document of the canon of the Judaism of the dual Torah.

By understanding the world as sages portrayed it in the Mishnah, we may penetrate into that economic rationality that, in their system, corresponds, point by point, with the rationality of economics as presently understood. It follows, therefore, that for the initial statement of the Judaism of the dual Torah, economics is systemically not inert but active and generative, indeed expressive of the basic message of the system of the Mishnah as a whole. That is the fundamental thesis of this book. Accordingly, I spell out and show the systemic significance of the economic theory of the initial document of the Judaism of the dual Torah, the Mishnah. Since that document defined the foundations for the principal Judaism from its time to ours, it marks the correct starting point for any inquiry into the way in which Judaism makes its cogent systemic statement through economics.

What is at stake here for learning is how a theory of economics forms an integral and coherent component of the larger theoretical statement of a social system. For no utopian design such as is given by the Mishnah, a classic political novel, or *Staatsroman,* in the tradition of Plato's *Republic* and Aristotle's *Politics,* can ignore the material organization of society. True, in modern times we are accustomed to view economics as disembedded from the political and social system, the market, for instance, as unrelated to kinship or institutions of culture. But until the eighteenth century economics was understood as a component of the social system and a formative constituent of culture. It follows that those religious systems, such as Judaism, Islam, and Christianity in its medieval phase, that propose to prescribe public policy in the earthly city and design a social world will integrate into their systems theories of (correct) economic behavior and accounts of systemically correct economic policy. Then precisely how does a religion make its systemic statement through its economics? That is the question I answer here in the case of the Judaism that begins with the system of the Mishnah.

A useful definition of economics directs our attention to the meaning of the word in antiquity and today. In Greek antiquity, *oikonomia* meant a formal administrative art directed toward the minimization of costs and the maximization of returns, with the prime aim of efficient management of resources for the achievement of desired objectives; "it was an administrative, not a market approach, to economic phenomena. . . . *Oikonomia* was an early predecessor of political economy."[3] Economics today is defined as the theory of rational action with regard to scarcity. In this book I propose to spell out the economics of a principal statement of a Judaism, namely, the economics of the Mishnah as a mode of rational action with regard to scarcity.[4] What I shall show is that the Mishnah treats subjects ordinarily addressed in antiquity by documents generally deemed to bear upon issues of economics and does so within the economic theory of Aristotle.[5]

In chapter 1 I place this book into the context of the study of both Judaism and economics. Reviewing prior treatments of this subject, I explain both what I propose to set forth and also, more important, what I do not believe can or should be done in treating this subject.

In chapter 2 I set forth the indicative traits of the document on which I have chosen to focus. I claim that the Mishnah does present a cogent system, a Judaism, a conception I explain. I briefly describe the systemic traits of the Mishnah, so that the components of the system that may be defined as economic are set forth in the correct context. I characterize the document as a statement of the Torah—and that as a matter of premise, established by context rather than contents—in the categories and modes of thought of philosophy, in the literary form of Greco-Roman legal codification, but in what I think is a simply unique idiom of symbol and metaphor. Accordingly, asking about the economics of the Judaism presented by the Mishnah on the surface forms a perfectly reasonable question; that is the point of chapter 2. In that same chapter, moreover, I propose to place the Mishnah into relationship with writing on economics and thought of an economic character that took place in the Greco-Roman world. I take up a document entitled *Economics* and, more broadly, survey the economics of the age, as this is portrayed in standard works. In this way we are able to grasp both the character of the Mishnah and its program's points in common with quite different kinds of writing of the same period. In both we see a concern for the same range of economic issues, though what matters about these economic issues in one document will radically differ from the aspects of those issues found important by another.

In chapter 3 I survey the main ideas of economic theory, as these are set forth in the relevant scholarly literature. This leads us to the center of the book, chapters 4, 5, and 6. Here I place into the Greco-Roman context important conceptions of economics presented by the Mishnah. I cover the principal means of production (the household), the medium of rationing scarce resources (the market, governed by supply and demand), and, finally, the definition of wealth. Then, having surveyed matters within the theory of market economics, I revert and reconsider these same classifications within the theory of distributive economics. In this way I show that two distinct theories of economics are in play in the economics of the initial statement of Judaism. By defining economics in the accepted way ("economics is the theory of rational action with regard to scarcity"), therefore, I demonstrate that the Judaism set forth the Mishnah encompasses a theory of economics and, as I have stressed, makes its systemic statement through what it says about material relationships and transactions as much as through what it sets forth about God in heaven and humanity on earth—indeed, not as much but even more fully and more amply. The reason, of course, is that the framers of the Mishnah proposed to design, for time to come, a world in which, with God, humanity might endure.

We shall find it possible to understand the economics of Judaism in its initial statement only when we appeal to two distinct economic theories, first, the market and market economics as against, second, the Temple and distributive economics. Distinguishing the one from the other in actual practice of course is no concern of ours; no one any longer doubts that from remote antiquity onward markets, and therefore the germ of a market economy, coexisted with a distributive economy.[6] But as a matter of theory, market economics and distributive economics cannot discover substantial grounds for compatibility, and the framers of the Mishnah along with Aristotle did not even try. Rather, they imagined a distributive economy while legislating for a market one. For, as we shall see at some length, the framers of the Mishnah joined together the premises of two distinct economic theories, market economics (chapters 4, 5, and 6) and distributive economics (chapter 7).[7] And these two distinct theories, moreover, coexisted on the foundations of an economics of reciprocity, joining heaven to earth.[8] And as we shall see in chapter 7, the conception of God's enjoying standing and power within the domain of economic life formed not a theological but an economic fact, on the basis of which decisions on the allocation of scarce resources and on the nature of wealth and ownership were reached and carried out in law. That simple fact constitutes the single indicative trait of the Judaism of the Mishnah, its power to translate theological conviction into exquisitely detailed rules for everyday life.

In framing issues as I do, that is, in terms of a particular Judaism and the economic theory portrayed in its documents, read in sequence one by one, I believe I commence a line of inquiry hitherto unexplored. That is in two ways.

First, in the study of the economics of Judaism I cannot find a literature of books and articles that closely define the Judaism under study and that identify the relevant sources and explain their pertinence to that particular Judaism. Ordinarily we find "Judaism" deemed the same thing as "the Old Testament," or various sayings deemed economic, always treated out of all documentary (let alone systemic) context. The consequent confusion obscures any useful results that might have been forthcoming.

Second, the study of the place and task of economic theory within the context defined by the larger statement of the system of a Judaism begins, so far as I know, in this book. True, we do have scholarship on topics that bear upon issues of economics in a Judaism and also upon Jews' economic behavior. So far as the law of Judaism (*halakhah*) deals with an economic topic or subject, extensive expositions of that law spell matters out quite nicely; these may serve, also, for an inquiry into economics.[9] But they do not address, and are not even relevant to, the issue at hand in this book, the place of economics in the system and the initial statement of the Judaism set forth by the first document of the Judaism of the dual Torah, which is the Mishnah.[10]

It remains to spell out, also, what I do *not* propose to do in this book. I do not discuss either the Jews' economic history or the role of any Judaism in the shaping of Jews' economic behavior. The reason is that I do not see that Jews have had a single history, unitary, continuous, internally cogent, and they also have not formed a single economy. I also know no evidence that Jews wherever they lived conducted economic action in one way, rather than in some other, nor wrote a single, unitary, linear, and harmonious economic history. Nor do we now know how Judaism has affected Jews' economic behavior, if, indeed, the role of ideology, or theology, in economic action in general has been conceded or even clarified. The allegation that Judaism formed an independent variable in accounting for Jews' society and economy is more commonly made than demonstrated.

Jews have formed social groups in a variety of circumstances of place and time, and these groups have conformed to no single pattern, nor have they constituted among themselves a single, continuous, and ongoing entity. The conception of "Israel" is a construct of theology, not a fact of social history.[11] Accordingly, Jews have never formed, and do not now form, a single economic unit, and therefore the economics or the economies of "the Jews" under all circumstances and in all periods of their histories, while subject to cataloguing, is not accessible to description, analysis, and interpretation. A cogent account of Jews' economic behavior and beliefs requires what Jews' groups do not exhibit, which is continuity and coherence in time and space. Not only so, but such an account by nature will have to distinguish Jews' economic action and thought from that of others in similar circumstances; otherwise all we know is an example of the conduct of a group that (as a matter of hypothesis) stands at the margins of an economic unit defined beyond its social limits. Just as Jews have made not a single unitary, continuous, and internally cogent history but only diverse and discontinuous histories, linked by ideology but not by politics, geography, culture, and the other structural components of a single and singular history, so they also have not constituted an economic entity subject to sustained analysis as to action and intellect. But we can identify and define a Judaism, a coherent statement consisting of a world view, a way of life, and an address to a clearly defined "Israel" meant to form the social entity that realizes that way of life and expresses as a group that world view. And if that Judaism contains a body of doctrine corresponding to what we now know as economics, we certainly can describe, analyze, and interpret that economics of that Judaism. And that is precisely what I propose to do in this book for the economics of the Judaism of the dual Torah, which took shape between the first and the seventh centuries A.D. and predominated thereafter.

I mean therefore to open many doors, but to close only one. It is the conception that, to define what "Judaism" says about a subject, we merely collect, arrange, and so compose into a neat collection defined by the topic at hand all typically pertinent sayings from all times and places and documents, hence from all Judaisms and all groups of Jews. But that is very commonly how people proceed, and not only in the study of Jews' and Judaisms' economics—that is, without regard to the always determinative dimension of context, let alone to inner logic and systemic discipline and setting. So they present dissertations on topics generally deemed to be, as in the present instance, those of economics. These dissertations may assemble little more than bits and pieces of uninterpreted data about Jews in the spice trade or in department stores, about slave traders or diamond merchants, about brokers or junk dealers. But on that basis we know nothing at all about "Jewish economic history," the economics of "Judaism" (whatever in context that can mean), let alone about economic actions characteristic of Jews or normative for Jews—and the reasons therefor. Even rather glib judgments about Jews' economic "marginality" stand for premises scarcely accessible to rational analysis.

It follows that mere hunting and gathering form no model for learning, since even data of the hardest kind require a context or remain mere gibberish. Sayings about the value of work, about agronomics, currency, commerce and the marketplace, correct management of labor—by themselves these too tell us nothing about economics as a theoretical construct and as a component of a still larger construction of a world, and they certainly do not inform us about what people actually did. Only a systematic reading of such sayings in the encompassing context of a full statement on the theory of economics made by a given Judaism in its well-crafted sources and their well-composed and cogent statement supplies the correct setting in which these discrete and episodic sayings gain meaning and yield consequence.

Let me briefly place this project into the larger progress of my work. As I said, I see three basic issues in the study of any Judaic, or other religion's, theory of a social system, namely, the place of politics, economics, and science within that system, with special attention to the ways in which that system makes its statement through what it offers as a design for these three pillars of social construction. I have already made my initial inquiry into the matter of science, treating science as a subfield of philosophy, specifically the specialty of natural philosophy as it was until modern times. In my commentary to Mishnah-tractate Tohorot I show that the framers of the Mishnah addressed issues of mixtures, an important component of Stoic physics.[12] In other parts of my Mishnah commentary, as well as in *Judaism: The Evidence of the Mishnah* (Chicago: University of Chicago Press, 1981), I show that perennial issues of philosophy, e.g., concerning being and becoming, will and intention, underlie substantial syllogistic constructions of the Mishnah, stated in a rather odd idiom to be sure. Consequently, I have shown that the Mishnah's authors concerned themselves with problems of natural philosophy and, more broadly, of philosophy, as these were framed in their world.[13] In my *The Making of the Mind of Judaism: The Formative Age* (Atlanta: Scholars Press for Brown Judaic Studies, 1987), I have taken as one premise the simple fact that the Judaism of the Mishnah contained within itself a considerable component of philosophical, including scientific, thought. The companion volume, *The Formation of the Jewish Intellect: The Traditional System of Formative Judaism* (in press) expands by comparing the process of thought exhibited by canonical writings of the Judaism of the dual Torah with those in the writings of other Judaisms of the period. Now, as is clear, I proceed to the matter of economics. This work forms the beginning of a sequence of parallel studies of the social science of the Judaism of the dual Torah, with special reference to the Mishnah as the initial statement, which I plan as follows:

The Politics of Judaism: The Formative Age. [Dealing with the comparison of the Mishnah's political theory with Aristotle's *Politics.*]

The Philosophy of Judaism: The Initial Statement. [Dealing with the Mishnah in the context of Greco-Roman philosophy.]

It may represent merely the envy of a tourist from a less refined society, but I point to the field of economics as the model of an academic science and its society. I have always found special pleasure in friendships with colleagues in the social sciences in general, and economics in particular. With gratitude I happily acknowledge the counsel of some of those colleagues. The definition of economics I owe to my friend and colleague Professor George Borts, Department of Economics, Brown University. Professor Peter Garber, of the same department at Brown, helped with bibliography and also presented me with questions I found quite stimulating. Others in that department, as well as in history, sociology, and anthropology, at Brown have taught me about their work and the rationality that animates it even when they did not realize.

In my own field, history of religion, with specialization in Judaism, I discussed problems of this book every day with Professors William Scott Green, University of Rochester, Ernest S. Frerichs, Wendell S. Dietrich, and Calvin Goldscheider of Brown University, and Professor Paul V. Flesher, Northwestern University. I express special thanks to my dear friend, teacher in social history, and comrade in everything but politics, Professor Eugene Genovese, University of Rochester, for supplying six pages of extremely valuable criticisms and suggestions, all of which I studied, and most of which I adopted. I have added some footnotes that bear his suggestive comments. His close and careful reading of this book forms only one of the many acts of generosity that have placed me, among many in the academic world, in his debt. Finally, I wish every serious academic author the pleasure of dealing with the director and staff of the University of Chicago Press.

Let me conclude on a personal note. I always enjoy learning new things, approaching a new problem or studying and translating a new text. My work moves in a steady rhythm from text to context to matrix. It is the substance of my life. In that context, I say I have not derived greater enjoyment from any text or any problem of establishing and analyzing context than I did in reading some of the great work on the history of economic theory and on the economic history of ancient times that this project brought me to know. Economics is a field that has attracted many truly first-rate intellects, and I found not only enlightenment and insight, but sheer pleasure at the encounter with marvelous minds, in my reading for this book. Among the impressive figures, three of course stand out, Polanyi, Schumpeter, and Finley; but they are merely the brightest stars in a well-illuminated firmament. Even though Polanyi's basic theses have now gone their way, it is clear that he raised the fructifying questions and directed the field of economic history, and the history of economic theory, from his day forward. And that is what a person can do.

I celebrate them and their colleagues, both the original minds and also those who present for us lesser beings in popular books and articles and in textbooks the results of their thought. This modest tribute to a great social science contains within itself a trace of envy, to be sure, but mostly the heartfelt thanks of the last and least among the followers of the history of the theory of economic science. In so stating, I hasten to disclaim any merit that makes me worthy of giving such a compliment; I mean only to express appreciation for the achievements of others. I do not stand in judgment upon work that exceeds my capacity to accomplish or even fully to grasp; but I can appreciate intellectual excellence and admire those who exemplify it.

This book was just going to the printer when my friend and fellow-traveler, Aaron Diamond, died. A lawyer by trade, an intellectual by vocation, he read voraciously on every possible subject. We met in Port Moresby, in Papua–New Guinea, where, with our families, we were embarking on a tour of that remote land. The tour was not a very successful one, except for the happy accident of discovering in a distant country a kindred spirit, a New York Jew of the kind I most appreciate: witty, mordant, not easily fooled, not readily disheartened, of unquenchable spirit and (justifiably) unlimited self-confidence. Aaron's wife, Elinor Ross Diamond, and my wife, Suzanne Richter Neusner, and our sons, Samuel and Eli, turned my (and Elinor's) bad gamble into a good time, mainly through the enchantment of Aaron's contentious wit and unfailing insight into fakery and quakery.

This is one book of mine that I know Aaron would have enjoyed; he was as unsentimental as I try to be. And he was as unapologetic; and as unimpressed with pretense, as engaged by truth and by the quest for understanding, as were our sages of blessed memory. If, in the yeshiva in heaven, there is a room set aside for the truly brilliant and the truly rigorous, the intellectually aggressive people, I think Aaron will be sitting at the head of the table. I never knew anyone with whom it was more fun to argue. This dedication is my memorial to him.

JACOB NEUSNER

The Institute for Advanced Study
Princeton, New Jersey

and

Program in Judaic Studies
Brown University
Providence, Rhode Island

1

The Economics of Judaism

When we place the political economics of the Mishnah into the context of Greco-Roman economic thought, we gain a clearer picture of the power of economics to serve in the expression and detailed exposition of a utopian design for society. For, as Robert Lekachman states, "We see the economics of Plato and Aristotle somewhat differently when we realize that what they were discussing above all was the good life, the just state, and the happy man." [1] They sought a unified science of society. And that serves as a suitable definition, also, for the program of the framers of the Mishnah. The authors of the Mishnah covered every important problem that any treatise on economics, dealing with not only the rules of household management covered in an *oiko-nomikos,* but also the law of money making, found it necessary to discuss, and on that basis, I claim to describe in some modest detail what I conceive to have been the economics of Judaism as the Mishnah's authors defined Judaism and as the ancient world understood the science of economics, or, in its context, political economy. But let me start from the beginning, and that means turning to the familiar definition of our subject.

The economics of Judaism is hardly an unexplored field of inquiry. Evidence of the interest that the subject now has attracted derives from two wildly disparate bodies of scholarship, both by economists. The first is Meir Tamari, represented by his widely circulated study, *"With All Your Possessions:" Jewish Ethics and Economic Life* (New York: The Free Press, 1987), a collection of sayings, organized by topics, culled from a variety of sources of Judaism, from antiquity onward. He treats as pertinent to "ethics and economic life" these subjects: the challenge of wealth; competition, prices, and profits; wages and labor; money, banking, and interest; taxation; welfare, environmental issues and the public good. All of these subjects are treated entirely out of historical and social context, of course, with the result that Tamari's work serves no interesting purpose. He proposes to show "that there does indeed exist, as a result of the Jewish value system, a separate and distinct 'Jewish economic man,' molded by religious law and communal practice" (p. 1). But all he shows is that there are lots of sayings on topics of economic relevance.

On the basis of this compilation we learn nothing about either ethics or economics in Judaism, since, out of context, sayings yield no insight.

The second, also Israeli, is the only scholar to have studied with requisite knowledge of economic theory the economics of Judaism in late antiquity, Ephraim Kleiman of the Hebrew University, Jerusalem. Kleiman's work is unique among studies of economic topics in the context of talmudic literature and sets the standard by which all work other than his simply fails. His principal articles are as follows:

"Bi-Metallism in Rabbi's Time: Two Variants of the Mishna 'Gold Acquires Silver,'" *Zion* 38(1973): 48–61.

"Markets and Fairs in the Land of Israel in the Period of the Mishnah and the Talmud," *Zion* 51 (1986): 472–486.

"'Just Price' In Talmudic Literature," *History of Political Economy* 19 (1987): 23–45 (with an excellent bibliography, pp. 44–45).

"Opportunity Cost, Human Capital, and Some Related Economic Concepts in Talmudic Literature," *History of Political Economy* 19 (1987): 261–287.

Public Finance Criteria in the Talmud (Jerusalem: Department of Economics, Hebrew University of Jerusalem, Working Paper # 192, 1988).

Kleiman's bibliography of books and fifty-seven published papers (as of July 25, 1988) is otherwise made up of studies in contemporary economics. He is the only trained economist ever to work in a sustained and responsible way on talmudic literature, and the character of his writing shows what is wrong with all others who, collecting and arranging sayings read out of all critical context in the manner of Tamari, have purported to tell us about the economics of Judaism in its formative age.

Other writing on the general theme, besides Tamari's and Kleiman's, is voluminous.[2] Indeed, any study of pertinent topics, whether of the Jews' role in various economies or of the Jews' own economy or of the economics of Judaism, takes its place in a long if somewhat irregular line of works on the subject.[3] Among them, the most important and best-known statement on the economics of Judaism purports to account, by appeal to the economics of Judaism and the economic behavior of Jews, for the origins of modern capitalism. Writing in the tradition of Weber's *Protestant Ethic and the Spirit of Capitalism,* Werner Sombart, in *The Jews and Modern Capitalism* (1911), set the issues of the economics of Judaism within a racist framework, maintaining that Jews exhibited an aptitude for modern capitalism deriving in part from the Jewish religion, in part from the Jews' national characteristics.[4] Jewish intellectuality, the teleological mode of thought of Judaism, the Jews' energy, mobility, adaptability, affinity for liberalism and capitalism—all of these accounted for the role of Jews in the creation of the economics of capitalism, which dominated. Sombart appealed, in particular, to the anthropology of the Jew, maintaining that the Jews comprise a distinct anthropological group. Jewish qualities persist throughout their history: "constancy in the attitude of the Jews to the peoples among whom they dwelt, hatred of the Jews, Jewish elasticity. . . . The economic activities of the Jew also show a remarkable constancy." Sombart even found the knowledge of economics among the rabbis of the Talmud to be remarkable. In the end Sombart appealed to the fact that the Jews constitute a "Southern people transplanted among Northern peoples." The Jews exhibited a nomadic spirit throughout their history. Sombart contrasted "the cold North and the warm South" and held that "Jewish characteristics are due to a peculiar environment." So he appealed to what he found to be the correlation between Jewish intellectuality and desert life, Jewish adaptability and nomad life, and wrote about "Jewish energy and their Southern origin," " 'Sylvanism' and Feudalism compared with 'Saharaism' and Capitalism," and ended, of course, with the theme of the Jews and money and the Jews and the ghetto.

The romantic and racist view of the Jews as a single continuing people with innate racial characteristics which scientific scholarship can identify and explain of course formed the premise for Sombart's particular interest in the economic characteristics of the Jew and the relationship of these racial traits to the Jews' origin in the desert. While thoroughly discredited, these views have nonetheless generated a long sequence of books on Jews' economic behavior.[5] Today people continue to conceive "Jewish economic history" as a cogent subject that follows not only synchronic and determinate, but also diachronic and indeterminate, lines and dimensions. Such books have taken and now take as the generative category the Jews' constituting a distinct economy, or their formation of a social unit of internally consistent economic action and therefore thought, the possibility of describing, analyzing, and interpreting the Jews within the science of economics. But that category and its premise themselves still await definition and demonstration, and these to this day are yet lacking. Consequently, while a considerable literature on "the Jews' economic history" takes for granted that there is a single, economically cogent group, the Jews, which has had a single ("an") economic history and which, therefore, forms a distinctive unit of economic action and thought, the foundations for that literature remain somewhat infirm.

The conception of Jews' having an economic history, part of the larger, indeed encompassing, notion of the Jews' having had a single history as a people, one people, has outlived the demise of the racist rendition of the matter by Sombart. But what happens when we take seriously the problems of conception and method that render fictive and merely imposed a diachronic history of the Jews, unitary, harmonious, and continuous, and when we realize that the secondary and derivative conception of a diachronic economics of the Jews is equally dubious? Whether or not it is racist, that unitary conception of the Jews as a single, distinctive, ongoing historical entity, a social group forming also a cogent unit of economic action, is surely romantic. Whatever the salubrious ideological consequences, such an economics bypasses every fundamental question of definition and method. If the Jews do not form a distinct economy, then how can we speak of the Jews in particular

in an account of economic history? If, moreover, the Jews do not form a distinct component of a larger economy, then what do we learn about economics
when we know that some Jews do this, others that? And if Jews in a given
place and circumstance constitute a distinct economic unit within a larger
economy, then how study Jews' economic action out of the larger economic
context which they help define and of which they form a component? The
upshot of these questions is simple: how shall we address those questions concerning rational action with regard to scarcity that do, after all, draw our attention when we contemplate, among other entities, the social entities that
Jews have formed, and now form, in the world? In my judgment, the answer
is to turn from "the Jews"—too diverse a social entity to sustain cogent description—to a Judaism, that is, a cogent system, made up of an account of
the way of life, world view, and social entity ("Israel") that the system
builders propose to construct. A given Judaism appeals to its canonical writings. These have been selected by the authorities of that Judaism because they
are deemed authoritative and hence may be treated as cogent—by definition.
The economics of a Judaism will then find definition in the economic theory
presented by principal canonical documents of that Judaism.

Now to the case at hand: the Mishnah, the initial statement of the Judaism
of the dual Torah, not only encompasses but integrates economics within its
larger system. That particular Judaism, indeed, makes its statement in part
through the exquisite details of rules and regulations governing the householder, the market, and wealth. In this regard, the Mishnah scarcely finds a
comfortable place within the age in which it was framed. For its remarkably
successful capacity to make its systemic statement through the concerns of
economics, its capacity to accomplish the detailed exegesis of economics
within its larger social vision and system—these lack a significant counterpart
in the generality of philosophy and theology in ancient times. Only in Aristotle do we find a great system builder who encompassed economic theory
within his systemic statement, and who did so (as we shall see) in a solid and
cogent way. Plato forms no important counterpart; as to Christianity, down to
the end of late antiquity, in the seventh century, economics as a matter of theory enjoyed no position whatsoever. For one example, we find slight interest
in, or use of, theories on the household, markets, and wealth in the framing of
the Christian statement, which bears no judgment that we may identify as a
statement upon, or of, economics. Only when we turn to Aristotle do we find
a counterpart to the truly remarkable accomplishment of the authors of the
Mishnah in engaging economics in the service of their larger systemic statement. Indeed, as the Mishnah's authors' power of the extraordinarily detailed
exegesis of economics as a systemic component becomes clear to us, we shall
conclude that, among the social theorists of antiquity, the framers of the Mishnah take first place in the sophistication and profoundity of their thought
among political economists.

But the fact that both Aristotle and the authors of the Mishnah appealed to economic theory in spelling out their ideas does not by itself require us to bring into juxtaposition, for purposes of comparison and contrast, the economic thought of the two writings. What requires that work is the simple fact that the Mishnah came forth in the age of the Second Sophistic and, in diverse ways, adheres to the attitudes and agenda of that movement. Not only so, but when we do read Aristotle's thought on economic theory, we find clear and detailed propositions in common between him and our authors. But there is yet a third reason for the central exercise of this book, which is the argument that the mishnaic sages present an economics congruent point by point with that of Aristotle. It is that both Aristotle and the sages of the Mishnah thought deeply and sustainedly about economic issues. The power of economics as framed by Aristotle, the only economic theorist of antiquity worthy of the name, was to develop the relationship between the economy and society as a whole.[6] And, as we shall see, the framers of the Mishnah did precisely that: they incorporated issues of economics, even at a profound theoretical level, into the system of society as a whole, as they proposed to construct society. That is why, in this book, to paraphrase Polanyi's judgment of Aristotle, the authors of the Mishnah will be seen as attacking the problem of man's livelihood within a system of sanctification of a holy people with a radicalism of which no later utopian religious thinkers were capable. None has ever penetrated deeper into the material organization of man's life under the aspect of God's rule. In effect, they posed, in all its breadth, the question of the critical, indeed definitive, place occupied by the economy in society under God's rule. That is what we shall see in the remarkable statement, within an even more subtle idiom, of the economics of Judaism as the framers of the Mishnah defined that economics.

Now it is time to ask: what precisely do I mean by "economics," and why do I claim that the Mishnah's economics *is* economics in the classic (though not the modern) sense of the word? By economics I mean what everybody means: systematic doctrines on rational action in regard to scarcity, encompassing a definition of wealth, and systemically rational rules on the increase and disposition of wealth. Economics from Aristotle to Quesnay and Riqueti, in the eighteenth century, dealt with not the science of wealth but rather "the management of the social household, first the city, then the state."[7] Economics formed a component of the larger sociopolitical order and dealt with the organization and management of the household (*oikos*). The city (*polis*) was conceived as comprising a set of households. Political economy, therefore, presented the theory of the construction of society, the village, town, or city, out of households, a neat and orderly, intensely classical, and, of course, utterly fictive conception. One part of that larger political economy confronted issues of the household and its definition as the principal unit of economic production, the market and its function within the larger political structure, and the nature and definition of wealth. I shall demonstrate that the framers of the Mishnah set forth, in acute detail and not as generalities, a theory of the household, the market, and wealth, indeed, that they joined two distinct and incompatible theories of all three. In that way I shall justify my claim that there is an economics of formative Judaism. Not only so, but I shall demonstrate point by point that the economics of this Judaism conformed in its principles to the economics of Aristotle.

In due course, moreover, we shall see that just as, through economics, Aristotle made the larger point that animated his system as a whole, so through economics did the framers of the Mishnah. The theory of both, moreover, falls into the same classification of economic theory, namely, the theory of distributive economics. Before proceeding, let me define market and distributive economics, since these form the two economic theories at issue in antiquity. In market economics merchants transfer goods from place to place in response to the working of the market mechanism, which is expressed in price. In distributive economics, by contrast, traders move goods from point to point in response to political commands. The far more ancient, the distributive, shaped the economic thought of the two important systems of antiquity that made their statement through economics, those of Aristotle and the Mishnah. In market economics, merchants make the market work by calculations of profit and loss. In distributive economics, there is no risk of loss on a transaction.[8] In market economics, money forms an arbitrary measure of value, a unit of account. In distributive economics, money serves as a medium of barter and bears only intrinsic value, as do the goods for which it is exchanged. It is understood as "something that people accept not for its inherent value in use but because of what it will buy."[9] The idea of money requires the transaction to be complete in the exchange not of goods but of coins. The alternative is the barter transaction, in which, in theory at least, the exchange takes place when goods change hands. In distributive economics money is an instrument of direct exchange between buyers and sellers, not the basic resource in the process of production and distribution that it is in market economics. In the Mishnah's conception of the market and of wealth, distributive, not market, economics shapes details of all transactions.

That distributive mode of economics, rationalized within theology and also fully realized in the detail of law, would not have astonished the framers of social systems from ancient Sumerian times, three thousand years before the time of the Mishnah, onward. For from the beginning of recorded time, temples or governments imposed the economics of distribution, and market economics, where feasible at all, competed with the economics of politics, organization, and administration. From remote antiquity onward, a market economy coexisted with a distributive economy.[10] The distributive economics characteristic of ancient temples and governments, which served as the storage points for an economy conceived to be self-supporting and self-sustaining, involved something other than a simultaneous exchange of legally recognized rights in property and its use; one party gave up scarce goods, the other party did not do so, but received those goods for other than market considerations. Free disposition of property, in distributive economics, found limitations in rules of an other-than-market character, e.g., taboos with no bearing upon the rational utilization of resources and individual decisions on the disposition of assets.

If, for example, the private person who possesses property may not sell that property to anyone of his choice, or may not sell it permanently, then the possessor of the property does not exercise fully free choice in response to market conditions.[11] The reason is that he cannot gain the optimum price for the land at a given moment, set by considerations of supply and demand for land or (more really) for the produce of land of a particular character. Another, a co-owner, in addition to the householder in possession of a piece of property, has a say. The decisions of that other owner are not governed solely (or at all) by market considerations. In the case of temple communities or communities having god-kings, land ownership and control fall into the hands of an entity other than the private person, whether we call it the temple, the priesthood, the government, the guild, or even the poor (!). Then, with private property and its use placed under limitations and constraints of an other-than-market origin, market trading is not possible: "While there could be a considerable development of governmental status distribution and some marginal barter, there could not develop a price-making market."[12] Private property in land, not merely in control of production, was required for the formation of a market economics in the conditions of antiquity, when ownership of production derived from ownership of land.

A further mark of the distributive economy—we shall see time and again— is that transactions are made in commodities of real value, that is, barter, and not of symbolic value, that is, money. In ancient Mesopotamia, with its distributive economics, while silver was the medium of exchange, it was used in ingots and required weighing at each transfer.[13] We shall repeatedly notice in our survey of the working of the market that that conception dominates in the Mishnah. Finally, in distributive economics, profit is a subordinate consideration, and, by minds so sophisticated as Aristotle's and the Mishnah's authors', profit is treated as unnatural. We need hardly review the positions already established to claim that competing with market economics in the Mishnah is a fully developed and amply instantiated, if never articulated, distributive economics. The Mishnah's author took over the economics of the Priestly Code, itself a restatement, in the idiom of the Israelite priesthood, of the distributive economics of temples and kings beginning with the Sumerians and Egyptians and coming down to the Greeks. Market economics was an innovation, its economics not fully understood, at the time of the Priestly Code, and, for reasons of their own, the framers of the Mishnah fully adopted and exhaustively spelled out that distributive economics, even while setting forth a plan for the market life of "Israel" in the market enclaves of the larger society.

In the received Scriptures, that old and well-established theory of economics is accurately represented by the Priestly Code spelled out in the rules of the biblical books of Leviticus and Numbers, upon which the Mishnah's authors drew very heavily. The economic program of the Mishnah, as a matter of fact, derived its values and also its details from the Priestly Code and other priestly writings within the pentateuchal mosaic. Indeed, at point after point, those authors clearly intended merely to spin out details of the rules set forth in Scripture in general and, in economic issues such as the rational use of scarce resources, the Priestly Code in particular. The Priestly Code assigned portions of the crop to the priesthood and Levites as well as to the caste comprising the poor; it intervened in the market processes affecting real estate by insisting that land could not be permanently alienated but reverted to its "original" ownership every fifty years; it treated some produce as unmarketable even though it was entirely fit; it exacted for the Temple a share of the crop; it imposed regulations on the labor force that were not shaped by market considerations but by religious taboos, e.g., days on which work might not be performed, or might be performed only in a diminished capacity.

The Priestly Code stated in the Israelite priestly idiom and in matters of detail the long-established principles of distributive economics and so conformed to thousands of years of that distributive economics that treated private property as stipulative and merely conditional and the market as subordinate and subject to close political supervision. Market economics came into being in Greece in the very period—the sixth century B.C.—in which the Priestly Code was composed. Aristotle, as we have seen, theorized about an economics entirely beyond anyone's ken and stated as principle the values of an economics (and a social system, too) long since transcended. Market economics, moreover, had been conveyed in practice to the Middle East a century and a half or so later by Alexander. By the time of the Mishnah, seven centuries after the Pentateuch was closed, market economics was well established as the economics of the world economy in which, as a matter of fact, the land of Israel and Israel, that is, the Jews of Palestine, had been fully incorporated. Theories of fixed value, distribution of scarce resources by appeal to other than the rationality of the market—these represented anachronisms. But the framers of the Mishnah developed a dual economics, partly market, partly distributive (but, as we shall see at length, with the distributive in the normative position). That is the fact that permits us to treat as matters of economic theory a range of rules that, in market economics, can have no point of entry whatsoever. Here an important qualification must register. It is an overstatement to claim that the Mishnah (or Scripture) set forth a theory of market economics. In the Mishnah what we have is an account of economics in which there was room left for market action, so that the seeds for such a theory were planted; not more than that.

Only when we have grasped the general terms within which those concrete rules are worked out shall we understand the mixed economics characteristic of the Judaism of the Mishnah. A distributive economics, we now realize full well, is one that substitutes for the market as the price-fixing mechanism for the distribution of goods the instrumentality of the state or some other central organization; in the case of Scripture's economics, set out in the Priestly Code of ca. A.D. 500, this agency was the temple. In such an economics, in the words of Davisson and Harper, "such an organization will involve people's giving and receiving, producing and consuming, according to their status." [14] Substituting for the market as a rationing device, the distributive economy dealt with "the actual things that are distributed," while in markets, "purchases and sales are usually made for money, not directly for other commodities or services." [15]

The definition of market economics cited above calls to our attention the contrary traits of distributive economics, in particular, the intervention of authority other than the market in controlling both production and distribution of scarce goods. In the case of the Mishnah, the Temple requires the recognition of the status of certain individual participants—in addition to the householder—in the transaction of distributing the material goods of the economy particularly portions of the crop. Priests, Levites, and the poor have a claim on the crop independent of their role in the production of the crop, e.g., in labor, in land ownership, in investment of seed and the like. Not only so, but the market is not the main point of transfer of value. For material goods of the economy are directed to the Temple—so in the theory of the Mishnah—without any regard for the working of the market. When it comes to the claim of the Temple and the priesthood upon the productive economy, there is no consideration of the exchange of material value for material value, let alone of the intervention of considerations of supply and demand, the worth of the goods as against the worth of the services supplied by the Temple, and the like. [16] Davisson and Harper state of the market, "Even politically powerful interests and corporations must agree to accept the market decisions whether or not the outcome of a particular market transaction favors a person of high status." [17] But in the Mishnah, that simply is not so. And, we shall further observe, the Temple taboos imposed upon the productive economy considerations of a nonmarket, nonproductive character, in consequence of which the maximization of productivity forms only one among several competing considerations, and not the most important one, in the planning of production.

This brings us to the fundamental and necessary trait of market economics, private property. Davisson and Harper further state:

> Private ownership of property . . . is an essential condition of the market, but its existence does not guarantee that a market will exist or that contractual exchanges will occur [that can reach a conclusion with a simultaneous exchange of legally recognized rights in property and its use]. To be sure, in the absence of private property in the ancient Near East and early medieval Europe, we find a distributive economic order. Is there, then, some relation of cause and effect between private property and the operation of a market? It seems that insofar as there is monolithic

owernship and control of property (as in the Sumerian temple communities or with the god-king pharaoh of Egypt) there can be no development of a market. When private property was so limited, there could be no market trading. While there could be a considerable development of governmental status distribution and some marginal barter, there could not develop a price-making market.[18]

That statement again draws our attention to the datum of the Mishnah, which informs, by the way, its economics as well: that God owns the land and that the household holds the land in joint tenancy with God. Private ownership does not extend to the land at all.[19] That simple fact imposes upon the Mishnah's economic theory the principles of distributive economics, even while the framers of that theory address a world of market economics. It accounts for the mixed economics—market, distributive—of the Mishnah. Not only so, but as we just noted, the mortal owner-partner with God in the management of the household is not free to make decisions based solely on maximizing productivity; other considerations as to the use of land, as much as to the disposition of the crop, intervened.

Both Aristotle and the framers of the Mishnah addressed economic theory not only within the framework of distributive economics. They also acknowledged the facts of market economics, even while reaffirming (each party in its own terms and context) the higher (Aristotle: "natural," thus more natural; Mishnah authors: "holy," hence holier) value associated with distributive economics. For Aristotle, therefore, the criterion of correct economic action derived from a larger concern with uncovering natural, as against unnatural, ways of conducting affairs, and for the sages of the Mishnah, the counterpart criterion appealed to the theology of the Priestly Code, with its inception of the magical character of the land the Jews held as their own, which they called (and still call) "the land of Israel." This land was subject to particular requirements, because God owned this land in particular and through the Temple and the priesthood constituted the joint owner, along with the Israelite householder, of every acre. But in so saying, I have jumped far ahead in my story. It suffices to note, at this point, that in what follows I therefore focus upon how the economics of the Mishnah fits into the larger world view and way of life set forth by the authors of that document and, further, upon how important components of that world view and way of life in the context of the Mishnah correspond to what we know as economics today, a twofold inquiry.[20]

The framers of the Mishnah understood the market to mean the marketplace, in which goods were transferred from one to another.[21] But that correct conception has no bearing upon market economics. For the market as an economic theory finds definition in its function as the price-making mechanism, the system of rationing scarce goods and services, that forms the centerpiece of economics. A price-making market regulates the supply of goods in relation to demand and channels demand in relation to supply.[22] The self-regulating market is a closed system; considerations of supply and demand operate without intervention of other matters, e.g., status, noneconomic claims upon the supply of goods and services, and the like. To the self-regulating market system personal life is irrelevant: "Religious faith, social status, political belief, family life, loving, hating, gossiping, do not decide what will be done, except as they are part of the complex of motives and emotions creating demand for products." [23] When, however, considerations of caste status interfere with demand and supply, the self-regulating market can no longer function, and a different economics comes into play. Then we may have a marketplace, but no market, that is to say, no market economics. In order to understand what is at stake in the Mishnah's economic system seen as a function and aspect of its theological conviction, we have therefore to understand what we mean by market economics as against distributive economics (in the case of the Mishnah's system, a distribution that takes place from the Temple and through the priesthood).

In a (mere) marketplace (as distinct from a market economy) the supply-demand-price mechanism is not free to operate. Price may be fixed, for example, or merely traditional, and hence does not determine either the amount supplied or the amount demanded. It may not even involve a price; it can be a meeting place for the transfer of goods from group to group, and even barter is not required, since equivalence may be determined on entirely different principles. [24] Supply is unaffected by price, demand unregulated, produce distributed by considerations not defined by the supply-demand-price mechanism at all. When the rights of the priesthood or the poor to a share of the crop affect the distribution of the crop, then the supply-demand-price mechanism is no longer in play, and a different one, which we have called distributive, governs. Neale lays out these choices, therefore:

> [a] Self-Regulating Markets, where demand, price and cost mutually and exclusively determined what shall be produced, how it shall be produced, and to whom it shall be distributed.
> [b] Market Places, which have nothing in common with Self-Regulating Markets except that goods move from person to person. . . .
> Between these two types are other markets having some of the characteristics of Self-Regulating Markets. They may be price-making markets in which considerations other than demand, price, and cost affect what is produced, how it is produced, and to whom it goes. They may be essentially market places which happen to make use of money but fix the prices. [25]

A mixed market characterized the economics of Judaism, a conclusion that supports the view that the self-regulating market forms the exception, rather than the rule: "For most of its span man has lived with fixed price markets, non-price-making Market Places, and perhaps mostly with economic systems best treated in terms of reciprocal or redistributive institutions whose essential character must be established independently of orthodox economic theory and with the help of other disciplines more familiar with nonmarket institutions." [26]

This brings us to the distributive economy in its own terms. In discussing what he calls "marketless trading," Polanyi states that where we do not have the market, "the lack of functioning markets calls for a substitute for markets." [27] Babylonia, he says, "possessed neither market places nor a functioning market system of any description." Nonmarket trade, which characterized antiquity, "is in all essentials different from market trade. This applies to personnel, goods, prices, but perhaps most emphatically to the nature of the trading activity itself." [28] The main point is simple:

> Prices took the form of equivalencies established by authority of custom, statute, or proclamation. The necessaries of life were supposed to be subject to permanent equivalencies. . . . The chief difference between administrative or treaty trade on the one hand and market trade on the other lies in the trader's activities themselves. In contrast to market trade, those activities are here risk-free, both in regard to price expectation and debtor's insolvency. Under such circumstances of no-risk business along administrative lines, the term 'transaction' hardly applies; we will therefore designate this type of activity as 'dispositional.' [29]

The determinative economic power lay not in the market but in "the interaction between the two independent variables, palace and city, [which] determined the entire course of the economic—and political—history of Babylonia." [30]

Enough has been said even at this initial stage in the exposition to place the Mishnah's economic theory well within the framework of distributive economics, even while it accords in concrete terms with the requirements of market economics. It follows that we must now recognize the Mishnah's economics as a thoroughgoing mixture, in a single economic theory, of two incompatible theories of economics, and we shall have to explain how the two contradictory theories are drawn into a cogent whole and why, systemically, that was deemed necessary. For the Mishnah's economic theory introduces principles of distributive economics at odds with the workings of the market, and it does so in an age in which, in point of fact, market economics prevailed. Our task therefore is to describe the indications of the mixed character of the theory and to explain, in the Mishnah's details and by uncovering the Mishnah's system's premises, the relationship between the mixed economics of the system and the larger systemic principles of politics and social theory. For our ultimate goal is to explain the relations between the system of production and distribution of scarce resources and other institutions in the society imagined by the Mishnah's authors, that is, the workings of the political economy in the interplay and balance between the market and society, relations of production, investments in capital goods and in consumer goods, and between merchants and producers, as these relationships are set forth in the Mishnah's vision of "Israel." When we can account for these matters, as I claim to be able to do in chapter 7, we shall know in its entirety and cogency the economics of Judaism in the Mishnah's system of Judaism.

If, therefore, we propose to describe, analyze, and interpret the economics of Judaism, we have to invoke the other of the two economics that have shaped the Mishnah's, that is, the economics of the palace or temple complex. That other mode of economics organized the rationing of scarce commodities around the palace or temple, which exercised a monopoly on production and trade, and which also organized the economic, military, political, and, of course, religious life of the society.[31] Distributive economics, resting on status and preferment, competed with market economics because of the advent, in the Near and Middle East, of Greek, then Roman, government. The Greco-Roman world was one of private ownership, while the Near Eastern world for many centuries had emphasized not private trade and private manufacture but the organization of affairs by bureaucracy. Whether or not we should appeal for explanation of the difference to the requirement of large-scale social organization to make possible the river-valley civilizations of the Nile, Tigris, and Euphrates (not to mention the Indus and Yellow) rivers is not pertinent here.[32]

For our purposes the simple point is that ancient Israel's priesthood set forth in its singular system principles of economic organization familiar for more than two thousand years before ca. 500 B.C., when the priestly conception (attributed to Moses at Sinai) reached written form in the Priestly Code and further drew together and made into a single statement what we now have as the Pentateuch. The conception of the market, the free market, is the innovation and came from without. The economics of the Mishnah, then, is the economics of the Temple in a world in which the rules were made by the market, a world in which, indeed, market economics in fact had predominated and in the aggregate had governed for some seven hundred years—indeed, the economics of a temple that then lay in ruins.

I said earlier that the Mishnah's economics *is* economics only in the classic, and not in the modern, sense of the word. For economics from the eighteenth century became a distinct science on its own, treating economics not as a chapter in politics ("political economy") but as a disembedded corpus of knowledge and a distinct component of social reality. On economics as the science has evolved from its eighteenth-century origins, of course, the Judaism studied here has nothing whatsoever to say.[33] My analysis therefore treats not the issues of economics broadly construed, e.g., how the framers of the Mishnah understood the difference between a commodity and specie, or how they defined the fundamental unit of production. Nor do the Mishnah's authors tell us anything at all about the economy of the Jews in the time of the Mishnah or even reveal economic attitudes that demand attention.

What those authors tell us, in grand scope and acute detail, is the answer to a different question. It is, specifically, what we learn about the Judaism of the dual Torah in its initial statement when we ask those questions that economics instructs us to ask. So the issue is systemic analysis: economics as an indicator of the character of a system in context. From economics as conceived in antiquity, we gain perspective on the Mishnah. What we shall learn is that the Mishnah is a document of political economy, in which the two critical classifications are the village, *polis,* and the household, *oikos.* Since, however, the Mishnah's framers conceived of the world as God's possession and handiwork, theirs was the design of a universe in which God's and humanity's realms flowed together. Their statement bears comparison, therefore, to Plato's *Republic* and Aristotle's *Politics* as a utopian program (*Staatsroman*) of a society as a political entity, encompassing its economics; but pertinent to the comparison also is Augustine's conception of a city of God and a city of man. In the Mishnah we find thinkers attempting, in acute detail, to think through how God and humanity form a single *polis* and a single *oikos*, a shared political economy, one village and one household on earth as it is in heaven.[34]

Systemic analysis is the sole correct approach when we deal with the initial statement of any particular Judaism, and especially the Judaism of the dual Torah, which developed its literary expression as a systematic exegesis of the Mishnah, viewed as "the oral Torah," and of Scripture, "the written Torah." Obviously, in the unfolding of the canonical corpus of that Judaism, economics developed in diverse ways, and any account of the economics of that Judaism will encompass more than the initial statement treated here. But if I insist, as I do, upon the centrality of context and deem context to begin with the identification of the particular Judaism, then I must start at the first and the foundation document and work outward from there. And no incongruity is committed in joining "economics" to "Judaism," for any Judaic system, consisting of a world view, a way of life, and an address to a particular and defined "Israel" makes its judgment along the way upon economics, as upon politics, as much as upon philosophy and theology and right conduct and diverse other components of the world under systemic construction.[35]

The Mishnah's sages placed economics, both market and distributive, in the center of their system, devoting two of their six divisions to it (the first and the fourth, for distributive and market economics, respectively), and succeeded in making their statement through economics in a sustained and detailed way far beyond the merely generalizing manner in which Aristotle did. And no one in antiquity came near Aristotle, as I said. So we shall see, at least, I claim, that it was with remarkable success that the sages of Judaism presented an economics wholly coordinated in a systemic way with a politics. In this study, therefore, we find ourselves on the border between sociology and economics, and therefore this inquiry places us squarely into the middle of the ongoing discourse on political economy. Compared to the work of Plato and Aristotle, the Mishnah's system presents the single most successful political economy accomplished in antiquity. That is no small claim, and the rest of this book serves to validate that claim. But let us start at the beginning: the conception of the Mishnah as not merely a collection of rules but a cogent system and a coherent statement.

2

The Initial Statement

The System of the Mishnah and Its Economics

Let us turn back now to the beginning, the initial statement of the Judaism of the dual Torah presented by the Mishnah.[1] In the form of a law code, the Mishnah sets forth a theoretical statement of a Judaism or Judaic system—a way of life and world view addressed to a particular "Israel." The document was produced under the sponsorship of Judah the Patriarch, ethnarch of the Jews of the land of Israel ("Palestine") under Roman authority and sponsorship. The document, absorbing within its systematic statement whatever of Scripture its authors found urgent, served as the basic law of the Jews of the holy land. It rapidly was adopted as the constitution, also, of the Jews in Babylonia and other of the western satrapies of the Iranian empire of the Sasanians.[2] The Mishnah is divided into six divisions: Agriculture (producing crops and handing over God's share in them to the scheduled castes), Seasons (holy days, conduct of the cult and the village on appointed times), Women (laws of the family, personal status, betrothal, marriage, divorce, vows, and some special problems), Damages (civil and criminal law, the organization and procedures of the courts), Holy Things (the Temple, conduct of the sacrificial rites on an everyday basis, the upkeep of the Temple buildings), and Purities (taboos affecting the Temple cult, uncleanness in respect to persons, and cultic cleanness effected, also, in the home).

These six divisions cover six principal topics: sanctification of the agricultural economy by conduct of farming in accord with the taboos of Scripture and support of the priesthood, the holy caste; sanctification of time, with reference to special occasions, appointed times, and the Sabbath; sanctification of the family and the individual; the proper conduct of points of social conflict, the political life of the people and the regulation of the economy in regard to trade, commerce, real estate, labor relations, and the like; the sanctification of the Temple and its offerings, with special emphasis on everyday and routine occasions; and, finally, the protection of the Temple from uncleanness and the preservation of cultic cleanness. All together, they cover the everyday life of the holy people in the here and now. The Mishnah generated systematic study and commentary in both the land of Israel and Babylonia, with two Talmuds, or systematic amplifications of the Mishnah, emerging. Among the six divisions of the Mishnah, the Talmud of the Land of Israel, or Yerushalmi, addresses four (Agriculture, Women, Seasons, and Damages), and the Talmud of Babylonia, or Bavli, treats four (Women, Seasons, Damages, and Holy Things). The Mishnah is a systemic, and not a traditional, statement and document. While using received facts from Scripture and other sources, the Mishnah constitutes a cogent and autonomous statement, using received materials for its authors' own purposes, rather than merely handing on the increment of an inherited set of sayings or rules.[3] The Mishnah in form and system alike emerged as a whole and complete statement, deriving but using for its own purposes information from earlier generations that had been preserved in a variety of ways.

The importance of the systemic, not traditional, character of the Mishnah for the study of the economics of the Mishnah is simple. It is only in the context of the system as a whole that the economics of the Judaism of the Mishnah is to be described. Like all other important topics of the system, therefore, economics will in its detail speak for the system as a whole and therefore will have to be read in the context, and as exemplary, of the system as a whole. In more general terms, the point pertains to every topic in the document. Specifically, the system of philosophy expressed through concrete and detailed law presented by the Mishnah consists of a coherent logic and topic, a cogent world view and comprehensive way of living. Any subject addressed by the authors of the Mishnah will permit the restatement of essentially the same fundamental proposition. That is the upshot of the Mishnah's character as a systematic statement, not a mere agglutination of received information. In this connection, we do well to remember the point at which we started, which was with Joseph Schumpeter's observation about the difference between an inert and a systemically important fact, stated in his language as follows: "In economics as elsewhere, most statements of fundamental facts acquire importance only by the superstructures they are made to bear and are commonplace in the absence of such superstructures."[4] We turn, therefore, to that superstructure built upon the facts that the authors of the Mishnah assemble.

The Mishnah's is a world view which speaks of transcendent things, a way of life in response to the supernatural meaning of what is done, a heightened and deepened perception of the sanctification of Israel in deed and in deliberation. Sanctification means two things: first, distinguishing Israel in all its dimensions from the world in all its ways; second, establishing the stability, order, regularity, predictability, and reliability of Israel in the world of nature and supernature, particularly at moments and in contexts of danger. Danger means instability, disorder, irregularity, uncertainty, and betrayal. Each topic of the system as a whole takes up a critical and indispensable moment or context of social being. Through what is said in regard to each of the Mishnah's principal topics, what the halakhic system as a whole wishes to declare is fully expressed. Yet if the parts severally and jointly give the message of the whole, the whole cannot exist without all of the parts, so well joined and carefully crafted are they all. In defining the Mishnah, we lay stress upon the document's topical program, because the document in excruciating detail presents a sustained exegesis of a single theme, and that is, as noted, the sanctification of Israel, the people, in its everyday life. Indeed, in the history of Judaism(s), after the book of Leviticus but even including the Essenic library of Qumran and the New Testament Letter to the Hebrews, the Mishnah provides the single most extreme statement of the centrality of sanctification. Sanctification bears a specific meaning. It is the ordering of all things on earth in conformity with, and in relationship to, the model and pattern of heaven, meaning God's realm. To the authors of the Mishnah, the here and now of everyday life, in the natural world, forms the counterpart and opposite of the supernatural world of God in heaven, and the ordering and regularizing of the one in line with the main outlines of the other constitutes, for the system of the Mishnah, the labor of sanctification. That is the overriding topic, and the Mishnah's system finds cogency in the exegesis of that topic.

The Mishnah's topical program throughout thus focuses upon the sanctificaton of the life of holy Israel, the Jewish people.[5] No wonder, then, that the economics of the Priestly Code, an idiomatic statement of the absolutely standard and established distributive economic theory of temples from Sumerian times onward, dominated in the economics of the Judaism that the Mishnah would set forth. Just as the authors of the Mishnah invoked the priestly conceptions of the holiness of Israel in answering the question of the age, so they adopted for their own use, with only negligible adaptation, the economic theory of the priesthood behind the pentateuchal Priestly Code and related writings. The question taken up by the authors of the Mishnah, in the aftermath of the destruction of the Temple, is simple. It concerns whether and—more to the point—how Israel is still holy. And the (to the authors, self-evidently valid) answer is that Israel indeed is holy, and so far as the media of sanctification persist beyond the destruction of the holy place—and they do endure— the task of holy Israel is to continue to conduct that life of sanctification that had centered upon the Temple. Where now does holiness reside? It is in the life of the people, Israel, there above all. So the Mishnah may speak of the holiness of the Temple, but the premise is that the people—that kingdom of priests and holy people of Leviticus—constitutes the center and focus of the sacred. The land retains its holiness too, and in raising the crops, the farmer is expected to adhere to the rules of order and structure laid down in Leviticus, keeping each thing in its proper classification, observing the laws of the sabbatical year, for instance. The priesthood retains its holiness, even without the task of carrying out the sacrificial cult. Therefore priests must continue to observe the caste rules governing marriage, such as are specified in Leviticus.

Four of the six principal parts of the Mishnah deal with the cult and its officers. These are, first, Holy Things, which addresses the everyday conduct of the sacrificial cult; second, Purities, which takes up the protection of the cult from the sources of uncleanness specified in the book of Leviticus (particularly chapters 12 through 15); third, Agriculture, which centers on the designation of portions of the crop for the use of the priesthood (and others in the same classification of a holy caste, such as the poor), and so provides for the support of the Temple staff; and, fourth, Appointed Times, the larger part of which concerns the conduct of the cult on such special occasions as the Day of Atonement, Passover, Tabernacles, and the like (and the rest of which concerns the conduct in the village on those same days, with the basic conception that what is done in the cult forms the mirror image of what is done in the village).[6]

In its quest for the rules of order and regularity such as heaven has laid down and a truly sanctified earth will follow, the authors of the Mishnah classify and compare, finding the right rule for each matter, each important situation, by determining whether one case is like another or not like another. If it is like another, it follows the rule governing that other, and if not, it follows the opposite of that rule.[7] In this way an orderly and logical way to sort out chaos and discover the inner order of being generates the balanced and stable, secure world described by the Mishnah. Historical events, when they enter at all, lose their one-time and unprecedented character and are shown to follow, even to generate, a fixed rule; events therefore are the opposite of eventful. This age and the age to come, history and the end of history—these categories play little role. Even the figure of the Messiah serves as a taxon, that is, a classification; namely, designation or anointment (as the word *mashiah* means) distinguishes one priest from another. An anointed priest—a messiah-priest—is a priest of one kind or classification, not of some other. So, in all, the Mishnah's method and process dictate the results of its authors' thought on any given topic, including the one of salvation, which is the proposition before us.

The dominant stylistic trait of the Mishnah, imposed in the process of ultimate closure and redaction, is the acute formalization of its syntactical structure, specifically in its intermediate divisions ("chapters," or composites of two or more paragraphs on exactly the same theme and problem and principle), which are so organized that the limits of a theme correspond to those of a formulaic pattern. Stress on the formalization of language corresponds to the Mishnah's inner structure, based as it is on regularization and order in the logic of being. The balance and order of the Mishnah are particular to the Mishnah.[8] A remarkably coherent, cogent, and exceedingly limited corpus of literary devices and redactional conventions characterizes the document throughout. A significant single norm of agglutination predominates, which is reliance upon distinctive formulaic traits imposed on a sequence of sentences and upon distinctive thematic substance expressed by these same patterned sentences. That is how intermediate units were put together and accounts also for the formalization of small ones—without reference to the diversity of authorities cited therein. Four distinctive syntactical patterns characterize all, with the fifth, the simple declarative sentence itself, so shaped as to yield its own distinctive traits. The Mishnah forms a closed and completed system not only in both topical program and inner, cogent logic, but also in language and syntax.[9]

I have already pointed out that the Priestly Code and other important priestly writings provide authoritative sources for the authors of the Mishnah. The topical program of the priestly strands of the Pentateuch predominates, providing answers to the now urgent question of whether and how Israel remains holy. We should therefore ask whether, in the Mishnah, we have nothing more than a reprise of a viewpoint and corpus of rules framed in an earlier age altogether (in the same time, more or less, as the birth of Greek philosophical interest in economics, as a matter of fact). That is why, in describing the Mishnah and the place of economics within its system, we have now to investigate the fundamental character of the document in relationship to received traditions. Let me frame the question I think determinative. Does the Mishnah derive from an agglutinative process of traditional formulation and transmission of an intellectual heritage, facts and thought alike? Or does that document make a statement of its own, cogent and defined within the requirements of an inner logic, proportion, and structure, imposing that essentially autonomous vision upon whatever materials its authors have received from the past?

The answer to that question will guide us in interpreting the data on economics that we shall review. If the Mishnah forms a cogent statement on its own, then we have to interpret the facts of economic theory as part of that larger statement and, therefore, within the logic of the mishnaic system as a whole. It will follow that the part—economics—forms a component of a larger composition, the needs of which, and the interests of which, have imposed their logic upon that component. If, on the other hand, the Mishnah simply collects and arranges received materials, then we err in reading economics as a systemic component and have to interpret the data of an economic character item by item, episodically and individually, not systemically and coherently. So at stake in our reading of the character of the Mishnah—statement or collection, system or tradition—is the same fundamental and generative problematic we shape in the interpretation of the economics of the document: part of a larger system or not, systemically active or inert. To state the answer simply: on the one side, the authors of the Mishnah do make use of received materials. But on the other, in literary terms the Mishnah is not traditional, for it is not formed out of the increment of received materials, the form of the reception of which governs in the syntax and wording of statements, but is—in the sense now implied—in syntactic and grammatical terms, highly systematic, therefore also systemic. That is, as literature it is orderly, systematic, laid out in a proportion and order dictated by the inner logic of a topic or generative problem and authoritative by reason of its own rigorous judgment of issues of rationality and compelling logic.

We turn, first of all, to the origin of the laws of the Mishnah, since the simple fact is that the authors of the Mishnah made up very few of the laws that they present. That fact will point toward the characterization of the Mishnah as traditional and agglutinative, not systematic and systemic. To explain the history of the Mishnah's laws, we have to recall a simple fact. Apart from the scriptural law codes, in antiquity no single system of law governed all Jews everywhere. So we cannot describe "Jewish law" as one encompassing system, everywhere handed down as tradition from generation to generation. The Scripture's several codes of course made their impact on the diverse systems of law that governed various groups of Jews, or Jewish communities in various places. But that impact never proved uniform. In consequence, in no way may we speak of "Jewish law," meaning a single legal code or even a common set of encompassing rules everywhere held authoritative by Jewry. The relationship between the legal system of one distinct group of Jews to that governing some other proves various.[10]

But all Jews opened the same holy Scriptures, and the framers of the Mishnah, having worked out the topical program of interest, did the same. The fact is that much of the law of the Mishnah derives from the age before its final closure. In that sense, the Mishnah presents us with the results of a process of tradition. In the Mishnah we see how a group of philosophical jurisprudents drew together a rich heritage of legal and moral traditions and facts and made of them a single system. From Scripture onward, no other composition compares in size, comprehensive treatment of a vast variety of topics, balance, proportion, and cogency.[11] That fact yields one incontrovertible result. The Mishnah's rules have to come into juxtaposition, wherever possible, with the rules that occur in prior law codes, whether Israelite or otherwise. That is the case, even though it presently appears that only a small proportion of all of the rules in the Mishnah fall within the frame of prior documents, remote or proximate. For every rule we can parallel in an earlier composition, the Mishnah gives us dozens of rules that in topic, logic, or even mere detail bear no comparison to anything now known in a prior composition, from Sumerian and Akkadian to Essene and Christian writers alike. (The sole exception, the Hebrew Scripture's law codes, comes under analysis presently.) While, therefore, we know as fact that the Mishnah's authors drew on received information, we have to ask, did they formulate their document as a restatement of that information, that tradition? That is a separate question. And the answer is fundamental.

The authors of the Mishnah did use available, sometimes very ancient, materials, reshaped for the purposes of making their own statement in their own way. The document upon close reading proves systematic and orderly, purposive and well composed. It is no mere scrapbook of legal facts, arranged for purposes of reference. Let me state with emphasis the criterion for that judgment. *The Mishnah is a document in which—just as in the traits of rhetorical and formal composition—the critical problematic at the center always exercises influence over the peripheral facts, dictating how they are chosen, arranged, utilized.* So even though some facts in the document prove very old indeed, on that basis we understand no more than we did before we knew that some facts come from ancient times. True law as the Mishnah presents law derives from diverse sources, from remote antiquity onward. But the law as it emerges whole and complete in the Mishnah in particular, that is, the system, the structure, the proportions and composition, the topical program and the logical and syllogistic whole—these derive from the imagination and wit of the final two generations, in the second century, of the authors of the Mishnah.

A simple exercise will show that, whatever the antiquity of rules viewed discretely, the meaning and proportionate importance of rules taken all together derive from the perspective and ecompassing theory of the authors of the Mishnah themselves. That is what will show that the history of law as the Mishnah presents the law can be traced, whole and cogent, only within the data of the Mishnah itself: systemically, not episodically. The desired exercise brings us to the relationship of the Mishnah to Scripture. For, as noted just now, that is the one substantial source to which the authors of the Mishnah did make reference. Accordingly, to demonstrate the antiquity of more than discrete and minor details of law of the Mishnah, we turn to Scripture. There, it is clear, we can find out whether the Mishnah constitutes merely a repository of ancient law.[12] Knowing how the authors of the Mishnah addressed Scripture tells us whether their work comprises a cogent system or a mere repository of available information, an exercise of selection and construction or one of collection and arrangement.

Let me now state the simple fact that settles the issue. The authors of the Mishnah to begin with read Scripture, as they read much else, in terms of the system and structure they proposed to construct. Their goals and conceptions told them what in Scripture they would borrow, what they would expand and articulate, what they would acknowledge but neglect, and what they would simply ignore. That fact shows that law in the Mishnah, even though shared here and there with other codes, and even though intersecting with still other systems, constitutes a distinct and autonomous system of law, a law on its own. So the Mishnah does not absorb and merely portray in its own way established rules of law out of a single, continuous, and cogent legal system, the law. Why not? Because, as we shall now see, the Mishnah's authors turn out to have taken from Scripture what they chose in accord with the criterion of the one thing they wished to accomplish. This was the construction of their system of law with its distinctive traits of topical and logical composition: *their* law, not *the* law. The pertinence of that result to the inquiry of chapters 4 through 8, we remind ourselves, is clear: we shall have to read their economics within their larger system, for we have not economics (also) in the Mishnah, but *the* economics of the Mishnah.

In order to show the preeminence, in the encounter with Scripture's laws, of the perspective and purpose—the system—of the authors of the Mishnah, we simply review the Mishnah's tractates and ask how, overall, we may characterize their relationships to Scripture. Were these wholly dependent, wholly autonomous, or somewhere in between? That is, at the foundations in fact and generative problematic of a given tractate, we may discover nothing more than facts and interests of Scripture's law; the tractate's authors may articulate the data of Scripture. Or when we reach the bedrock of a tractate, the point at which the articulation of the structure of the tractate rests, we may find no point of contact with facts, let alone interests, of Scripture's laws. And, third, we may discover facts shared by Scripture but developed in ways distinctive to the purposes of the framers of the Mishnah tractate at hand. These three relationships, in theory, encompass all possibilities. The reality is simple. The authors picked and chose, rejected and selected, made things up as their purpose required, did everything but one thing: merely repeat, merely paraphrase, merely summarize an inherited system or received facts.

Let us turn to the facts. First, there are tractates which simply repeat in their own words precisely what Scripture has to say and at best serve to amplify and complete the basic ideas of Scripture. For example, all of the cultic tractates of the second division, Appointed Times, which tell what one is supposed to do in the Temple on the various special days of the year, and the bulk of the cultic tractates of the fifth division, Holy Things, simply restate facts of Scripture. There is no way to understand Mishnah-tractate Yoma, on the Day of Atonement, without a point-by-point reference to Leviticus 16. For another example, all of those tractates of the sixth division, Purities, which specify sources of uncleanness, depend completely on information supplied by Scripture. Every important statement in Niddah, on menstrual uncleanness, and the most fundamental notions of Zabim, on the uncleanness of the person with flux referred to in Leviticus 15, as well as every detail in Negaim, on the uncleanness of the person or house suffering the uncleanness described at Leviticus 13 and 14—all of these tractates serve only to restate the basic facts of Scripture and to complement those facts with other important ones.

There are, second, tractates which take up facts of Scripture but work them out in a way which those scriptural facts cannot have led us to predict. A supposition concerning what is important *about* the facts, utterly remote from the supposition of Scripture, will explain why the Mishnah tractates under discussion say the original things they say in confronting those scripturally provided facts. For one example, Scripture takes for granted that the red cow will be burned in a state of uncleanness, because it is burned outside the camp, meaning the Temple. The priestly writers cannot have imagined that a state of cultic cleanness was to be attained outside of the cult. The absolute datum of tractate Parah, by contrast, is that cultic cleanness can be attained outside of the "tent of meeting." The red cow was to be burned in a state of cleanness exceeding even that cultic cleanness required in the Temple itself. The problem which generates the intellectual agendum of Parah, therefore, is how to work out the conduct of the rite of burning the cow in relationship to the Temple: is it to be done in exactly the same way, or in exactly the opposite way? This mode of contrastive and analogical thinking helps us to understand the generative problematic of such tractates as Erubin and Besah, to mention only two.

And third, there are, predictably, many tractates which either take up problems in no way suggested by Scripture or begin from facts at best merely relevant to facts of Scripture. In the former category are Tohorot, on the cleanness of foods, with its companion, Uqsin; Demai, on doubtfully tithed produce; Tamid, on the conduct of the daily whole offering; Baba Batra, on rules of real estate transactions and certain other commercial and property relationships, and so on. In the latter category are Ohalot, which, on the pretext of applying the taboos about the corpse in a tent of Numbers 19, spins out its strange problems concerning the comparison of a utensil and a tent (!) within the theory that, viewed as utter abstractions, that is, two forms of contained space, one large, one small, a tent and a utensil are isomorphic in essence ("idea"); Kelim, on the susceptibility to uncleanness of various sorts of utensils; Miqvaot, on the sorts of water which effect purification from uncleanness; Makhshirin, on the power of water to impart susceptibility to uncleanness in line with Lev. 11:34, 36; and many others. These tractates draw on facts of Scripture, whether many or, as in the case of Miqvaot and Makhshirin, few. But the problems confronted in these tractates in no way respond to problems important to Scripture. Nor on the basis of Scripture could we have predicted the shape of the generative problem explored in the Mishnah tractate at hand. What we have here is a prior program of inquiry, which will make ample provision for facts of Scripture in an inquiry generated essentially outside of the framework of Scripture.

It follows that we have everything and its opposite. Some tractates merely repeat what we find in Scripture. Some are totally independent of Scripture. Some fall in between. Scripture confronts the framers of the Mishnah as revelation, not merely as a source of facts. But the framers of the Mishnah had their own world with which to deal. They made statements in the framework and fellowship of their own age and generation. They were bound, therefore, to come to Scripture with a set of questions generated elsewhere than in Scripture. They brought their own ideas about what was going to be important in Scripture. This is perfectly natural. The philosophers of the Mishnah conceded to Scripture the highest authority. At the same time what they chose to hear, within the authoritative statements of Scripture, in the end formed a statement of its own. And that is the mark of their paramount trait: system builders, who selected what they needed for their purposes and who knew, when they came to Scripture, precisely what information made a difference in the composition of their structure. To state matters simply: all of Scripture is authoritative. But only some of Scripture is relevant. And what happened is that the framers and philosophers of the tradition of the Mishnah came to Scripture when they had reason to. That is to say, they brought to Scripture a program of questions and inquiries framed essentially among themselves. So they were highly selective. Their program itself constituted a statement upon the meaning of Scripture. They and their apologists of one sort hastened to add that their program consisted of a statement of, and not only upon, the meaning of Scripture.

Scripture provides indisputable facts. It is wholly authoritative—*once we have made our choice of which part of Scripture we shall read and what question we find compelling, even urgent, when we read that selected passage.* Scripture generated important and authoritative structures of the community, including disciplinary and doctrinal statements, decisions, and interpretations—once people had determined which part of Scripture to ask to provide those statements and decisions. Community structures envisaged by the Mishnah were wholly based on Scripture—when scripture had anything to lay down. But Scripture is not wholly and exhaustively expressed in those structures which the Mishnah does borrow. Scripture has dictated the character of formative structures of the Mishnah. But the Mishnah's system is not the result of the dictation of close exegesis of Scripture, except after the fact. And to that fact, the history of the law of the Mishnah while interesting, is essentially beside the point.[13] The reason is clear. The legal system presented by the Mishnah consists of a coherent logic and topic, a cogent world view and comprehensive way of living. It is a world view which speaks of transcendent things, a way of life in response to the supernatural meaning of what is done, a heightened and deepened perception of the sanctification of Israel in deed and in deliberation. Each topic of the system as a whole takes up a critical and indispensable moment or context of social being. Through what is said in regard to each of the Mishnah's principal topics, what the legal system as a whole wishes to declare is fully expressed. Yet if the parts severally and jointly give the message of the whole, the whole cannot exist without all of the parts, so well joined and carefully crafted are they all.[14]

Viewed as a whole, therefore, the Mishnah's system has no history, though it makes use of received, that is, "historical," materials. The system therefore cannot and does not derive from an incremental process of tradition. Theories of economics, no less than purity taboos, therefore must serve a larger systemic purpose, and the reason that a theory of economics finds a place in the structure is that the framers of the system, to accomplish their goals, found economics pertinent and systemically useful.

That paramount and definitive position of the system as a whole, emerging all at once, whole and complete, is the fact, even though, seen piece by piece, some of the principal components of the system do emerge from such a traditional process. The Mishnah, all together, all at once, emerged from a process of formulation and transmission accomplished by a cogent social group, which knew exactly the topics important in their construction and also knew precisely the rules of rhetoric and logic they wished to impose on the presentation of any topic at hand. The predominance of the rules of rhetoric and logic in the framing of the whole, in nearly all of its parts, expresses also the counterpart: the hegemony, over the whole, of the system—urgent question, self-evidently valid answer. The Mishnah therefore is systemic, stating a philosophical system, whole and complete. The authors worked, at the outset, *de novo*. They were philosophers in the deepest and richest sense of the tradition of philosophy. The Mishnah's authors present a profoundly reasoned view of a rational and well-proportioned world, a world of rules and order and reason and rationality. That constitutes their religious statement: the affirmation of creation as a work of logic and order and law, to which the human mind, with its sense of logic, order, and rule, conforms, as it was created to conform. Now to the place of economics in that system.

We begin with the fundamental question of whether or not we may hope to describe the economics of a Judaic religious system.[15] For, in general terms, that issue—does every social system by definition have, also, an economics—remains subject to debate. On the one side, some deem "all forms of society" subject to objective analysis "into a finite number of immutable elements," so that we may address the same system of analytical classifications to any society, ancient or contemporary.[16] On the other hand, others hold that economics, e.g., a market-centered analysis, simply does not apply where there is no market, and, more broadly, that economics is an inquiry into a particular kind of society and its system of exchange. Further, the inaccessibility of reliable statistics makes conventional economic analysis parlous indeed. How then to proceed to describe the economics of Judaism? Let us first consider what, in antiquity, people thought economics comprised, then review the range of opinion on how, for our part, we may think about economics in antiquity.

When for antiquity, we read the writings of a Greek author who wrote on "economics," meaning the art of household management, we find that he indeed covered rules for what we may reasonably call, without vastly stretching matters, "allocation of scarce resources," both tangible and intangible, as well as regulations for increasing wealth, all accomplished thorugh sound agronomics. He further dealt with policy concerning that extended family that we know as the household, conceived to constitute the fundamental unit of economic life and action, as well as labor policy in regard to slaves, the politics of economic action, and a familiar program of economic thought in theory and in policy.[17] The Judaism the initial statement of which we consider here assuredly does the same.[18] But when it treats economics, it means not only the household management, but the management of "house" in a much richer and deeper sense, as we shall see at the end.

The Judaic religious system before us in the Mishnah encompasses, within its systemic statement and construction, an account of rational action in regard to scarcity and, further, to the formation and disposition of wealth, and that account constitutes its economics. But we shall see that that economics is not exactly the same as the market economics conventionally covered within the definition at hand. For if economics encompasses all systemic doctrines on rational action in regard to scarcity, a definition of wealth, and systemically rational rules on the increase and disposition of wealth, then economics in theory cannot accept the limitation to the consideration of only agriculture or agronomy at all. Quite to the contrary, when the Mishnaic system addresses issues of production, e.g., rules governing the correct mode of planting crops, the proper disposition of corps, that is, in context, agricultural production, it raises questions, most certainly and explicitly deemed important in respect to scarcity, that for our part we should regard as hardly economic in any conventional sense. But theirs was a different convention, deriving from a different rationality. And understanding the economics of their Judaism, we also search out the rationality that, at the deep structure of the system as a whole, accounts for that economics.[19] It was, as I have already pointed out, a distributive economics, an economics commonplace in antiquity but with a rationality particular to the system at hand.

Let us begin with the conventional meanings imputed to economics, particularly in theory. The Mishnah presents precisely what any ancient work on economics was expected to provide, namely, a full account of the virtue of rationality as realized in the household and its management, encompassing issues of family and property which confronted the householder (the master of the house, *paterfamilias* in Latin) *baal habayit* in Hebrew. Take, for one fact, the meaning of the word economics, made up of two Greek words, *nomos*, that is, law, and *oikos*, household. A work on the law, *nomos*, of the household, *oikos*, in the context of antiquity in which the household formed the fundamental unit of economic production, constituted an exercise in economic thought, that is to say, a theory on the rational action with regard to scarcity that, in the aggregate, then and now defined economics.[20] Such a work therefore will counsel on avoiding scarcity through rational action, by allocating scarce goods and services through prudent management, increasing production, preserving scarce goods through wise action, and otherwise rationally conducting the affairs of the *oikos*. It follows that the household defined the principal unit of economic production. In covering these subjects, a treatise in concrete terms, for instance, in agronomy, will provide an overall theory of applied economics in accord with the conventional definition of economics and the received rationality entirely familiar to us in the West. By following the received topical program of treatises or episodic discourse on economics, we can construct an account of the program of the economics of the Judaism of the Mishnah in a simple way.

Let us take for our model of a treatise on economics—the art of household management—a well-known piece of writing bearing precisely that title and therefore explicitly treating that topic, then ask whether the Mishnah, wholly or in large part, falls into the same classification of writing. Before the middle of the fourth century an Athenian philosopher, Xenophon, better known for his *Anabasis,* also wrote a treatise called *Oeconomicus,* a discourse on estate management, as Cicero, who admired the work and translated it into Latin, described it.[21] Framing matters in the contemporary mode, as a socratic dialogue, Xenophon viewed economics as a practical and applied science only. In his economics he simply explained the management of an estate, the rules governing the preservation of wealth in the form of the land, the crafts of the household, land development, and agriculture. The work begins with the claim that estate management is the name of a branch of knowledge, like medicine, smithing, and carpentry: "the business of a good estate manager is to manage his own estate well" (1.2). One who understands this art, even if he has no property of his own, can "earn money by managing another man's estate . . . and he would get a good salary if, after taking over an estate, he continued to pay all outgoings and to increase the estate by showing a balance."

Xenophon goes on to ask the abstract questions of theory that, in our world, we regard as economics, e.g., the definition of "estate," which we may render "wealth:"

> "But what do we mean now by an estate? Is it the same thing as a house, or is all property that one possesses outside the house also part of the estate?"
> "Well, I think that even if the property is situated in different cities, everything a man possesses is part of his estate" (1.5).

Land is wealth if it is worked in such a way as to produce a profit; the same is so of sheep: "The same things are wealth and not wealth, acccording as one understands or does not understand how to use them" (1.9). Xenophon then proceeds to ask how to increase one's estate (2.1ff.). The way, of course, is to spend less than one's income. And the way to do that is through sound estate management. Xenophon's advice is to keep everything in the right place.

One should train for the job all those who are employed on the estate, whether slaves or children or women:

> Estate management is the name of a branch of knowledge . . . by which men can increase estates, and an estate appeared to be identical with the total of one's property; and . . . property is that which is useful for supplying a livelihood, and useful things turned out to be all those things that one knows how to use (6.4).

What is involved in all this is good organization and cooperation. Of critical importance in all this is the right training of the wife (7.7ff.). Her duty is "to remain indoors and send out those servants whose work is outside and superintend those who are to work indoors. . . . When wool is brought to you, you must see that cloaks are made for those that want them. You must see too that the dry grain is in good condition for making food" (7.36), and on and on. She is to train slave-girls in spinning and weaving, produce children, and, in general, perform the wifely part in the work of running the estate. And what of the day to day conduct of the estate: "And by what kind of work do you endeavor to keep your health and strength? . . . What diligence do you use to have a surplus from which to help friends and strengthen the city?" (11.13). The householder (if I may call him that) does his business in town, then super-intends the details of the work of the estate: planting, clearing, sowing, har-vesting (11.14–18). In all, one who is to be successful in the management of a farm must learn what to do and how and when to do it (15.6). Xenophon's observations on economic activity, as distinct from economic analysis, led him also to recognize the division of labor:

> In small towns the same man makes couches, doors, ploughs and tables . . . and still he is thankful if only he can find enough work to support himself, and it is impossible for a man of many trades to do all of them well. In large cities, however, because many make demands on each trade, one alone is enough to support a man. . . . Of necessity he who pursues a very specialized task will do it best.[22]

Specialization improves quality; Xenophon is not interested in increasing pro-ductivity and cannot be regarded as a precursor of Henry Ford.

Can we deem Xenophon's thought to compare to economic theory as we know it? Hardly. The art of household management is not economics: "though that may involve 'economic' activity, it is misleading, and often flatly wrong, to translate it as 'economics.' "[23] We shall have to await our en-counter with Aristotle to find discourse to which "economics" appropriately pertains. Aristotle joins *oikonomia* and *chrēmatistikē,* the art of acquiring property, when he presents us with something we may read as an economic theory. In all, therefore, if we wish to invoke the word "economics," we will have to discuss farming, not, however, as mere agronomics, but as the central action in the production of wealth by the unit of production comprising the household. To put matters simply, in the Greco-Roman world, a doctrine of economics will tell us how to manage wealth so as to increase it. And, since the same is so today, we must conclude that the Greeks and Romans under-stood economics just as we do: the theory of the management and increase of wealth.

So far as, in antiquity, we have a theory of economics, therefore, we shall have to turn to the model of the work at hand. A book on economics focused upon the regulation of the household. Xenophon's *Oeconomicus,* addressed to the householder, deals with the good life, the use of wealth, the virtues of the householder, the training and managment of slaves, wifely virtues and the training of a wife, and agronomy.[24] Sections on marriage and divorce under-line the focus, for economics in the received sense, upon the life of the family. But "family" had its own sense, richer in meaning than we today imagine. Finley explains the Latin *familia* as "all the persons, free or unfree, under the authority of the *paterfamilias,* the head of the household; or all the descendants from a common ancestor; or all one's property; or simply all one's servants."[25] We shall now see a simple correspondence. The economics of Judaism set forth in the Mishnah covers precisely those topics that, in antiquity, a book on economics was expected to treat. Clearly the mishnaic Hebrew for *paterfamilias* can only be *baal habayit,* householder, head of the house, and the economics of Judaism, set forth in the Mishnah and related writings, concerns the *baal habayit,* the master, or head, *baal,* of the house, *bayit,* the one who manages and controls the personnel and property of the house, without distinction as to economic or personal or social behavior.

To claim, however, that either the Mishnah's economics or Xenophon's corresponds to economics as we know the science exceeds the limits of the evidence. As Finley notes, "In Xenophon . . . there is not one sentence that expresses an economic principle or offers any economic analysis, nothing on efficiency of production, 'rational' choice, the marketing of crops."[26] But we shall see in due course considerable thought, in the Mishnah and related writings, on precisely that: what brings about increased production or causes scarcity. A theory of economics, absent in Xenophon and in other Greco-Roman writers on agronomics, encompasses and makes into a whole diverse observations on the right conduct of the household. Finley explains the absence of economics in a way important for our study.[27] He first cites Erich Roll's definition of economics: "If then we regard the economic system as an enormous conglomeration of interdependent markets, the central problem of economic enquiry becomes the explanation of the exchanging process, or, more particularly, the explanation of the formation of price." Finley then states, "But what if a society was not organized for the satisfaction of its material wants by 'an enormous conglomeration of interdependent markets'? It would then not be possible to discover or formulate laws . . . of economic behavior, without which a concept of 'the economy' is unlikely to develop, economic analysis impossible."[28]

We shall find out that the framers of the Mishnah conceived interdependent realms that formed a single, mutually interacting world of economic activity, in which scarcity found rational explanation and economic action found reasoned guidance by laws subject to testing and replication. Finley explains that ancient society produced no economic theory because "ancient society did not have an economic system which was an enormous conglomeration of interdependent markets. . . . There were no business cycles in antiquity; no cities whose growth can be ascribed, even by us, to the establishment of a manufacture; no 'Treasure by Foreign Trade,' to borrow the title of Thomas Mun's famous work stimulated by the depression of 1620–24. . . ."[29] But for their part sages recognized cycles of abundance and scarcity, if they did not call them business cycles; they explained the growth of cities by appeal to what was done in them, and understood a process of exchange between economic entities that by no grand leap of metaphor we may readily identify as foreign

trade. Sages most certainly understood the principles of market economics as
they affected the market mechanism and manipulated those principles to
achieve their own goals, as the following story indicates:

A. A pair of birds in Jerusalem went up in price to a gold denar.
B. Said Rabban Simeon b. Gamaliel, 'By this sanctuary! I shall not rest
    tonight until they shall be sold at silver denars.'
C. He entered the court and taught, 'The woman who is subject to five
    confirmed miscarriages or five confirmed fluxes brings only a single
    offering, and she eats animal sacrifices, and the rest of the offerings
    do not remain as an obligation for her.'
D. And pairs of birds stood on that very day at a quarter-denar each, one
    hundredth of the former price, [the demand having been drastically
    reduced].

(M. K. 1.7K–Q)

The story shows that sages recognized the effect upon prices of diminished
demand and were prepared to intervene in the market. For, as in the present
case, cultic rules could create "artificial" demand, demand not related to the
production efficiency of the household. For example, if a rule for the selection
of a sacrificial animal set forth requirements difficult to meet with ordinary
beasts, e.g., a particular color, or a beast that had never worked, then such
beasts would command a far higher price than otherwise. And that is one way
in which the noneconomic considerations of the cult intervened in the normal
working of the market. Good examples of this phenomenon derive from the
red cow, to be burned for the creation of ash for purification water, Num.
19:1ff./tractate Parah. The rules are various, e.g. as to age, color, condition,
and the cost of such a beast is measured in gold. At the same time, sages
legislated for the market in such a way as to intervene and set aside the market
mechanism altogether. They favored one that, in due course, we shall identify
as distributive.

There was exchange, the exchange bore concrete economic consequences,
and understanding the world as sages portrayed it in the Mishnah, we may
penetrate into that economic rationality that, in their system, corresponds,
point by point, with the rationality of economics as presently understood. To
claim that economics takes place only when people invoke our explanations
for phenomena, e.g., of trade, perceived by both them and us seems to me to
construe economics in a needlessly limited framework.

When Edgar Salin, cited by Finley, dismisses as null the economic explanations of antiquity, it is in my judgment a misunderstanding of correspondences.[30] Salin contrasted modern cyclical crises, which he called "rational
disturbances of a rational process," as Finley says, "with ancient crises, always attributed to natural catastrophes, divine anger, or political distur-
bance." But when the ancient thinkers invoked divine anger, they dealt, in
their setting, with facts of life, and they also proposed rational explanations—

that is, appealed to laws that described rational disturbances of a rational process. Such laws, they held, can be discovered and invoked. Their theory of rational action in regard to scarcity, its causes and its cures, addressed phenomena comparable to those we take up; that same theory yielded systematic action, in accord with rules; and for the system, the rules formed part of a larger, cogent construction of the social world. The subject matter, scarcity, the mode of thought, rational consideration of rational action—these remain constant for ancient and modern economists. What differs is the rationality in structure and contents, but not in process and not in application. The emphasis, therefore, must rest upon the inner rationality of a system, and the task, to uncover what, within the system, made the systemic rationality rational: how did economics in its realm express the rationality of the system as a whole and contribute to that system? To state matters in a way I find more appropriate: how does a detail of the system attest to the rationality of the whole? And how does the system as a whole impose its inner structure upon the detail at hand? In addressing the economics of the Mishnah as an economics, I mean to see how, in this matter too, the system of the Mishnah does its work on an important component of the world subject to composition and construction by the Mishnah—but also by the world of the West.

At issue is the discovery and explanation of patterns, whether of weather or of the market economy, whether of good health or of scarcity or of abundance. Systemic rationality explains in a manner amply demonstrated within the system why things happen one way, rather than some other. To deny to explanations of the weather the classification of meteorology, or to the working of the economy as the system describes and explains it the classification of economics, or to counsel on health and sickness the classification of medicine or therapy, hardly finds justification in the appeal to mere difference. True, their economics, meteorology, and medicine differed from ours. And no one can expect today to learn anything important about economics, meteorology, or medicine from ancient writings. But if we hope to understand the systems made by others, we have to grasp that in their systems economics, meteorology, and medicine found a place—indeed, I should maintain, had to find a place for the systems to compose the world that they proposed to construct.

Now, before we turn to the received theoretical writings on ancient economics, let me review my program. I do not pretend to describe the Jews' economy in the land of Israel in the second century, to which the Mishnah testifies in some measure. While the Mishnah contains important facts, in the form of premises and inert presuppositions, about the conduct of economic affairs, what makes the Mishnah interesting for economic theory is its utilization of topics of economic theory in the formation of its larger system. To that matter how things actually were is not very important, except after the fact. Nor can I pursue the inviting path opened by Polanyi and his co-workers, which we shall presently survey.[31] Aided by accounts of how ancient writers thought about economics as a matter of theory, I ask a somewhat different question of the Mishnah, which is, as is clear, in two parts. First comes the descriptive question. What are the components of the Mishnah's framers' theory of economics, defining economics in a conventional way, but allowing the definition to encompass (to us) unconventional topics? These, we shall see, encompass the two distinct theories, distributive and market economics. And that fact leads me to my second question. How can I account for the appeal to these two distinct theories?

If we ask what the system says through its economic theory, we frame a question concerning economics that seems to me accessible and indicative for the larger study of the Judaism of the dual Torah. For in that way, from the standpoint of systemic analysis of economics, we see the dimensions of that household, that *oikos* or *bayit,* on earth but also transcending this world, that the framers of the Mishnah proposed to describe. We now realize that, in a general way, the topical program of the Mishnah corresponds in important tractates to the topical program of an ancient treatise on economics. But that rather general observation only opens the question. To locate the conventional side to the Mishnah's authors' economics, we have now to find out how their economics fit into ideas on economics characteristic of the ancient world.

they valued, and money wealth, liquid capital and movables, which they did not value so highly. The war against Troy, for Thucydides, involved the wealth of the community measured in land and its products, quantities of arms, treasures, utensils, metal, and large houses and slaves. In the time of the Peloponnesian War wealth was in the form of coin, which could command all forms of real wealth.[16] But the economic theory of the important philosophers was primitive and unimportant in their larger work, which concerned politics, not economics. General principles with bearing on economic theory or policy, of course, can be identified, e.g., the recognition of the subjective and relative character of utility by Democritus.[17] Plato's ideas on economic subjects are random.[18] Joseph A. Schumpeter introduces Greco-Roman economics with these words: "rudimentary economic analysis is a minor element—a very minor one—in the inheritance that has been left to us by our cultural ancestors, the ancient Greeks."[19] The reason for that fact, many maintain, is that prior to the development of the market, economic activities were insufficiently differentiated to attract particular attention.[20] As we already have observed, when writers such as Xenophon, all the more so the Romans later on, spoke about economics, they provided rules for household management, observation rather than analysis.[21] When Aristotle refers to *chrēmatistikē*, he discusses pecuniary aspects of business activity.[22] Economic thought forms a small part of a larger general philosophy of state and society. Plato envisaged an essentially steady-state economy within a stationary population. In that context each person would have an inalienable allotment of land, given to a single heir, so as to keep the family intact and its property intact as well.[23] He sought in general to preserve a social equilibrium, with a limited, and not increasing, number of citizens. Plato proposed to describe economics within the context of the ideal state, which was to be large enough "to allow appropriate scope for the play of each man's natural talent."[24] That is why a small state was adequate. In that context, Schumpeter describes Plato's perfect state:

> Plato's Perfect State was a City-State conceived for a small, and, so far as possible, constant number of citizens. As stationary as its population was to be its wealth. All economic and non-economic activity was strictly regulated—warriors, farmers, artisans . . . being organized in permanent castes, men and women being treated exactly alike. Government was entrusted to one of these castes, the caste of guardians or rulers who were to live together without individual property or family ties.[25]

Schumpeter explains the "rigid stationarity" by appealing to Plato's dislike of "the chaotic changes of his time. . . . Change, economic change, was at the bottom of the development from oligarchy to democracy, from democracy to tyranny."[26] (We shall find a remarkable counterpart in the stasis, the steady-state world, which the framers of the Mishnah envision for themselves, in the setting of the second century, after the catastrophic war of 66–73 and 132–135.) Plato's caste system rests upon the perception of the necessity of some division of labor. The emphasis lies upon the "increase of efficiency that results from allowing everyone to specialize in what he is by nature best fitted for." Plato's theory of money is that the value of money is on principle independent of the stuff it is made of.[27]

Aristotle, the important economic thinker in antiquity, proposed to think through the requirements of the state, and it is in that context, as with Plato, that his economic thought went forward, once more that political economy that characterizes the Mishnah's system as well. In that context, he dealt with property and the art of managing the household that we should find in Greek called by the word economics. The fundamental of Aristotle's economics is the distinction between *oikonomikē*, economics, and *chrēmatistikē*, the former involving wealth consumed in the satisfaction of wants and the use of commodities or goods for that purpose, the latter, wealth-getting, money-making, and exchange.[28] As to "chrematistics," there are both natural and unnatural ways of doing things, the former, barter, the latter, through retail trade and money making. Exchange is natural, therefore. Things have a primary and a secondary use; the primary use of a shoe is for wearing, the secondary, for trading or exchanging. As to value, Plato had maintained that one "should not attempt to raise the price, but simply ask the value," while Aristotle introduces the notion of subjective value and the usefulness of the commodity: "In the truest and most real sense, this standard lies in wants, which is the basis of all association among men."[29]

So Haney: "An exchange is just when each gets exactly as much as he gives the other; yet this equality does not mean equal costs, but equal wants."[30] In book 5 of the *Nicomachean Ethics* and book 1 of the *Politics,* economic analysis, a subsection of other matters, comes to the fore. In the *Ethics,* Aristotle treats economics in the context of justice. Aristotle concerns himself with distributive justice, e.g., involving honors, goods, and other possessions. Justice means equality. Corrective justice involves private relations between individuals, in which "it may be necessary to 'straighten out' a situation, to rectify an injustice by removing the (unjust) gain and restoring the loss."[31] Aristotle had in mind fraud or breach of contract, not an "unjust" price.[32] In the *Politics,* Aristotle addresses as the context in which (fair) exchange is discussed the forms of human association, which are the household and, made up of households, the *polis.* Here he deals with issues of authority—dominance and subjection—which form the center of political theory. And in that context he treats, also, property and acquiring it, asking whether "the art of acquiring" property is the same as "the art of household management," that *oikonomikē* which we met earlier.[33] What Aristotle contributed to economic theory covers the economic organization of society, the matter of communal versus private property, and value and exchange.[34] On this latter topic, Spiegel states:

> Aristotle makes the important distinction between use and exchange, which later was to be expanded into the distinction between value in use and value in exchange.

The true and proper use of goods . . . is the satisfaction of natural wants. A secondary or improper use occurs when goods are exchanged for the sake of monetary gain. Thus, all exchanges for monetary gain are labeled as unnatural. This includes specifically commerce and transportation, the employment of skilled and unskilled labor, and lending at interest. The exchange of money for a promise to pay back the principal with interest is considered the most unnatural one. . . . Lending at interest yields gain from currency itself instead of from another exchange transaction which money as a medium of exchange is designed to facilitate. Money begets no offspring; if nevertheless there is one—interest—this is contrary to all nature.[35]

The essential point, Spiegel notes, is the emphasis on the mutuality of give and take. Each gives to the other something equivalent to what he receives from the other.

Aristotle defines wealth as "a means, necessary for the maintenance of the household and the *polis* (with self-sufficiency a principle in the background), and, like all means, it is limited by its ends." [36] Money makes possible exchange, and, as we just noted, Aristotle regards usury, e.g., consumer loans, as the practice of the art of money-making in an unnatural way: interest makes money increase, and that violates the purpose of money, which is merely for the sake of exchange. Exchange by itself is natural: "shortages and surpluses . . . were corrected by mutual exchange. . . . When used in this way, the art of exchange is not contrary to nature, nor in any way a species of the art of money making. It simply served to satisfy the natural requirements of self-sufficiency." [37] Profit is made not according to nature but at the expense of others. Aristotle in general insists on the "unnaturalness of commercial gain," and Aristotle therefore does not consider the rules or mechanics of commercial exchange: "Of economic analysis there is not a trace." [38]

As Finley notes, we cannot translate the abstraction "the economy" into Greek—any more than, as we shall see, we can into the Hebrew of the Mishnah (though we can into contemporary Hebrew). And Finley's judgment of Xenophon as an economist is already before us: "In Xenophon there is not one sentence that expresses an economic principle or offers any economic analysis, nothing on the efficiency of production, 'rational' choice, the marketing of crops." [39] The argument of Lowry is that "the ancient Greeks developed many of the analytical formulations basic to modern economic theory and that the discipline of economics is heavily indebted to them." [40] We need not take up a position on that disagreement. It is clear that Finley's judgment pertains to what we have in hand, not what the Enlightenment economic theorists made of what the Greeks left, which, it would appear, was more than meets the eye.

Aristotle simply divided the art of acquisition into *oikonomia* and money making, and what survived was the manual of the household such as that of Xenophon's, which we noted above. From that kind of writing, economics could not come, for the reason given by Finley: "Without the concept of relevant 'laws' (or 'statistical uniformities' if one prefers) it is not possible to have a concept of 'the economy.'" [41] Finley's explanation for that fact is of interest to us, since it will in due course provide perspective on the document of our concern. He sees it as a consequence of the idea of *koinonia*, a perspective already familiar to us in Polanyi's reading of matters. *Koinonia* was

> a heavy encroachment by political and status demands on the behavior of ordinary Greeks. . . . If we consider investment, for example, we immediately come up against a political division of the population that was unbridgeable. All Greek states . . . restricted the right of land ownership to their citizens. . . . They thereby . . . erected a wall between the land, from which the great majority of the population received their livelihood, and that very substantial proportion of the money available for investment which was in the hands of non-citizens.

The upshot was that money-holding citizens turned to the land "from considerations of status, not of maximization of profits," while "the non-citizens [kept off the land] of necessity lived by manufacture, trade and moneylending."[43] The consequence—to abbreviate Finley's interesting argument—is that "what we call the economy was properly the exclusive business of outsiders."[44] Aristotle favors private property over communal property on five grounds: progress, peace, pleasure, practice, and philanthropy.[45] None of these has any bearing upon economic theory or policy, except for progress: "Private property is more highly productive than commual property. . . . Goods that are owned by a large number of people receive little care. People are inclined to consider chiefly their own interest and are apt to neglect a duty that they expect others to fulfill."[46]

This rapid review of Aristotle on economics in hand, we turn to the interesting analysis of Aristotle's economics by Joseph Schumpeter. Aristotle impressed Schumpeter as a figure of "more than slightly pompous common sense."[47] But the analytic intention makes him an interesting figure. As to economic problems, the interest was subordinate; social and political analysis predominated in his program. Schumpeter said of Aristotle's general contribution to social science:

> [1] that not only was Aristotle, like a good analyst, very careful about his concepts but that he also coordinated his concepts into a conceptual apparatus, that is, into a system of tools of analysis that were related to one another and were meant to be used together. . . ; [2] that . . . he investigated processes of change as well as states; [3] that he tried to distinguish between features of social organisms or of behavior that exist by virtue of universal or inherent necessity and others that are instituted by legislative decision or custom; [4] that he discussed social institutions in terms of purposes and of the advantages and disadvantages they seemed to him to present.[48]

Aristotle's economics, in *Politics* I.8–11 and *Ethics* 5.5, present an economic analysis based upon wants and their satisfactions. "Starting from the economy of self-sufficient households, he then introduced division of labor, barter, and, as a means of overcoming the difficulties of direct barter, money—the error of confusing wealth with money duly coming in for stricture. There is no theory of 'distribution.'"[49]

As to value, Aristotle distinguished value in use and value in exchange and saw the latter as derivative of the former. But there was no theory of price and the ethics of price. This theory of an intrinsic or fixed value, which will concern us, is treated by Schumpeter in these words:

> Aristotle . . . sought for a canon of justice in pricing, and he found it in the "equivalence" of what a man gives and receives. Since both parties to an act of barter or sale must necessarily gain by it in the sense that they must prefer their economic situations after the act to the economic situations in which they found themselves before the act—or else they would not have any motive to perform it— there can be no equivalence between the "subjective" or utility values of the goods exchanged or between the good and the money paid or received for it.[50]

Schumpeter denies that Aristotle has in mind "some mysterious Objective or Absolute Value of things that is intrinsically inherent in them and independent of circumstances or human valuations or actions." He argues that Aristotle "simply thought of the exchange values of the market, as *expressed* in terms of money, rather than of some mysterious value substance *measured* by those exchange values." Schumpeter sets forth his reading of matters as follows: "his concept of the just value of a commodity is indeed 'objective,' but only in the sense that no individual can alter it by his own action."

We find ourselves on familiar ground. For example, Schumpeter explains that an equality in every act of exchange or sale involves the following:

> If A barters shoes for B's loaves of bread, Aristotelian justice requires that the shoes equal the loaves when both are multiplied by their normal competitive prices; if A sells the shoes to B for money, the same rule will determine the amount of money he ought to get. Since . . . A would actually get this amount, we have before us an instructive instance of the relation which, with Aristotle himself and a host of followers, subsists between the logical and the normal ideal and between the "natural" and the "just."[51]

In denying the notion of an objective or absolute or intrinsic value, Schumpeter calls that notion "a metaphysical entity most welcome to people with philosophical propensities and most distasteful to people of a more 'positive' type of mind."[52] In due course, we shall see how that notion comes to expression in the economics of Judaism. There, the conception of a true value is not murky or obscure but expressed in simple and plain words: concrete rules, which people (merchants in the market) had to observe.

Taking the view of money opposite to that of Plato, Aristotle took the position that the exchange of goods and services in barter is not always possible. People may not have what other people want, and so have to offer in exchange, or accept in exchange, "what one does not want in order to get what one does want by means of a further act of barter (indirect exchange)." But money is not wealth, it is merely a medium of exchange; money does not satisfy the necessities of life.[53] It is merely the inconvenience of barter that yields the development of money as a medium of exchange. Some commodities, such as metals, may serve better than others.

As Schumpeter presents the matter, Aristotle's theory of money therefore regards money as principally a medium of exchange. In order to serve as a medium of exchange in markets of goods, money itself must be one of those goods:

> It must be a thing that is useful and has exchange value independently of its monetary function, . . . a value that can be compared with other values . . . . Thus the money commodity goes by weight and quality as do other commodities; for convenience people may decide to put a stamp on it in order to save the trouble of having to weigh it every time, but this stamp only declares and guarantees the quantity and quality of the commodity contained in a coin and is not the cause of its value.[54]

Money then takes the place of barter, but it is a kind of barter.[55] Money was a medium of exchange eliminating the need to barter. That was the natural use of money:

> There are two sorts of wealth-getting: . . . one is a part of household management, the other is retail trade. The former is necessary and honorable, while that which consists in exchange is justly censured; for it is unnatural, and a means by which men gain from one another. The most hated sort . . . is usury, which makes a gain out of money itself, and not from the natural object of it. For money was intended to be used in exchange, but not to increase at interest.
>
> (*Politics* 1258a–b)[56]

Since Plato held, as Schumpeter reads him, that the value of money is independent of the stuff of which it is made, we have here a point of difference to direct to the Mishnah's authors as well: do they understand the value of money, in our terms, to be intrinsic to the coin, as with Aristotle, or to be functional and imputed, therefore extrinsic, as with Plato? The third point of interest in Aristotle, besides the question of true value and the theory of money, concerns interest. Schumpeter states, "Aristotle accepted the empirical fact of interest on money loans and saw no problem in it." [57] He made no effort to classify loans by their purposes and saw no difference between a consumer loan and a producer loan. He simply condemned interest ("usury" in all cases), "on the ground that there was no justification for money, a mere medium of exchange, to increase in going from hand to hand. . . . But he never asked the question why interest was being paid all the same. Aristotle had no theory of interest." [58]

The Mishnah came forth in a Greek-speaking world, and its framers appear to have known little or no Latin. Lekachman sums up the opinion of all historians of economic theory: "Rome developed nothing new in the sphere of theoretical economics. . . . There was much the same relation between their economic writings and economic analysis as between the art of business management and the abstruse economic theory of the graduate school." [59] His survey of maxims makes the point full well. Lekachman and others find little of theoretical interest in the economics in the sense of household management left by Cato, Cicero, and others. While well informed as to the facts of the agricultural economy in the narrow sense just now introduced, namely, rules of household management and agronomy, they presumably had no access to technical treatises on the rural economy, e.g., producing wine and oil and grain, such as were written by Cato, Varro, and Columella, in the tradition of Xenophon.[60] When we consider the economic thought upon which the Mishnah's authors drew, the premises that guided concrete decisions, we shall not find reason to regret their slight knowledge of the then ruling state and its economics, for, in Schumpeter's judgment, all that has to be explained in Roman economics is the absence of analytic work.[61]

Roman law, which is quite another matter than Roman economics, dealt with economic issues only episodically: "jurists analyzed facts and produced principles that were not only normative but also . . . explanatory. They created a juristic logic that proved to be applicable to a wide variety of social patterns." True, the law warned buyers to take measures to avoid being cheated but the buyer had no recourse except in the case of misrepresentation: "it was the doctrine of the jurists that each might seek to overreach the other in the matter of price."[62] But we find no interest in defining overreaching or its causes. There was, however, the concept of a just or real price, *verum pretium*.[63] So far as their facts were economic, their analysis was economic analysis. "Unfortunately, the scope of this analysis was strictly limited by the practical purposes they had in view, which is why their generalizations yielded legal principles but not also economic ones."[64] We cannot therefore speak of an economic theory of the *corpus juris*.

On the other hand, writings on agriculture covered economic subjects, as we noted with Xenophon. None of these writers produced economic theory or appealed to theory at all, even though they made practical observations that economic analysis could have precipitated, e.g., profitable use of land depends on distance from the market or center of consumption.[65] Cynicism, Stoicism, and Epicureanism all contained episodic remarks on such subjects as possessions and their loss, slavery and exile, and the like; Cynicism aimed at "freedom from want" by "extinguishing desire and relinquishing possessions," but this has nothing to do with a theory of economics.[66] Stoicism, for its part, accepted the acquisition and care of property. The Epicureans for their part had profound remarks to make concerning pleasure, including the uses of wealth, but nothing to say about such critical issues as the household, markets, prices, and the like.[67]

The same may be said of Christianity. Since Jesus told his disciples to give up occupations and possessions (Mt. 4:18–22), and in numerous other passages showed indifference to economic considerations and disapproval of wealth, we should look in vain to Christian thinkers for systematic theories concerning the workings of the (or an) economy.[68] Condemnation of the rich, as at James 2:2–7, hardly qualifies as an economic theory. True, wealth may serve God's purpose, as Clement of Alexandria argues in "Who Is the Rich Man That May Be Saved?"[69] Some fathers of the church denounced private property; John Chrysostom, in the fourth century, "praised the economy of God, which made certain goods common to be shared equally by men as brothers. . . . As to wealth, it is questionable whether it can be acquired without injustice either on the part of the owner or of those from whom he inherited it." [70] Augustine saw wealth as a gift of God and a good; he held that private property was a creation of the state, a human, not a divine right. God really owns the world. [71] We find opinions concerning the workings of the economy, but no economics.

Schumpeter observes that Christian thought of the first six centuries produces no economics: "The opinions on economic subjects that we might find—such as that believers should sell what they have and give to the poor, or that they should lend without expecting anything . . . from it—are ideal imperatives that form part of a general scheme of life and express this general scheme and nothing else, least of all scientific propositions." [72] But even when we examine the great intellectuals of the tradition, we find no analysis of an economic character. The church fathers did preach against wanton luxury, in favor of charity and restraint. True, too, there may have been a theory behind such advice as that of Tertullian, "to content oneself with the simple products of domestic agriculture and industry instead of craving for imported luxuries or a theory of value behind his observation that abundance and rarity have something to do with price." [73] But if there was a theory, it never comes to expression or sustained exemplification.

While the great intellectuals of the church addressed the political problems of the Christian state, they did not attend to economics, so Schumpeter: "the How and Why of economic mechanisms were then of no interest either to its [the church's] leaders or to its writers." [74] When we turn to the Mishnah, therefore, we shall address to its authors the questions that are framed for us by the classic Greek theorists concerning economics, covering a variety of meanings for the word: the art of household management, making money, and the broader and more interesting questions of market, money, and the like, on which we find important ideas in Aristotle in particular. What we shall find is that, on economic issues defined conventionally, the sages of the Mishnah would have found a comfortable position alongside Aristotle and entirely within his program of topics for the theory of the economy.

We come now to the contemporary debate on the theories we have reviewed. The issue before modern scholarship is in two parts. First, can we speak of economics at all, in the sense in which today we use the word? In our context, was there such a thing as an economics of Judaism at all? Second, can we maintain, in the tradition of Polanyi, that prior to the time of Aristotle, there was anything like a market economics? Polanyi holds, as I pointed out in chapter 1, that for three thousand years distributive economics predominated. The contrary view, which, as I pointed out, has come to prevail, is that there was a dual economics through that long period, distributive economics, centered, for instance, on temples, priesthoods, governments, and bureaucrats, and also a market economics. The two were, of course, not of equal stature; distributive economics will be seen to have dominated thought of an economic character. My entire analysis rests on two premises. First, we can indeed describe an economics of Judaism, defining as its principal components a theory of the household, the market, and wealth. Second, that economics fits well into the established pattern of a mixed theory, distributive and market economics, and forms a striking example of how two theories coexist, side by side. Let me now spell out the terms of the first of the two debates.

On the one side, we find what Finley, citing Georgescu-Roegen, calls "a chemical doctrine of society," which claims "that all forms of society can be objectively analyzed into a finite number of immutable elements." [75] In that case, classifications of economic belief and behavior serve equally for all societies everywhere and at all times. That accounts for the numerous works on the economies of Greece and Rome. Finley rightly criticizes the best of them for omitting all reference, within the economic analysis, to the household, or *oikos,* the fundamental unit of production, e.g., in Mitchell, *The Economics of Ancient Greece* (New York: Macmillan, 1940). Michell covers these topics: agriculture, mining and minerals, labor, industry, commerce, trade in various products, money and banking, public finance, and the like, standard categories of fact gathering for economic analysis, to be sure. But how the economy worked, as distinct from how diverse components of an economy function, seems to me to emerge from the interplay of the irreducible and fundamental unit of production which also was the unit of society, the household, and other units of the economy. Without understanding the household, we do not know anything about the economy, even though large segments of the economy were conducted outside of the household.

Within that thesis, however, that all forms of society can be objectively analyzed into a finite number of immutable elements, we as a matter of fact find many chapters in the Mishnah that by any standard and definition fall into the classification of applied economics, e.g., on real estate law, on labor relations, on market transactions, on true value, on assigning a fixed price to goods, and on other issues of market relationships, and so for a long list of matters of theory conventionally deemed economics. But we misunderstand our data if we construe them as all that our system has to say about issues conventionally within the definition of economics. And, more to the point,— and let me state with emphasis—*when we have collected these data, we do not understand the economy envisaged by the framers of the Mishnah.* For that purpose, we have to invoke the categories of market economics to deal with one set of rules set forth by the Mishnah, those in the fourth division, on civil law, and also reread those same categories as they are recast by distributive economics, in the first division of the Mishnah, on agriculture. And that places me into opposition to Polanyi.

For, on the other side, we do contend with those who maintain that we cannot apply to antiquity a market-centered analysis, as Weber and Polanyi have argued.[76] That conception makes economics a theory defined by function and relative to the social world in which the theory is framed. It clearly represents a mode of thought congenial to the project at hand, covering as it does both conventional and unconventional components of a theory of the *oikos,* the household, and its laws, not to mention the meaning of wealth and how to assemble it. Let me cite, for example, the introductory statement of Karl Polanyi, Conrad M. Arensberg, and Harry W. Pearson, in *Trade and Market in the Early Empires.*

> Most of us have been accustomed to think that the hallmark of the economy is the market. . . . Similarly, our inquiries into general economic history have usually been concerned with market activities or their antecedents. What is to be done, though, when it appears that some economies have operated on altogether different principles, showing a widespread use of money and far-flung trading activities, yet no evidence of markets or gain made on buying and selling? It is then that we must reexamine our notions of the economy. The conceptual problem arises in market-less economies where there is no 'economizing,' i.e., no institutional framework to compel the individual to 'rational' and 'efficient' economic activity or 'optimum' allocation of his resources. . . . In that case the economy would not be subject to economic analysis, since this presumes economizing behavior with supporting institutional paraphernalia, e.g., price-making markets, all-purpose money and market trade. (p. xix)

I cannot imagine a more stunning statement of the position contrary to that of all who have written on Greek and Roman economic history and, by extension, economics (since the contents of economic history surely rest on a premise of an economics).[77] At the same time, the authors maintain that there are only a small number of alternative patterns for organizing man's livelihood.[78]

That is why we can consider diverse theories of economic organization. The inquiry of Polanyi is defined by Carney:

> Polanyi first identified the concepts, institutions, and processes which economists have shown to make up a self-regulating market system. He then asked: Do the societies of antiquity have words for these things? Do these societies have any institutions and processes which resemble those of this particular market system? It emerged that the societies of the ancient Near East had not, but that fifth-century (B.C.) Greece had evolved the beginnings of some such system. The next question was: What did the ancient Near East have, then? It emerged that exchanges of goods and services were handled by a redistributive system. A hint of a system of reciprocity also appeared in the Polanyi study.[79]

Carney notes that what Polanyi did was to draw a contrast "between three types of exchange systems—those involving the market, reciprocity, and redistribution." Reciprocity involves gift giving and related sanctions, e.g., the exchange of subsistence goods. Redistribution "involves a central institution which organizes production, then stores, redistributes, and trades . . . produce." "The most advanced form of exchange is that of the market," involving a marketplace and "an institutionally protected arena wherein goods and services are bartered to maximize the returns to buyers and sellers." The fourth type of exchange is "mobilization exchange[,] . . . taking of control over, and disposition of, a society's goods and services[,] . . . conducted by a society's elite . . . in the overall interests of that society. This takeover was liable to happen in any society in antiquity that was organized beyond the tribal level and was faced with a war or social crisis." As to money and barter, defined as "the direct exchange of real wealth," barter "goes with the household economy and subsistence farming. . . . The monetization of an economy depends upon 'the extent of the market,' the number and kinds of people who use money and the things which money can buy." A market is not a discrete entity "but rather just another such complex of attitudes and functions, varying over time. The range of goods and services purchasable increases over time. . . . So does the 'marketization' of thought—the extent to which activities are conceived in terms of a calculus of anticipated utilities."

Carney further notes, of special interest here:

> The development of marketization can only proceed as far as the basic institutions of the market matrix allow. And two basic economic building blocks were lacking in the economies of antiquity: the firm and the public service instrumentality. Instead, these economies relied upon the household or estate economy of the extended household and the regulative apparatus bureaucracy. . . . The dominant economic unit in ancient society was not the firm but the extended household, with its estate and household economy.[80]

We see that an economics of an ancient society becomes possible within the categories and classifications worked out by Polanyi and his co-workers. Whether or not the economics will have defined its classifications and assembled its data in the way in which those catalogued did the work I cannot claim to know; but we see a fresh and fundamental rethinking of matters of economics.

Finley for his part seeks "different concepts and different models, appropriate to the ancient economy, not (or not necessarily) to ours."[81] But it is hard for me to discern that Finley has learned a great deal from Polanyi and his colleagues. In general, my sense, from the rest of *The Ancient Economy,* is that Finley has given us not an economics but a fairly standard repertoire of economic topics, e.g., "orders and status," "masters and slaves," "landlords and peasants," "town and country," "the state and the economy." I am not clear on why Finley maintains that these represent anything other than the received categories into which information on economic topics is organized. "The state and the economy," for example, goes over such matters as the expenses of liturgical activity, decisions made by the state on economic matters, maritime commerce and the food supply, and so on and so forth. Finley refers to "the ancient economy," but so far as I can see, in the book he discusses details of this and that, but no large-scale description of a working economy, such as justifies appeal to the word "economy," in more than a very concrete sense of "this and that about wealth or scarcity, always construed in acute and concrete detail, and never subject to generalization." I see no economics without generalization, and here there is precious little. My sense is that Finley found it exceedingly difficult to move from detail to generalization.[82] But that, after all, is the problem that others have tried to work out, whether or not it was to Finley's satisfaction. To state matters simply, the problem of his opening chapter is not addressed in the rest of the book: where and how can we locate "the ancient economy" (and how it worked), as distinct from details of an economic character? My task at hand hardly demands that I respond to those questions. For this survey of the contemporary debate suffices to set the conditions for my two-stage description, analysis, and systemic interpretation of the economics of Judaism in its initial statement, treating the same categories, household, market, wealth, first one way, within the framework of market economics, then the other way, seen as components of a distributive economics.

In seeing matters in this way, I do not mean to suggest that the sages of the Mishnah knew what Greek philosophers or Roman legislators had to say about economics or about transactions of an economic character, respectively. For it remains to make the simple and obvious observation that the authors of the Mishnah did not have to go to an academy to study philosophy or to a law school to learn economics, such as the field, in theory, consisted of in Greco-Roman antiquity. They had only to open Scripture to find a variety of rules and regulations of an economic character.[83] A very brief reminder of the well-known topics calls to the fore recognition of how much within Scripture would have found resonance for the Greek and Roman philosophers and legislators. Mosaic law recognized usury and forbade it within Israelite life (Dt. 23:19–20). One might not lend money upon usury nor lend commodities for increase (Lev. 25:37). Usury meant lending things over time and getting back three shekels for two or three bushels for two.[84] Lending was a kind of charity (Dt. 15:7–9). Scripture also provided evidence for the conception of a just price, at least so far as just weights and measures are concerned. A well-regulated market does not permit adulteration of produce. The notion that real wealth meant real estate came to expression, e.g., in the saying, "He who tills the soil will have plenty of food" (Prov. 12:11). Trade and commerce were deemed things outsiders, e.g., Canaanites, did (Hos. 12:7–8).

That economic gain formed only one consideration in the organization of society is shown by the institution of the Sabbath, on which people had to cease from productive labor, and of the seventh, or sabbatical, and the jubilee years, in which the land had to be left fallow. Yet these rules were persistently explained as part of the economic plan governing the world, and, in consequence of keeping these rules, people would prosper, while, not keeping them, they would suffer want. Accordingly, we have to take account of taboos, particularly as these affected production and the organization of units of production, as part of the economics of the system. Take for example the effects of the seventh year, perceived to reduce agricultural production, but not presented as part of the natural economy. In the seventh year the land had a Sabbath; leaving the fields fallow, we know, restored fertility. But in that same year debts were remitted (Dt. 15:4). That had nothing to do with the fertility of the soil, and the social utility of the remission of debts was not self-evident to lenders, who declined to lend money as the seventh year approached, so the Mishnah's authors claim. Not only so, but, like Plato, the pentateuchal legislators imagined that land was to remain within its "original" family, so that at the fiftieth year, everyone might return to his possession (Lev. 25:13). Land was to be rented, not permanently sold.

Reflection on these and similar rules, however, viewed as systematically not inert but active, will have led to such conceptions as that "stationarity" of society so important to Plato and, as a matter of fact, also to the framers of the Mishnah, and that broader spectrum of thought about the question of intrinsic or true value that interested Aristotle and his successors. But these rules did not yield economics, in the sense in which Aristotle presented something very like the economics, as a matter of theory, that such exemplary minds as Schumpeter and Finley take to form a counterpart of interest to modern economic theory. They yielded only ethics, and, as we have seen in our swift glance at the New Testament and the fathers of Christianity, ethics is not the same thing as economics. There was no Christian economics, but as I shall now show, point by point, there assuredly *was* in the initial statement, set forth by the Mishnah's authors, an economics of Judaism, that is to say, an economic component, of considerable theoretical sophistication, of the Judaism of the dual Torah.[85] And, in light of the common and correct judgment, framed for us here by Edwin Cannan, that fact must win our attention: "But though much of economic interest might be found in those old legends and records, I doubt if the most patient research even if combined with a fairly active imagination would find in them much with which to fill a doctoral dissertation on 'Ancient Jewish Economic Theory.'"[86] In the next four chapters I shall try to prove him wrong—if not by much.

4

The Mishnah's Market Economics

The Household

In terms, then, of our modern speech Aristotle's approach to human affairs was sociological. In mapping out a field of study he would relate all questions of institutional origin and function to the totality of society.

Karl Polanyi[1]

The encompassing and ubiquitous householder, a technical classification defined presently, is the Mishnah's authors' most characteristic invention of social thought. Ancient Israelite thinkers of the same order, e.g., the priestly authors of Leviticus, the prophetic schools that produced Isaiah's and Amos's conceptions, discerned within, and as, "Israel" classes identified by their sacerdotal and genealogical traits and functions, in relationship to other classes, or a mixed multitude of poor and rich.[2] We look in vain in the imagination of the deuteronomist writers in their several layers for a conception of an "Israel" composed of neatly arranged farms run by landowners, of families made up of households, an Israel with each such household arrayed in its hierarchy, from householder on top to slave on bottom. But that is how the authors of the Mishnah see things, a vision unique in the context of thought on society and economy in all Judaic writings of antiquity.

Indeed, while the pentateuchal composite encompasses issues of political economy, its focus is not upon those issues. By contrast, critical to the system of the Mishnah is its principal social entity, the village, comprising households, and the model, from household to village to "all Israel," comprehensively describes whatever of "Israel" the authors at hand have chosen to describe. We have therefore to identify as systemically indicative the centrality of political economy—community, self-sufficiency, and justice—within the system of the Mishnah. It is no surprise, either, that the point of originality of the political economy of the Mishnah's system is its focus upon the society organized in relationship to the control of the means of production—the farm, for the household is always the agricultural unit.

We realize, in the context of social thought of ancient times, that this systemic focus upon political economy also identifies the Mishnah with the prevailing conventions of a long-ago and a far-away land. For, as we recall from the preceding chapter, it was a world in which thinkers represented by Aristotle took for granted that society was formed of self-sufficient villages, made up of self-sufficient farms: households run by householders. But, we know, in general, nothing can have been further from the facts of the world of "Israel," that is, the Jews in the land of Israel, made up as it was of not only villages but cities, not only small but larger holders, and, most of all, people who held no land at all and never would.

Let us now turn, in the context of a world of pervasive diversity, to the Mishnah's authors' fantastic conception of a simple world of little blocks formed into big ones: households into villages, no empty spaces, but also, no vast cities (for a reason characteristic of the system as a whole, as I shall specify presently). In this conception community, or village (*polis*), is made up of households, and the household (*bayit/oikos*) constituted the building block of both society, or community, and economy.[3] It follows that the household forms the fundamental, irreducible, and, of course, representative unit of the economy, the means of production, the locus and the unit of production.

We should not confuse the household with class status, e.g., thinking of the householder as identical with the wealthy. The opposite is suggested on every page of the Mishnah, in which householders vie with craftsmen for ownership of the leavings of the loom and the chips left behind by the adze. The household, rather, forms an economic and a social classification, defined by function, specifically, economic function. A poor household was a household, and (in theory; the Mishnah's authors know none such in practice) a rich landholding that did not function as a center for a social and economic unit, e.g., a rural industrial farm, was not a household.[4] The household constituted "the center of the productive economic activities we now handle through the market."[5] Within the household all local (as distinct from cultic) economic (therefore social) activities and functions were held together. For the unit of production comprised also the unit of social organization and, of greater import still, the building block of all larger social, now also political, units, with special reference to the village.

In the conception at hand, which sees Israel as made up, on earth, of households and villages, the economic unit also framed the social one, and the two together composed, in conglomerates, the political one, hence a political economy (*polis, oikos*), initiated within an economic definition formed out of the elements of production. The Mishnah makes the single cogent statement that the organizing unit of society and politics finds its definition in the irreducible unit of economic production. The Mishnah conceives no other economic unit of production than the household, though it recognizes that such existed; its authors perceived no other social unit of organization than the household and the conglomeration of households, though that limited vision omitted all reference to substantial parts of the population perceived to be present, e.g., craftsmen, the unemployed, the landless, and the like.

The social foundation of the economy of the Mishnah therefore rested on the household.[6] The household in turn formed the foundation of the village, imagined to comprise the community of households, in the charge of small farmers who were free and who owned their land.[7] In fact, the entire economics of Judaism in its initial statement addresses only the social world formed by this "household." Time and again we shall find no economics pertaining to commercial, professional, manufacturing, or trading, let alone laboring, persons and classes. "The household" is a technical term, and landless workers, teachers, physicians, merchants, shopkeepers, traders, craftsmen, and the like cannot, by definition, constitute, or even affiliate with, a household: an amazingly narrow economics indeed. The definition of the market and its working, and the conception of wealth, viewed within both market and distributive economics, sort out affairs only as these pertain to the household. That is to say that the economics of Judaism omitted reference to most of the Jews, on the one side, and the economic activities and concerns of labor and capital alike, on the other. The system at hand simply treats these formidable components of the social entity "Israel," from an economic perspective, as null. In the pages of the Mishnah, as we shall see, no one else but the householder and his establishment plays a role in economic thinking—except in relationship to that householder. In passages in which proprietary responsibilities and obligations play no role, e.g., matters having to do with the cult, religious observance, the sacred calendar, and the like, by contrast, the Mishnah's authors speak not of the householder but of "he who," of "a man," or of other neutral building blocks of society, not defined in terms of proprietary status of landholding.

Whether, in fact, all "Israel," that is, the Jews in the land of Israel, lived in such villages or towns made up of a neat array of householders and their dependents, we do not know. But, self-evidently, it is difficult to imagine a reality composed of such a neat arrangement of building blocks, and the Mishnah's authors recognize that the village consisted of more than households and householders, while at the same time recognizing that "household" forms an abstract entity, not a concrete and material social fact. Not only so, but, even without such passages, we should find it exceedingly difficult to imagine a society made up wholly of small holders and people assembled in neat array around them, a society or community lacking such other social categories as large holders, landless workers in appreciable numbers, craftsmen laboring for a market independent of the proprietary one of householders, and numerous other categories of production and classifications of persons in relationship to means of production. That makes all the more indicative of the character of the mishnaic system and its thought the fact that we deal with a single block, a single mold and model. In imagining a society which surely encompassed diverse kinds of person, formed in various molds and in accord with a range of models, the authors of the Mishnah have made their statement of its vision, and that vision dictates the focus and requirements of analysis.

That "household" as the building block of the village (the two fundamental units of Israelite society) is an abstraction, not a concrete physical or social entity, e.g., a house separate from other houses, a family distinct from other families, is easy to demonstrate. It simply is not a concrete description of how people really lived, for instance, of the spatial arrangements of houses, or of the social units made up of distinct household-houses (or families as equivalent to households). The supposition of Mishnah-tractate Erubin, for example, is that households are in a village, that people live cheek by jowl in courtyards and go out into the fields from the village. So the notion of the isolated farmstead is absent here. That is important in relating the household to the village, *oikos* to *polis,* and it also shows how abstract is the conception of the household, since it is conceived as a unit, even though, in fact, the households were not abstract and distinct units at all.

The singularity of the household was not in its physical, let alone genealogical traits, but in its definition as a distinct unit of economic production. What made a household into a household was its economic definition as a whole and complete unit of production, and the householder was the one who controlled that unit of production; that economic fact made all the difference, and not that all of the household's members were related (that was not the fact at all), nor that all of them lived in a single building distinct from other single buildings. What made the household into a social unit was the economic fact that, among its constituents, all of them worked within the same economic unit and also worked in a setting distinct from other equivalently autonomous economic units. In the idiom of the Mishnah, they ate at the same table, and eating should be understood as an abstraction, not merely as a reference to the fact that people sat down and broke bread together. That seems to me an interesting point. Nor is the household of which courtyards are composed necessarily only Jewish: "He who dwells in the same courtyard with a gentile, or with an Israelite who does not concede the validity of the *erub*" (M. Er. 6:1). This concession of householder status to the gentile neighbor in a courtyard once more underlines the economic, and functional, definition of the household, rather than its genealogical and cultic meaning.[8] The premise of the household as an autonomous unit and building block of society contradicts the realities described by the Mishnah's framers. The social unit of the courtyard has numerous cultic implications, but it is not an econoomic unit and is not recognized as such. "The householder" has no counterpart in "the shareholder of a courtyard." The one forms an economic unit, the other does not; e.g., in M. Er. 6:3–4, the courtyard is a cultic unit, bearing no economic weight whatsoever. This again shows us the precision in use of the terms "household" and "householder"—the precision, but also the utter abstraction of the conception.

Two divisions, the first and the fourth (Agriculture and Civil Law, Zeraim and Neziqin, respectively), alone form the center of discourse on the householder. These are the divisions that take up transactions in property and the disposition of wealth. In the divisions that attend to cultic considerations (the fifth, sixth, and second) and in the third division (on the conduct of family affairs, Women), "the householder" is not the subject of a great many predicates. The reason is that at issue in the Agriculture and Civil Law divisions are the disposition of wealth, which is agricultural, on the one side, and commercial transactions, real estate and farming exchanges, and the like, on the other. These form the center of discussion of issues we should today deem economic, such as marketing and prices, laws governing real estate transactions and labor law, selling and buying, disposition of wealth, and conduct in the use of material goods. The other divisions do not concern the disposition of material property and, it follows, also do not find occasion to speak frequently of householders in particular. They then find a different fixed subject for diverse predicates, one that is economically neutral and applicable to persons without reference to considerations of property holding. It follows that "householder" is a very specific classification of person, with a particular definition, playing a role in discourse mainly when issues of property and substance have to be sorted out.

Let me give a few examples of the foregoing generalization (omitting reference to the division on civil law). "The householder" or "proprietor" occurs in passages in which reference is made to: the farmer, in charge of his estate and disposing of the produce of his field (as at M. Pe. 3:5 and elsewhere in that tractate, and throughout other tractates in the division of Agriculture, e.g., Terumot, Maaserot, Maaser Sheni, Orlah); business partnerships among farmers (M. Er. 7:5); rights of householders to make use of their own houses (M. Bes. 3:5); provision of support for various persons at the table of a householder (M. Git. 5:4); the intention of the householder, here meaning the owner of a beast, hence, the farmer, concerning the disposition of his beast (M. Me. 6:1); household objects (M. Kel. 15:1); and the like. By contrast, we only rarely find allusions to the householder in such tractates as Shabbat, on Sabbath law, and Erubin, on the same (and here peoples' residences are very much in evidence, but the common point of reference is to dwelling in a courtyard, made up of many houses). These results of a very rough survey of ways in which the word *baal* is used in the Mishnah suggest that most, though not all, usages bearing the sense of householder, that is, *baal habbayit*, occur in the divisions Agriculture and Civil Law, with parallel usages to the ones in Agriculture occurring also in Holy Things, and for the same reason, namely, a concern with the farmer's disposition of his crop.[9]

By "household" the framers of the Mishnah meant one kind of unit of production, specifically, a landholder engaged in agriculture, essentially a subsistence farmer, but one with some relationships to a sheltering market beyond. The household must be understood as an abstraction, not as a concrete and material social entity. This is in two senses. First, while the household was assumed to be a farming unit, in fact the householder was imagined to live in town. There was no distinction between country and town that affected the definition of the householder. Second, while the household was treated as an autonomous entity, in fact, the law takes for granted that houses are formed into courtyards, and none is taken to be freestanding. While, therefore, the householder formed the autonomous and formative entity of economic life, and while the household was taken to constitute an identifiable entity, the household did not exist in separation from other households, and hence its autonomy and distinct status were a matter of theoretical, not concrete and material, reality—a systemic fact alone.

As to the actualities of social life, the fundamental premise of all social discourse in the Mishnah is that Israelites lived side by side in villages or towns, the latter different from the former only by size. For cultic reasons the system could not differentiate between small and large settlements, e.g., towns and cities, or villages and towns (except for adventitious purposes), but only between Jerusalem and everywhere else. For the system formed an exercise in the study of sanctification and its effects, and therefore, for systemic reasons, Jerusalem was *the* city, and its "city-ness" derived from its holiness.[10] "City" therefore formed a cultic, not a sociological, category. It follows that the distinction between town and village, or town and country, made no difference whatsoever to the authors of the Mishnah. It was a distinction that made no systemic difference. What mattered was solely that people are assumed to live in villages, small or large, and there alone.

Within the villages any Israelite male was assumed to be a potential householder, that is, in context, the master of a domain, a landholder.[11] The single most important difference between the conception of the householder in the Mishnah and the conception of landholding in the Greek thinkers who in theoretical economics formed the counterpart to the Mishnah's authors lies in that one fact, as Finley states it: "It was the Greeks who most fully preserved for citizens a monopoly of the right to own land, and who in the more oligarchic communities restricted full political rights to the landowners among their members."[12] While the householder by definition always is assumed to own land and command a domain, the Mishnah knows landless persons as full citizens of the kingdom for which it legislates, and when it speaks of cultic or ritual responsibilities, all the inhabitants of a town, or other categories to which landholding bears no point of relevance whatsoever, the Mishnah speaks of "a man," "he who," or "all the residents of the town," and not of "the householder."

In fact the householder is a classification serving solely economic components of the system of Judaism as a whole. It is a technical term, which occurs when we speak of either market or distributive economics, in the fourth and first divisions of the document, respectively. In most of the Mishnah, the differentiation between householder and any other Jew made no difference, and therefore the language of the document ignored that differentiation, invoking it only where for systemic reasons the distinction made a difference. Take, for instance, "And all the villagers nearby gather together there for the reaping of the first sheaf of grain for the *omer*" (M. Men. 10:3–4), a formulation which accords no differentiation to householders, because it is not relevant. Where the identification of a person as a householder does affect the law, the authors specify that an actor is a householder, as in the following: "The potter who brought his pots into the courtyard of the householder without permission, and the beast of the householder broke them—the householder is exempt" (B. B.Q. 2:3A–C). Here we must know that the householder is an actor, because the rights of ownership of a domain are involved. That point is critical to our understanding of the householder, who is not the same as any Israelite for the Mishnah's authors, but who is the center of interest, the principal unit of productive activity, the classification of person who forms the building block of the village. The political economy of the Mishnah is defined by the householder forming with other householders a village: *oikos* become *polis*.

The Mishnah's theoretical conception of its ("Israel's") political economy, that is, the village or *polis* comprising the household or *oikos,* therefore, is neat and orderly, with all things in relationship and in proper order and proportion. True, the political economy encompassed other economic entities, in particular craftsmen and traders, both of them necessary for the conduct of the household. But each was placed into relationship with the household, the one as a necessary accessory to its ongoing functioning, the other as a shadowy figure who received the crops in volume and parceled them out to the market. The relationships between householder and craftsman, or between householder and hired hand, are sorted out in such a way as to accord to all parties a fair share in every transaction. Responsibilities of the one as against the other are spelled out. The craftsman or artisan, to be sure, is culpable should he damage property of the householder, but that judgment simply states the systemic interest in preserving the present division of wealth so that no party to a transaction emerges richer, none poorer. Accordingly, I find no class interest expressed in the following:

A. If one gave something to craftsmen to repair, and they spoiled the object, they are liable to pay compensation.
B. If he gave to a joiner a box, chest, or cupboard to repair, and the latter spoiled it, he is liable to pay compensation.
C. A builder who took upon himself to destroy a wall and who smashed the rocks or damaged them is liable to pay compensation.

D. If he was tearing down the wall on one side, and it fell down on the other side, he is exempt. But if it is because of the blow that he gave it, he is liable.

(M. B. Q. 9:3)

All that is at stake here is the preservation of wealth in its established proportions, so that one party does not emerge richer, another poorer, from any transaction or encounter. Along these same lines, laws governing relations of employer to employee hold that each party must abide by its commitment and that the party which changes the terms of an agreement bears liability to the other. The prevailing custom must be observed in the absence of an explicit stipulation. One example of the care with which the rights of all parties are taken into account is at M. B.M. 9:12, which ensures that when the worker has laid claim on his wages, the claim is paid. But the employer may pay by giving a draft on a storekeeper or money changer.

The household therefore should be understood in three aspects. First, it marked a unit of production, and the householder was the master of the means of production: it was a farming unit in particular. That defines the household's indicative character and quality. Second, the household also marked a unit of ownership, and the householder was the master of a piece of property. Commanding means of production meant, in particular, running a farm. Third, the household also encompassed an extended family unit. But a household— affines living together in a house—without land simply was no household. For the term bore economic, not only social, valence: a family unit by itself did not constitute a household. That is one side of the matter. The other is equally critical. Merely owning a piece of property, without using the property for farming, also did not make a man into a householder. The routine and commonplace identification of the householder as a farmer in possession of land is expressed in the following, which derives from Mishnah-tractate Baba Mesia 5:2–3:

A. (1) The potter who brought his pots into the courtyard of the householder without permission,

B. and the beast of the householder broke them—

C. [the householder] is exempt.

D. (2) And if [the beast] was injured on them,

E. the owner of the pots is liable.

F. (3) If [however] he brought them in with permission,

G. the owner of the courtyard is liable.

H. (1) [If] he brought his produce into the courtyard of the householder without permission,

I. and the beast of the householder ate them up,

J. [the householder] is exempt.

K. (2) And if [the beast] was injured by them, the owner of the produce is liable.

L. (3) But if he brought them in with permission, the owner of the courtyard is liable.

(M. B.M. 5:2)

A. (1) [If] he brought his ox into the courtyard of a householder without permission,

B. and the ox of the householder gored it,

C. or the dog of the householder bit it,

D. [the householder] is exempt.

E. (2) [If] that [ox] gored the ox of the householder,

F. [the owner] is liable.

G. [If] it fell into his well and polluted its water, [the owner of the ox] is liable.

H. [If] his father or son was in [the well and was killed], [the owner of the ox] pays ransom money.

I. (3) But if he brought it in with permission, the owner of the courtyard is liable.

J. Rabbi says, "In all cases [the householder] is liable only if he undertakes upon himself to guard the ox."

(M. B.M. 5:3)

The triplet makes the same three points three times, as indicated. The insertions at 3G–H simply restate the principle of 3E–F. Rabbi differs at each point at which liability is assigned to the owner of the courtyard. The clause at 3C is a needless interpolation. The point of interest to us is simple. The householder is assumed to own a house in a courtyard, to conduct a farm, to bear responsibility for a particular bit of private domain. As we proceed, we shall gain a still more nuanced view of the meanings of the word and the social facts presupposed in usages of that word. But the main point is clear. To be a master of a household, one exercises ownership and control of real property, and real property of a particular kind, namely, a farm. Ownership is not an abstraction; it is defined and delimited by function.

For, to state matters negatively, the authors of the Mishnah cannot conceive of ownership in the absence of productive use of property and therefore call into question the permanence of absentee ownership, e.g., the organization of properties not manàged by their owners. That negative conception forms the underside of the positive conception of the householder in charge of a unit of production and in command (of course) of the means of production. We uncover the negative definition, specifically, when we consider how the authors of the Mishnah dispose of the absentee landowner who holds property but does not work it or oversee its productive utilization. It follows, as I just suggested, that ownership is not an abstract right, divorced from all material function, but entails management and productive utilization of property, and the householder embodies that command and everyday mastery of the means of production in a way in which the absentee landowner cannot. Ownership in the present context, identified as it is with supervision, utilization, and usu-fruct, derives from the premise of the householder as active manager and ad-ministrator of the means of production, and ownership finds its meaning in the command of the unit of production. That conception of ownership in such ma-terial terms makes its appearance only within the details of the law, to which we now turn.

To understand what follows, we have to note that one might demonstrate ownership of a property not only by presenting a valid deed but also by show-ing, without such a deed, that one has made use of the property for a span of uninterrupted time. Ownership is proved not only by documentary evidence, but also by testimony that a person has held, and enjoyed the usufruct of, a property for a given period of time. One therefore may lose his deed and re-tain the land, or, conversely, retain the deed and lose the land to a competing claim resting upon deed and usufruct. The upshot is to render impossible long-term investment in land held fallow and to render at least difficult absen-tee ownership of vast and essentially unsupervised properties. For if an ab-sentee owner, e.g., living in a distant city, held a valid deed but a claimant could show that, absent such a deed, he had full control of the usufruct of the field for a period of three years, the squatter had every possibility of gaining ownership of the land. The law at hand points toward the conception of usu-fruct, therefore, as a means of establishing ownership, with the concomitant notion that absentee ownership not joined by supervision, let alone usufruct, might prove parlous. That is not to suggest that a person with no valid claim to land might seize a property from an absentee landlord; the claimant-squatter had the obligation to establish a prima facie claim, e.g., the deed has been lost. But the upshot is the same. Let us consider the detailed exposition of the notion of ownership established through usufruct.

Mishnah-tractate Baba Batra 3 expounds the rules of acquiring or secur-ing title through usucaption, specifying the conditions under which such a claim may be made and effected, the sorts of things subject to that particular process for establishing ownership, and related questions of squatters' rights. M. B.B. 3:1–2 provide the basic principle of establishing title through usu-caption. The formal traits of M. B.B. 3:1 are somewhat complex, but its main point, that one secures title through usucaption after three years of un-harassed occupancy, is clear. M. B.B. 3:2 adds that the presumptive owner's absence from the province means he does not have the opportunity to com-plain, and so no title is secured unless he is present and able to object. That qualification protects the right of a legitimate owner to be away for a span of time, but at the same time secures for the squatter a claim against a permanent absentee owner. M. B.B. 3:3 greatly enlarges the rule. Its main contribution is to clarify the fact that mere squatting, without some legitimate claim, e.g., of having purchased the field or received it as a gift, is null. M. B.B. 3:4 adds the (for Mishnah) inevitable quibble about the assessment of damages against false witnesses, e.g., those who testify deceitfully in three groups about three

distinct years of occupancy. M. B.B. 3:5 goes over the ground of what constitutes an exercise of usucaption. M. B.B. 3:6, finally, lists aspects of a property which are, and are not, subject to usucaption at all. M. B.B. 3:7–8 form
a brief appendix on another aspect of customary use and control. One may not
change the existing patterns in a courtyard, e.g., by adding doors or windows.
One may not build a projection or balcony over the public way. If he has purchased a house with such a trait, he retains it, according to M. B.B. 3:8, in
line with M. B.B. 2:5.

A. [Title by] usucaption of (1) houses, (2) cisterns, (3) trenches, (4)
    caves, (5) dovecots, (6) bath-houses, (7) olive presses, (8) irrigated
    fields, (9) slaves,
B. and anything which continually produces a yield—
C. title by usucaption applying to them is three years,
D. from day to day [that is, three full years].
E. A field which relies on rain—[title by] usucaption for it is three
    years,
F. not from day to day [Danby: "And they need not be completed"].
G. R. Ishmael says, "Three months in the first year, three in the last,
    and twelve months in between—lo, eighteen months [suffice]."
H. R. Aqiba says, "A month in the first year, a month in the last, and
    twelve months in between—lo, fourteen months."
I. Said R. Ishmael, "Under what circumstances?
J. "In the case of a sown field.
K. "But in the case of a tree-planted field, [if] one has brought in the
    [grape crop], collected the olives, and gathered the [fig] harvest,
L. "lo, these [three harvests] count as three years."

(M. B.B. 3:1)

A. There are three regions so far as securing title through usucaption [is
    concerned]: Judea, Transjordan, and Galilee.
B. [If] one was located in Judea, and [someone else] took possession of
    his property in Galilee,
C. [or] was in Galilee, and someone took possession [of his property in
    Judea], it is not an effective act of securing title through usucaption—
D. unless [the owner] is with [the squatter] in the same province.
E. Said R. Judah, "They specified a period of three years only so that
    one may be located in Ispamia, and one may hold possession for a
    year, people will go and inform [the owner] over the period of a year,
    and he may return in the third year."

(M. B.B. 3:2)

The basic rule set out in M. B.B. 3:1 is somewhat complicated, because
there are some secondary issues inserted into the primary declaration of A and
C. The first is the consideration at B, the second that at D and F. F bears a
very heavy gloss at G–H; I–L further gloss A–C. The point is that anything

which is valuable and is allowed to remain in the hands of a person for a period of three years is assumed to belong to that person. If there were a valid claim against the squatter, any other party would have made it within the specified time. This principle is implicit at A, made explicit at B, and then restated by Ishmael at I–L. The difference between D and F is explained by G–H. The only reason that E is specified is so that the stated difference may be made explicit, since otherwise E belongs perfectly happily in the opening catalogue. It follows that a good bit of editorial work has been done to produce M. B.B. 3:1 as we have it. M. B.B. 3:2 contains no problems, because A is neatly spelled out by B–D. Then Judah, E, ties M. B.B. 3:1 and M. B.B. 3:2 together to make sense of both the specification of the period of years of usucaption and the stipulation on the location of the contesting owner of the property. It would be difficult to improve upon this spelling out of a complex set of materials, particularly through the exegetical sayings of Ishmael (M. B.B. 3:1I–L) and Judah (M. B.B. 3:2E).

A. Any act of usucaption [along] with which [there] is no claim [on the property being utilized] is no act of securing title through usucaption.
B. How so?
C. [If] he said to him, "What are you doing on my property,"
D. and the other party answered him, "But no one ever said a thing to me!"—
E. this is not usucaption.
F. [If he answered,] "For you sold it to me," "You gave it to me as a gift," "Your father sold it to me," "Your father gave it to me as a gift"—
G. lo, this is usucaption.
H. He who holds possession because of an inheritance [from the previous owner] requires no further claim [in his own behalf].
I. (1) Craftsmen, partners, sharecroppers, and trustees are not able to secure title through usucaption.
J. (2) A husband has no claim of usucaption in his wife's property,
K. (3) nor does a wife have a claim of usucaption in her husband's property,
L. (4) nor a father in his son's property,
M. (5) nor a son in his father's property.
N. Under what circumstances?
O. In the case of one who effects possession through usucaption.
P. But in the case of one who gives a gift,
Q. or of brothers who divide an estate,
R. and of one who seizes the property of a proselyte,
S. [if] one has locked up, walled in, or broken down in any measure at all,
T. lo, this constitutes securing a claim through usucaption.

(M. B.B. 3:3)

The principle of A is perfectly well spelled out by B–G. H glosses the fore-going. Mere squatting does not confer any rights; one has to have a valid claim of how he came to hold the land. The party of H cannot know how the father got the land. I–M list various people who may not to begin with lay claim of securing title through usucaption, because their right to enjoy the usufruct of a property is secured on grounds other than ownership. Referring back to M. B.B. 3:1, N–O introduce a secondary consideration. If one wishes to effect ownership of something acquired as a gift, through inheri-tance, or from an estate lacking heirs, one has only to acquire by securing possession, S, in order to gain a title through usucaption. Three years of occu-pancy are not required.

A. What are [usages] which are effective in the securing of title through usucaption, and what are [usages] which are not effective in the se-curing of title through usucaption?
B. [If] one put (1) cattle in a courtyard, (2) an oven, (3) double-stove, (4) millstone, (5) raised chickens, or (6) put his manure, in a court-yard—
C. this is not an effective mode of securing title through usucaption.
D. But [if] (1) he made a partition for his beast ten handbreadths high,
E. and so too (2) for an oven, so too (3) for a double stove, so too (4) for a millstone—
F. [if] (5) he brought his chickens into the house,
G. or (6) made a place for his manure three handbreadths deep or three handbreadths high—
H. lo, this is an effective mode of securing title through usucaption.

(M. B.B. 3:5)

The contrast between B–C and D–H is clear. In the latter instance we have signs of permanent occupation.

A. A gutterspout does not [impart title through] usucaption [so that the spout still may be moved], but the place on which it discharges does impart title through usucaption [so that the place must be left for its present purpose].
B. A gutter does [impart title through] usucaption.
D. An Egyptian window does not [impart title through] usucaption, but a Tyrian window does [impart title through] usucaption.
E. What is an Egyptian window? Any through which the head of a hu-man being cannot squeeze.
F. R. Judah says, "If it has a frame, even though a human being's head cannot squeeze through, it does [impart title through] usucaption."
G. A projection, [if it extends] a handbreadth [or more], does [impart title through] usucaption,
H. and one has the power to protest [its being made].

I. [If it projects] less than a handbreadth, it is not subject to [imparting title through] usucaption,

J. and one has not got the power to protest [its being made].

(M. B.B. 3:6)

A−B and C−D augment M. B.B. 3:5. One may move the gutterspout, but the right of discharge is permanent. The small ladder or window does not impart title; the large one does, to the one who uses it for a long time. E−F gloss this, and G−J make the same point about large and small projections.

This detailed survey of the exposition of the principle of usucaption has carried us far from our main point, but it also has shown us how, in exquisite detail, our authors will state the principle of owernship. What is relevant to our inquiry is briefly recovered. It is the notion that ownership is not abstract and not unconditional but concrete and related to ongoing and hands-on administration: usufruct, not merely deed, proves a right of ownership or functional access and use, as the case may be. And that definition of ownership draws us once more within the orbit of the household as a unit of production, distinct, on the one side, from the family, but different, on the other, also from the industrial-scale agricultural unit. What makes a household a household is possession *and usufruct* of land: both. And, I repeat, it is the household that defines the building block of the village, the *oikos* of the *polis,* and in the systemic statement of the Judaism of the Mishnah, the formation of households into villages comprises "all Israel."

What we see in the mass of details we have surveyed is a system in which a principal and generative consideration derives from control of the means of production. For, as a matter of fact, the political economy of the mishnaic system proves partial and highly selective, and the economic unit dictated the perception of the political.[13] The householders form a social group which also is an economic one, but, as a matter of fact, the householders comprise a group seen all in all as the basic productive unit of society, around which other economic activities function. That is the starting point for the politics of the system, but, more consequentially, the entire frame of reference of the system as a whole finds its definition in the issue of who controls the means of production that the system deems important. There is, after all, production of other than agricultural products, for example, goods and services. Production encompasses making pots and chairs, but the craftsman does not define an economic unit, e.g., a householder, if he does not also own and farm (perhaps through day laborers) land as well. The shopkeeper or tradesman, the merchant and capitalist also command wealth and engage in productive activities of all kinds. But they too do not control those means of production that make a difference to the system of the Mishnah. But in due course, when we consider the Mishnah's version of distributive economics, we shall understand why the framers of that system consider land, and only land, to form the productive entity society, so that only the householder, who is by a definition a landholder who farms, constitutes the focus of consideration and concern. And when we grasp the reason for that fact, we shall see precisely why the system delivers its message and makes its statement through economics, and why the framers of the system had no meaningful choice, given what they wished to say, but to address issues of production, in the household, as well as of market and of wealth.

It suffices at this point in the argument simply to grasp the centrality of the household in economy and society, forming the leitmotif of the system, governing its perspective and perceptions of all else. I doubt that a more thoroughgoing definition of society by the measure of its economic categories and building blocks, that is, by appeal to the means and unit of production, can be located in any other Judaism. And, as we shall see in the concluding chapter, other categories and classifications of society, other conceptions of the political economy, and, therefore, also a different, and substantially diminished, place for the household, that is, the economy, defined as the unit and medium of production, characterized even the Judaism that was ultimately to emerge from the Mishnah's system and defined the economics of the Judaism of the dual Torah.[14] Let me describe in general terms the householders as the framers of the Mishnah perceive them. Householders were farmers of their own land, proprietors of the smallest viable agricultural unit of production—however modest that might be. They stood at the center of a circle of a sizable corps of dependents: wives, sons and daughters-in-law, children and grandchildren, slaves, servants. At the outer fringes of the Mishnah's household were such ancillary groups as day laborers, craftsmen and purveyors of other specialties, wagon drivers, providers of animals and equipment for rent, moneylenders, shopkeepers, wholesalers of grain and other produce, peddlers and tradesman, barbers, doctors, butchers, scribes and teachers, and, of course, the ultimate dependents, the scheduled castes: priests, Levites, and the poor. This list tells us, as we shall observe presently, that in the system of the Mishnah the economic classes of traders and other purveyors of liquid capital ("capitalists") were essentially outside of the conceptual framework of the Mishnah's political economy.[15]

As principal and head of so sizable a network of material relationships, the householder saw himself as pivot of the village, the irreducible building block of society, the solid and responsible center of it all. In the corporate community of the village, other components, each with a particular perspective and program of pressing questions, surely existed, and the householder could have been only one of these. But in the perception of the Mishnah, he was the one that mattered. And the Mishnah's framers could not have erred, for the householder controlled the means of production and held the governance of the basic economic unit of the village as such. Traders, peddlers, and others outside of the economy of the household also functioned outside of the framework of the village as such; by definition they were not settled, landed, stable. Their economic tasks required them to travel from place to place, for instance, to collect produce and resell it at the market. But so far as the Mishnah's picture of society in its economic relationships and productive aspects is concerned, the whole held together through the householder. This is expressed in mythic terms: one who owns something is the only one who may sanctify it, and that is, in heaven, God, and, on earth, the householder, the farmer.

The householder for his part functioned as the principal economic actor, who made the decisions for himself and his dependents.[16] The household forms one of the two social constructs of the Mishnah's world, the other being the village, which is made up of households, thus the *oikos* and the *polis;* these are the foundations for the political economy envisaged by the document. By household, however, we must understand a considerably larger social unit than we do today. The household encompassed the householder, the head of the unit, his wives and children, and slaves, day workers, and other employees utilized as needed, as well as his livestock, movables, and real property. The householder's will reigned supreme, and his decisions governed. As an economic unit, the household aimed at a self-sufficiency of production, consumption, and exchange that we do not seek in the contemporary family, extended or nuclear, and household unit.

The definition of the householder in wholly economic terms, as the one who commands the means of production—or, more accurately, those means of production of which the framers of the system propose to take note— proves critical. When we see the household as an economic unit, the social side of matters loses all importance; indeed, it hardly matters whether or not we introduce considerations of kinship, and, as noted, co-residence is not always essential in designating a person a part of a household. Propinquity means only that one is within a reasonable distance, which is to say, is part of the village, but the village takes form out of households and is (merely) a construction of households, having no other independent social forms. Accordingly, the entire system knows as its basic social unit and building block what is also its basic economic unit, defined as the component of the whole that controls the means of production, the "farm" in all that "farm" entails.

While, in recent anthropological thought, the distinction between the household and the (mere) extended family has come under question, in the case of the Mishnah's world, the former is assumed to encompass the latter.[17] The framers of the Mishnah, for example, do not imagine a household headed by a woman; a divorced woman is assumed to return to her father's household. The framers make no provision for the economic activity of isolated individuals, out of synchronic relationship with a household or a village made up of householders. Accordingly, craftsmen and day laborers or other workers, skilled and otherwise, enter the world of social and economic transactions only in relationship to the householder. The upshot, therefore, is that the social world is made up of households, and, since households may be made up of many families, e.g., husbands, wives, children, all of them dependents upon the householder, households in no way are to be confused with the family.[18] The indicator of the family is kinship, that of the household, "propinquity or residence." [19] And yet, even residence is not always a criterion for membership in the household unit, since the craftsmen and day laborers are not assumed to live in the household compound at all. Accordingly, the household forms an economic unit, with secondary criteria deriving from that primary fact.

And the householder, then, stands for the economic unit encompassing families of a variety of relationships to the householder (or no blood relationship at all), and he controls the means of production and also constitutes the unit of production, as we noted at the very outset. [20] There is another side to it, to be sure. If brothers eat together at their father's house(hold) but live in separate houses, they are for cultic purposes regarded as distinct and not as a single household unit (M. Er. 6:7A–B). But that is a minor refinement. The point is clarified as follows: a father and his sons, wives, daughters-in-law, and manservants and maidservants, when no one else lives with them in the courtyard, do not have to prepare an *erub* (T. Er. 5:10A–C), since they are regarded for cultic purposes as a single unit. And that seems to me to be the basic conception of the family in relationship to the household.

But having defined the household as fundamentally the economic unit of Israelite society imagined by the Mishnah's authors, we should not obscure how the economic relationship penetrates into all other human relationships within that society. Quite to the contrary, only when we understand that control of the means of production bears consequence for the shape and structure of all other relationships in society shall we fully understand what is at stake in our understanding of the householder and his systemic position. The householder's will proves paramount in all matters, not only economic decision-making; this is shown most dramatically by the systemic opposite of the householder, the slave, whoose will is never effective. In this regard we should not confuse the rights of the male as householder with the male's rights and power as husband. To be sure, the householder, always a male, as husband has cultic rights over his wife, e.g., in confirming or nullifying her vows. But, more to the point, as master of the household, he controls all property, so that, for the duration of the marriage, the wife's and minor children's property is his to do with as he wishes. And his disposition of real property through gift or inheritance is equally autocephalic. True, biblical rules of primogeniture may apply as to the disposition of estates. But the householder may give away the property and in doing so may ignore the received rules of testamentary succession. That total control of real wealth, vested in the householder, then sets aside the inherited laws that dictate in some measure who gets what. In these and other ways, we see that, while the householder to begin with commands the economic unit, that same control bears secondary implications for his control of other than economic matters as well. We may therefore affirm that the one who controls the means of production and who defines and constitutes the unit of production effectively is in charge of all else.

This brings us at the end to the concrete, detailed description of the household within the system of the Mishnah, beginning with general observations, proceeding to concrete expressions of generalizations. The building block of mishnaic discourse, the circumstance, addressed whenever the issues of concrete society and material transactions are taken up, is the householder and his context. While the Mishnah's framers know about all sorts of economic activities, the center and focus of interest lie in the village, made up of households, each a unit of production in agriculture, perceived to be the economic activity that is normative and natural, for reasons already provided by Aristotle. The households are constructed by and around the householder, who is ordinarily also the father, the head of an extended family encompassing sons, wives, children, servants and slaves, and various dependents, some in residence, some not, as well as craftsmen in the village.

Let us revert to the simple question introduced at the outset: when do the authors of the Mishnah refer to the household, and in what contexts? The main point is that such references are by no means random. "The householder" (*baal habbayit*) is a term bearing particular meaning and occurring in only specific and appropriate contexts, with reference to a proprietary persona or relationship: one who possesses or is responsible for a household (*bayit*), just as a *baal mum* is one who possesses or is subject to a blemish, and a *baal qeri* is one who is subject to sexual impurity by reason of involuntary emission of semen. *Baal habbayit* is not merely another way of saying "a person" or "a man." On the negative side, when the authors wish to speak of liturgical obligations, e.g., in tractate Pesahim, or religious taboos, as in tractate Shabbat, the subject of most predicates is not the householder (*baal habbayit*) but "one who" or "a man." And conversely, as a matter of rule, when they wish to invoke the notion of domain or home ownership or proprietorship, even in those same cultic tractates, they allude to the householder; e.g., in M. Shab. 1 : 1ff., with reference to the specification of public and private domain, the person located in private domain is called "the householder," even though in the rest of that tractate there is no such reference at all.

An example of the care in defining and using the term "householder" may be noted in the sequence of subjects of sentences in M. Shab. 1 : 1–2. In the first of the two paragraphs, the author refers to the position of a beggar and a householder in the transfer of an object on the Sabbath from private domain, that of the householder, to public domain, where the beggar is standing, a transfer that on the Sabbath is forbidden. So the author makes use of the category that governs ownership of private domain, hence, householder: "If on the Sabbath the beggar stands outside and the householder inside. . . ." In the next passage the author wishes to speak of any individual, without reference to his status as to control of a private domain, and hence, land ownership. The subject shifts from "householder" to mere, undifferentiated "man": "A man should not sit down before the barber close to afternoon prayer" (M. Shab. 1 : 2). Other such individuals, not landholders and householders, come under discussion, e.g., M. Shab. 1:3: "A tailor should not go out carrying his needle, nor a scribe with his pen." Along these same lines, since others besides householders may hire day laborers, when the authorship wishes to discuss conditions under which, at the end of the Sabbath, one hires day laborers, reference is to "a man" and not "a householder"; so M. Shab. 23:3: "A man should not hire workers on the Sabbath or tell someone else to do so. They do not wait at twilight at the Sabbath limit to hire workers or to bring in produce." The householder is not the critical category in tractate Pesahim; here it is the head of the family, e.g., "He who says to his children, 'Lo, I shall slaughter the Passover offering in behalf of the one of you who will get up to Jerusalem first.'" (M. Pes. 8:3). This statement pertains not to the householder in particular but to the family head in particular, and is so phrased. That means where we do have "householder," the choice is deliberate and conveys meaning.

When collective action in the village is under discussion, e.g., tractate Taanit, there is no discussion of householder, nor, given what we know, should we have expected such a discussion. Everyone is involved equally, "they," as in, "When do they make mention. . . ." In relationship to heaven, all Israelites, so far as the means of production go, are the same. There is therefore no occasion for specification of class status or economic standing in these tractates. That encompasses Berakhot also. Where it is relevant, they do specify the caste or class standing, e.g., priestly courses in tractate Taanit 4, proprietary interests in the *baal habbayit* materials, and so on. M. Ta. 2:6–7, "members of the father's house . . . members of the priestly watch and the public delegation . . . ," presents an instance of the use of language in another situation in which the economic-social entity, the householder, is irrelevant: "My children, let one be ashamed before his fellow, but let a person not be ashamed on account of what he has done. It is better for a person to be ashamed before his fellow, but let him and his children not suffer from famine" (M. Ta. 2:1, and see T. Ta. 1:8E). The individual is not a householder as such but is mentioned as a person who is singular by reason of his piety, as in M. Ta. 1:3–7. And, further, the authors do differentiate the village from the town, but only by size, not by an essential difference in the social or economic units of which each of the two, respectively, is composed, e.g., "What is a large town? Any in which there are ten men available at all times to form a quorum. If there are fewer than this number, lo, it is a village" (M. Meg. 1:3A–C).

With exactly what proportion and component of Jewry in Palestine, that is, Israel in the land of Israel, did the economics of Judaism concern itself? In fact, as in the case of Aristotle as Finley sees his economics, so in the instance of the economics of the Mishnah; we have an economic theory that ignores most participants in the economy, which is supposedly subject to legislation and direction. In order to understand the true dimensions of the Mishnah's economics, we conclude by reverting to the question, who in the system of the

Mishnah could become a householder? The answer, given above, is self-evident: any Israelite. But that answer carries in its wake a certain disingenuousness. For, as we have already noticed, it is taken for granted that "Israel" stands for males, and, in the nature of things, males possessed of sufficient wealth to acquire land, however small their holdings, and it is further taken for granted that the Mishnah's entire system addresses Jews; gentiles are not represented as householders, though their presence in the neighborhood is persistently acknowledged. So the Mishnah's economics excluded gentiles, who formed a sizable part of the population of the areas of the land of Israel that Jews occupied, as well as areas of the same territory ("Palestine") that Jews did not occupy in appreciable numbers. The same economics, more to the point, also made slight provision for the regulation of the affairs of those Jews, as well as gentiles, who lived by pursuing crafts not in connection with the work required for the household, meaning the farm; who lived by trade and investment; who lived by the sweat of their brow as day laborers; and however many other sorts and classifications of persons and of manners of earning a living one can imagine.

In its identification of the householder as the building block of society, to the neglect of the vast panoply of "others," nonhouseholders, the Mishnah's authors reduced the dimensions of society to only a single component in it. But that is the sole option open to a system that, for reasons of its own, wished to identify productivity with agriculture, individuality in God's image with ownership of land, and social standing and status, consequently, with ownership and control of the land which constituted the sole systemically consequential means of production. Now if we were to list all of the persons and professions who enjoy no role in the system, or who are treated as ancillary to the system, we have to encompass not only workers—the entire landless working class!—but also craftsmen and artisans, teachers and physicians, clerks and officials, traders and merchants, the whole of the commercial establishment, not to mention women as a caste.[21] Such an economics, disengaged from so large a sector of the economy of which it claimed, even if only in theory, to speak, can hardly be called an economics at all. And yet, as we have seen and shall realize still more keenly in the coming chapters, that economics bore an enormous burden of the systemic message and statement of the Judaism set forth by the authors of the Mishnah.

Fair and just to all parties, the Mishnah nonetheless speaks in particular for the Israelite landholding, proprietary person. The Mishnah's problems are the problems of the householder, its perspectives are his. Its sense of what is just and fair expresses his sense of the giveness and cosmic rightness of the present condition of society. These are men of substance and of means, however modest, aching for a stable and predictable world in which to tend their crops and herds, feed their families and dependents, keep to the natural rhythms of the seasons and lunar cycles, and, in all, live out their lives within strong and secure boundaries on earth and in heaven. This is why the sense of landed place and its limits, the sharp line drawn between village and world, on the one side, Israelite and gentile, on the second, Temple and world, on the third, evoke metaphysical correspondences. Householder, which is Israel, in the village, and temple, beyond, form a correspondence. Only when we understand the systemic principle concerning God in relationship to Israel in its land shall we come to the fundamental and generative conception that reaches concrete expression in the here and now of the householder as the centerpiece of society.

In this regard, therefore, the Mishnah's economics finds within its encompassing conception of who forms the *polis* and who merely occupies space within the *polis* its definition of the realm to which "economics" applies. In the economics of Judaism the householder is systemically the active force, and all other components of the actual economy (as distinct from the economics) prove systemically inert. As such, of course, the economics of Judaism can hardly qualify as an economics at all, since the theory ignores most of the actuality. But in the context of Aristotle's conception of economics, the Mishnah's theory of the economy qualifies full well. In this context, we do well to point to what is at stake in an economics that treats as economically beyond the realm of theory the generality of participants in the actual economy. The stakes are well defined by Finley when he observes, "All Greek states . . . restricted the right of land ownership to their citizens. . . . They thereby . . . erected a wall between the land, from which the great majority of the population received their livelihood, and that very substantial proportion of the money available for investment which was in the hands of non-citizens." [22] In this setting of the Judaism of the Mishnah, we find ourselves in a theory of the political economy in which anyone might own land, even though few did, and the result is no different from that to which Finley points. If only an Israelite male may own land and exercise usufruct over it (wives who own land cede to their husbands usufruct of the bulk of their estates for the duration of the marriage), then we find ourselves entirely within Finley's framework; all we need do is change "citizen" to "free, male, adult Israelite," and the Greek economic theory proves entirely a comfortable fit.

But then what of the economically active members of the *polis,* the ones who had capital and knew how to use it? If they wished to enter that elevated "Israel" which formed the social center and substance of the Mishnah's Israel, they had to purchase land. Then matters again turn out as they did in the Greek cities described by Finley. For in both cases the upshot was that money-holding citizens turned to the land "from considerations of status, not of maximization of profits. . . . The non-citizens [kept off the land] of necessity lived by manufacture, trade and moneylending." [23] The consequence—to abbreviate Finley's interesting argument—is that "what we call the economy was properly the exclusive business of outsiders." [24] In the case of the economics of Judaism, by contrast, economic theory encompassed the market as much as the household. The same message pertained, the same statement resonated. We shall now see precisely what it was. For when we know what we now do about the household, we can describe a steady-state society, but we have not yet gained access to what the system, through its disposition of the household as the systemically active unit of economic activity, proposed to lay down as its statement concerning, and through the creation of, that steady-state, stationary world.

5

The Market

Exchange by itself is natural: 'shortages and surpluses . . . were corrected
by mutual exchange. . . . When used in this way, the art of exchange is
not contrary to nature, nor in any way a species of the art of money-
making. It simply served to satisfy the natural requirements of self-
sufficiency.'

M. I. Finley [1]

In everyday transactions as the framers of the Mishnah sorted them out, they
proposed to effect the vision of a steady-state economy, engaged in always
equal exchanges of fixed wealth and intrinsic value. Essentially, the Mishnah's authors aimed at the fair adjudication of conflict, so that no party
gained, none lost, in any transaction. The task of Israelite society, as they saw
it, is to maintain perfect stasis, to preserve the prevailing situation, to secure
the stability of not only relationships but status and standing. To this end, in
the interchanges of buying and selling, giving and taking, borrowing and
lending, in transactions of the market and exchanges with artisans and craftsmen and laborers, it is important to preserve the essential equality, not merely
equity, of exchange. Fairness alone does not suffice. Status quo ante forms the
criterion of the true market, reflecting as it does the exchange of value for
value, in perfect balance. That is the way that, in reference to the market, the
systemic point of urgency, the steady state of the polity, therefore also of the
economy, is stated. The upshot of their economics is simple. No party in
the end may have more than what he had at the outset, and none may emerge
as the victim of a sizable shift in fortune and circumstance. All parties' rights
to and in the stable and unchanging political economy are preserved. When,
therefore, the condition of a person is violated, the law will secure the restoration of the antecedent status.

To understand the economics at hand, we have to recall the two distinct
principles at play, market economics as against distributive economics. We
can identify two modes of carrying out the functions of the market: state or

temple intervention in the organization of production and in distribution, or the working of a market. The former invokes matters of status governing giving and receiving, producing and consuming; the latter, a free market exchange.[2] The third option, an utterly self-sufficient economy, was simply not available. But the Mishnah, with its keen interest in questions of price and its active intervention in production and distribution, simply ignores the working of the market, even while intervening in enormous detail in the determination of prices.

To begin with we distinguish the notion of a market from the theory of market economics, the economic theory in which the market works as a rationing device, responding to supply and demand through the mechanism of price so as to control the rational disposition of scarce resources. In antiquity, markets surely existed, much as MacMullen describes: "The peasants must have not too long a journey to bring their produce to the city. . . . They leave before dawn for the city, their donkeys laden with cereals, olives, grapes, or figs, depending on the season. Towards seven or eight o'clock the bazaar is full. . . . Towards ten o'clock time to think of one's own purchases—the few items of luxury which the land does not yield. . . . Towards eleven, the city is emptied and everyone starts home." [3] That description of the market as marketplace bears no relationship to the abstract mechanism, embodied to be sure in the market, we mean when we speak of market economics.

To understand the definition of the market as an economic category, we turn, as usual, to Davisson and Harper, who state:

> A market is a series of transactions by buyer and seller where prices measure the scarcity of a commodity on the market. A high price indicates that the quantity of a given commodity on a market is low when measured against buyer demand; lower prices indicate that the quantity is great when measured against buyer demand. . . . It is an essential point of market trading that the political authority of the society (government, temple, guilds) gives up control of production and distribution to this impersonal mechanism.[4]

The alternative to market economics is a system of redistribution, or distributive economics. In such a system scarce goods are collected and allocated not by the market but by some other authority, e.g., political and religious.

This alternative system is described very simply as follows: "Redistribution requires central collection and allocation by a higher authority, but can be seen as satisfying the basic unit's need for services and goods which it cannot produce alone by providing an institutionalized channel for the pooling of resources." [5] In the case of the Judaism of the dual Torah in the statement of the Mishnah, distributive economics is represented by the intervention of God's authority through the priesthood into the production and disposition of scarce resources. The rationality of distributive economics rests on the conviction that God is the co-owner with Israel, therefore with Israelite householders, of the holy land. Hence all farmers or householders are joint tenants, with God, in their fields and produce, and that consideration introduces the justification, within the system, for distributive economics, right alongside market economics. In due course we shall further examine the workings of this alternative to market economics. But the present definition serves to warn us that the representation of the market in the Mishnah will not wholly accord with the requirement of the market, since market decisions are based, for the Mishnah, upon nonmarket considerations. In fact, the Mishnah's framers invoked an economics of a wholly distributive character, even while legislating for a market economy, which they fully recognized and understood in its crucial points.

Accordingly, it is a simple fact that the systemic focus and emphasis of that Judaism contradicted the fundamental function of the market and also missed the point of the market as Greco-Roman philosophy understood it, even while reiterating, in the particular and singular idiom utilized to set forth the systemic context of the Judaism at hand, precisely the conceptions of Aristotle about trade and exchange in general, and the market in particular. The market is an instrument of rationing:

> The market is one of the ways in which a particular society acquires the production that it needs and allocates that production among the various groups in the society. The market is simply a rationing device. The significant difference between a market operation and the other methods of rationing is that the latter deal with real wealth, while markets deal with money wealth. Other methods of rationing deal directly with the actual things that are distributed. In market operations purchases and sales are usually made for money, not directly for other commodities or services.[6]

To understand what is at stake we have to identify the indicators of the market and how it is defined and described. For that purpose we turn to Davisson and Harper, who state:

> A market may be described in two ways, by its institutions and by its functions. . . . The market may be defined by looking at its component elements: private property and inheritance, money wealth and income, the profit motive, standardized commodities, and an exchange of price information within geographic limits.[7]

By this criterion, the authors of the Mishnah did set forth the institutional requirements of the market, since it took for granted the conceptions of private property (e.g., private domain, in real estate, as distinct from public domain), inheritance (a conception received, of course, from the Pentateuch, ca. 500 B.C.), wealth in the form of money, consideration of the classifications of commodities, and the like. In these important ways, the Mishnah's framers fully recognized the facts of the market economy with which, in reality, their country presented them.[8]

But in numerous ways, the framers of the system subverted the workings of the market in favor of a distributive system, which they imagined. For example, the authors of the Mishnah took for granted that price information within geographic limits was not to circulate freely but was to be kept under control to affect market price and supply, e.g., M. Ta. 2:9: "They do not decree a fast [in connection with the signs of a drought] for the community in the first instance for a Thursday [which was the market day] so as not to disturb the market prices," since people would assume a famine was coming and hoard, consequently disrupting the stability of prices. While sound public policy, that rule certainly indicates the intention to intervene in the working of the market and hardly attests to the conception of a market working in its conventional manner. Since a controlled market is no market, and the two words "free" and "market" are a redundancy, we find ourselves confronted by evidence that the framers of the Mishnah invoked considerations of an other-than-economic character even when thinking, for systemic purposes, about the market. And that tells us that the market formed a category of intense systemic concern and in no way an inert fact of life of no conceptual or generative consequence.

In the world envisioned by the authors of the Mishnah, markets exist and the requirements of market economics are certainly confronted. We know that fact from the simple story told about Simeon b. Gamaliel. The market mechanism, the centerpiece of market economics, assuredly was understood by sages; so the Mishnah testifies. The goal of our authors is to overcome the—fully acknowledged—facts of market economics. The tension between the working of the market and the way in which sages proposed to legislate for it imparts to the Mishnah's static portrait of a market a dynamic tension deceptively lacking on the surface.

But, in the face of clear evidence of knowledge of market economics, in the system of Judaism in its initial statement, market economics is set aside, so far as is possible, in favor of the principle of distributive economics, the conception of a fixed value or an intrinsic worth to an object or a commodity. For the framers of the Mishnah conceived of the economy as one of self-sufficiency, made up as it was (in their minds, at least) of mostly self-sufficient households joined in essentially self-sufficient villages. They further carried forward the odd conception of the priestly authorship of Leviticus that the ownership of the land is supposed to be stable, so that, if a family alienates inherited property, it reverts to that family's ownership after a span of time. The conception of steady-state economy therefore dominated, so that, as a matter of fact, in utter stasis, no one would rise above his natural or inherent standing, and no one would fall either. And that is the economy they portray and claim to regulate through their legislation. In such an economy, the market did not form the medium of rationing but in fact had no role to play, except one: to insure equal exchange in all transactions, so that the market formed an arena for transactions of equal value and worth among households each possessed of a steady-state worth. Since, in such a (fictive) market, no one emerged richer or poorer than he was when he came to market, but all remained precisely as rich or as poor as they were at the commencement of a transaction, we can hardly call the Mishnah's market a market mechanism in any sense at all.

The ideal market for the framers of the Mishnah therefore conformed to the larger principle of the system as a whole: equivalence of exchange must govern all transactions. Unlike the case of market economics, there could be no possible risk of loss. To understand that principle, we turn first to Aristotle, as expounded by Polanyi:

> Aristotle's argument on "natural trade" in his *Politics* . . . rests on the premise that, like other forms of exchange, trade stems from the requirements of self-sufficiency. . . . Natural trade is a gainless exchange. . . .
>
> The Mishnah is imbued with the Old Testament abhorrence of profit or advantage, derived from any transaction between members of the tribe. Its prescriptions show an obsession with the moral peril of profiteering, even if involuntarily or inadvertently. Equivalents are here deliberately employed as a safeguard against this danger.[9]

The notion of equivalency also predominates in Scripture, a point to which we shall return in due course.

For the system of the Mishnah the function of the market as a price-setting mechanism, as we saw, does receive recognition—but the market mechanism gets slight appreciation. Quite how the authors of the Mishnah imagined that production and distribution would be worked out, if not through the mechanism of the market, we do not know, though I shall show ample evidence of the operative fantasy. But I do not imagine that those authors asked themselves such a question in an articulate way, even while answering it fully and completely. To the Mishnah's statement, the operation of the market mechanism made a considerable difference, since the setting of prices formed a considerable concern. The absence of a conception of the function of the market as a price-fixing mechanism that distributes goods and forces people to economize is indicated in a simple way.[10] In a market economy, the framers of the Mishnah invoked the conception of true or inherent value, and that is an anti-market conception.

The fundamental notion operative for the Judaism of the Mishnah opposed market trading, since an authority independent of the market mechanism intervened in the setting of prices and, hence, the rationing of scarce goods and services.

> It is an essential point of market trading that the political authority of the society (government, temple, guilds) gives up control of production and distribution to this impersonal mechanism. The market mechanism of exchange must determine the use of resources regardless of the status of the individual participants to the transaction, regardless of the relation of the individuals to the transaction and to each other. Transactions on the market must result in prices which measure only the scarcity of standardized commodities in a given market at a given time. . . . Mar-

ket trading does not exist unless the elements within the society universally agree to accept the market as the method of allocating resources and commodities.[11]

By that definition, it is clear, we cannot identify in the economics of the Mishnah the working of the market, even though on the surface the system appeals to the market as its instrument of rationing and exchange.

This brings us to the centerpiece of the Mishnah's framers' conception of the fair exchange of goods and services outside of the market mechanism, which is the notion of inherent value or true worth. In line with this conception prices must accord with something akin to true value, and the market simply facilitates the reasonable exchange of goods and services by bringing people together. The market provides no price-setting mechanism that operates on its own, nor is the market conceived as an economic instrument, but rather, as one of (mere) social utility in facilitating barter, encompassing, of course, barter effected through specie or money. In the following dispute, we see what is at issue:

A. If one sold the wagon, he has not sold the mules. If he sold the mules, he has not sold the wagon. If he sold the yoke, he has not sold the oxen. If he sold the oxen, he has not sold the yoke.

B. R. Judah says, "The price tells all."

C. How so? If he said to him, "Sell me your yoke for two hundred zuz," the facts are perfectly clear, for there is no yoke worth two hundred zuz.

D. And sages say, "Price proves nothing."

(M. B.B. 5:1)

Judah's view is that there is an intrinsic value, against which the market does not operate. This notion of true value, though in the minority in the case at hand, in fact dominates in mishnaic thought about the market mechanism.[12] The notion that true value inheres in all transactions, so that each party remains exactly as he was prior to the engagement, comes to concrete expression in a variety of circumstances.

Not only price, e.g., in relationship to supply and demand, but also services are so negotiated that ideally no one benefits or loses. The point throughout is that one must so adjudicate disputes that no party emerges poorer or richer than he was when he entered the transaction. Here is an extreme example of keeping the measure equal:

A. He who stole something from his fellow or borrowed something from him or with whom the latter deposited something, in a settled area, may not return it to him in the wilderness.

B. If it was on the stipulation that he was going to go forth to the wilderness, he may return it to him in the wilderness.

(M. B.Q. 10:6)

The whole notion of preserving the status quo is expressed in many other ways, but the key is the insistence that the prevailing practice be followed:

A. "He who leases a field from his fellow, in a place in which they are accustomed to cut the crops, must cut them.
B. If the custom is to uproot the crops, he must uproot them.
C. If the custom is to plough after reaping and so to turn the soil, he must do so.
D. All is in accord with the prevailing custom of the province"

                                                    (M. B. M. 9:1A–D)

In this regard, Aristotle would have understood the premises of discourse concerning the market. For, we recall, the market was not perceived by Aristotle as a price-setting mechanism, but rather as the setting in which distribution took place in such a way that the principle of equivalence was enforced. In this context we review Schumpeter's judgment:

> Aristotle . . . sought for a canon of justice in pricing, and he found it in the "equivalence" of what a man gives and receives. Since both parties to an act of barter or sale must necessarily gain by it in the sense that they must prefer their economic situations after the act to the economic situations in which they found themselves before the act—or else they would not have any motive to perform it— there can be no equivalence between the "subjective" or utility values of the goods exchanged or between the good and the money paid or received for it.[13]

Since the framers of the Mishnah maintain that there is a true value, as distinct from a market value, of an object, we may understand the acute interest of our authors in questions of fraud through overcharge and not only through misrepresentation. Mishnaic law therefore maintains that, if a purchaser pays more than a sixth more than true value, or if a seller receives a sixth less than that amount, in the form of an overcharge, fraud has been committed. The sale is null. The defrauded party has the choice of getting his money back or of keeping the goods and receiving only the amount of the overcharge. This point is worked out with some care at M. B.M. 4:3–4. We shall review the entire chapter, since it is a systematic and orderly statement of a position on what is from our perspective a systemically crucial matter.

There is a little prologue at M. B.M. 4:1–2, having to do with the right of retraction of a sale under normal circumstances, not fraudulent ones. B.M. 4:1 makes the important point that a sale is regarded as final when the buyer has drawn into his own possession the commodity which is to be purchased, not merely when the seller has received the money. The importance of that rule should not be missed. The conception is that paying money, by itself, does not effect an exchange and acquisition of the purchased item. Only a symbolic act of barter does so, and that fact (not unique to the law of the Mishnah, to be sure) tells us that, within this system, the theory of money is set aside by the theory of barter, and the market is simply a mechanism for barter. The principles that all transactions are really acts of barter, that money has no meaning other than an instrument of barter, and, consequently, that money (e.g., silver, gold) is merely another commodity—all these conceptions express in detail the substitute, within distributive economics, for the notion of the market as the mechanism of exchange. And not one of them would have surprised Aristotle, who, as we recall, firmly maintains that money merely substitutes for grain or beasts in barter. Accordingly the,initial statement of the economics of Judaism imagined a barter economy and provided for the mechanism of the barter of commodities of an intrinsic value in equal measure from one party (no longer buyer) to the other (no longer seller). For that purpose, as Aristotle, but not Plato, would have understood, coins serve only as a bushel of corn served, having intrinsic, not merely symbolic, worth. This point is made in a somewhat complicated way, but it is not difficult to follow.

M. B.M. 4:2 then illustrates the matter of retraction along the lines of the theory set out in M. B.M. 4:1. As indicated, M. B.M. 4:3–4 then go on to retraction in a case of overcharge. M. B.M. 4:5 concludes this exposition with yet another important point on fraudulent coinage: a coin which diverges from the true weight of its denomination by a fixed proportion (one-twenty-fourth, one-twelfth, or one-sixth) is a fraud and may not be used. M. B.M. 4:6 specifies the time in which the transaction is null. M. B.M. 4:7–8 conclude this discussion with a large formal exercise, of marginal relevance to what has gone before.

From discussions of cases of fraud in commercial transactions, our chapter on the working of the market proceeds to three related matters. The first (M. B.M. 4:9) is transactions not covered by a claim of fraud by reason of overcharge. These involve sales of slaves, discounted notes of indebtedness, real estate, and consecrated items. M. B.M. 4:10, second, introduces the notion of fraud through verbal misrepresentation. M. B.M. 4:11–12, finally, turn to misrepresentation through adulteration of produce for sale. In general one may not mix one kind of produce with some other. But wholesalers may gather grain from various farms and mix the whole into a single bin. Wine may be diluted only if it is customary in the province where it is sold. At the end are some miscellaneoous rulings relevant to this theme.

Let us now turn to the pertinent statement of matters and follow its course as it makes a single point: there is no such thing as a market (within the definition just now supplied), but the economy rather works through barter, that alone. And, it must follow, barter requires a true and stable value to be imputed to all commodities, since no market working out the rationing of scarce commodities is conceivable. At the end I shall explain the larger systemic principle that requires the authors to reach these conclusions in the detail of economics.

A. (1) Gold acquires silver, but silver does not acquire gold.

B. (2) Copper acquires silver, but silver does not acquire copper.

C. (3) Bad coins acquire good coins, but good coins do not acquire bad coins.
D. (4) A coin lacking a mint mark acquires a minted coin, and a minted coin does not acquire a coin lacking a mint mark.
E. (5) Movable goods acquire coins, and coins do not acquire movable goods.
F. This is the governing principle: All sorts of movable objects effect acquisition of one another.

(M. B.M. 4:1)

A. How so?
B. [If the buyer] had drawn produce into his possession but not yet paid over the coins,
C. he [nonetheless] cannot retract.
D. [If] he had paid over the coins but had not yet drawn the produce into his possession, he has the power to retract.
E. Truly have they said:
F. He who exacted punishment from the men of the Generation of the Flood and the Generation of the Dispersion is destined to exact punishment from him who does not keep his word.
G. R. Simeon says, 'Whoever has the money in his hand—his hand is on top.'

(M. B.M. 4:2)

There are two separate matters, but the relationship is integral. The first makes the point that the commodity of lesser value effects acquisition of the commodity of greater value. The second makes the point that a (mere) transfer of funds does not effect transfer of ownership. The actual receipt of the item in trade by the purchaser marks the point at which the exchange has taken place. These two points together make a single statement. It is that barter of commodities, not exchange of (abstract) money, is what characterizes the exchange of things of value. Money is an abstraction. It does not merely represent something of value, nor is it something itself of value. The entire notion of trade other than as an act of barter of materials or objects of essentially equal worth is rejected. Trade now is merely (just as Aristotle thought) a way of working out imbalances when one party has too much of one thing but needs the other, while the other party has too much of the other thing but needs what the former has in excess. Such a conception of trade ignores most trading, which took place not because of the needs of a subsistence economy, but—by the second century, A.D.—formed an autonomous economic activity, independent of the requirements of mere survival.

The rejection of the conception of money as abstraction, a unit of value on its own, in favor of money as a commodity, is expressed in a simple way. What is at issue in the pericopae before us is how a purchase is effected. The datum is that transfer of funds alone does not complete a transaction. Only the transfer of the object—the commodity—does so. The consequences of that principle are what is spelled out. But we should not miss the centrality of the principle that exchanges take place only through barter. Then each party must maintain that he has received something of equivalent value to what he has handed over, with the further consequence that profit in trade is simply inconceivable. In a money market, such as characterized the world in which the framers of the Mishnah lived, establishing the premise of barter and the priority of commodity exchange, rather than purchase with money, demands a clear and detailed statement in concrete facts, yielding symbolic demonstration. And since the Judaism of the Mishnah makes its statement through symbolic demonstration, e.g., gesture and fact of behavior rather than (mere) verbal explanation or exposition, the point that barter and not the money market operates demands ample symbolic statement in detail. This point registers in a stunning and simple way: the demonetization of money, first of all, the principle of barter instead of a money transaction, second. The former point announces that precious metals are commodities, less precious, (mere) money. Then the more precious metal will acquire the less precious, since the commodity effects acquisition, the mere coin does not.

I cannot imagine a more stunning or subtle way of denying the working of the money market and insisting upon barter as the "true" means of effecting trade and therefore permitting exchange and acquisition. Since money does not effect a transaction, we have to determine that sort of specie which is (functionally) deemed to constitute currency, and that which is regarded as a commodity. In general, the more precious the metal, the more likely it is to be regarded not as money or ready cash, but as a commodity, subject to purchase or sale, just as much as is grain or wine. This notion is expressed very simply: "Gold acquires silver," meaning, gold is a commodity, and when the purchaser has taken possession of the gold, the seller owns the silver paid as money for it. But if the exchange is in the reverse—someone paying in gold for silver—the transaction is effected when the seller has taken possession of the gold. In an exchange of copper and silver, copper is deemed money, silver is now the commodity. All of this is neatly worked out for us at M. B.M. 4:1, which, in the light of these remarks, should pose no special problems.

Another way of making the same point is to insist that, in an exchange, the transfer of money does not mark the completion of the transaction. Only when the purchaser has taken over the object of purchase is the transaction final, at which point the purchaser becomes liable to pay over funds or money equivalents—and it does not matter which. It will follow that if the buyer has transferred the money, but the seller has not yet handed over, nor the buyer received, the object of purchase, then either party may retract. Once the buyer has taken up ("lifted up") or drawn into his own possession the object or purchase, the transaction is complete. The buyer now is liable to pay off the purchase price, if it has not already been paid; the seller may no longer retract. M. B.M. 4:2A–D then satisfactorily instantiate M. B.M. 4:1's point that the sale is complete when the buyer has made acquisition of the produce, and not when the seller has received the money. M. B.M. 4:2G is important. Simeon rejects the theory that, once money has been paid, the commodity has not been fully purchased until it has been drawn into the buyer's possession. On the contrary, so soon as money changes hands, while the seller still has the power to retract, the purchaser does not. Since Simeon rejects M. B.M. 4:12A–D, he must reject the theory of acquisition presented at M. B.M. 4:1 as well.

We continue this sequence of principles of economics, moving from the rejection of the conception of money as a unit of value to the affirmation of the principal notion, true value. The notion of true value logically belongs together with the conception of money as an item of barter or meant merely to facilitate barter, because both notions referred to the single underlying conception of the economy as a steady-state entity in which people could not increase wealth but only exchange it. Quite what true value can mean is not at all clear, since the notion is a rather murky one. But the point before us is that an object has a true or intrinsic value, which cannot be exceeded in payment or receipt by more than 18 percent. Fraud involves not adulteration of a product or misrepresentation of the character or quality of merchandise, such as we should grasp. We shall now see that fraud is simply charging more than something is worth. And that can only mean, more than something is worth intrinsically. This profoundly Aristotelian economic conception is now made explicit. (I cannot suggest where, in Scripture, sages could have come upon it)

A. Fraud [overreaching] is an overcharge of four pieces of silver out of twenty-four pieces of silver to the sela—
B. (one-sixth of the purchase price)
C. For how long is it permitted to retract [in the case of fraud]?
D. So long as it takes to show [the article] to a merchant or a relative.
E. R. Tarfon gave instructions in Lud:
F. "Fraud is an overcharge of eight pieces of silver to a sela—
G. "one-third of the purchase price."
H. So the merchants of Lud rejoiced.
I. He said to them, "All day long it is permitted to retract."
J. They said to him, "Let R. Tarfon leave us where we were."
K. And they reverted to conduct themselves in accord with the ruling of sages.

(M. B.M. 4:3)

The definition of fraud self-evidently rests on the conception of an intrinsic or true value, and there is no conception of fraud as mere misrepresentation of the character of merchandise. That comes later, and bears its own considerations. Fraud here is simply charge higher than the intrinsic worth of the object permits. That definition rejects the conception of "free" and "market," that redundancy that insists upon the market as the instrument of the rationing of scarce resources. If an object has a true value of twenty-four and the seller pays twenty-eight, he has been defrauded and may retract. Tarfon gave and took, E–K. In this connection we recall our earlier review of the counterpart views of Greek, particularly Aristotle's, economics. The just price derives from good will, *philia*, as a matter of reciprocity: "In such exchange no gain is involved; goods have their known prices, fixed beforehand."[14] So Haney: "An exchange is just when each gets exactly as much as he gives the other; yet this equality does not mean equal costs, but equal wants."[15] Schumpeter's statement on the same matter reminds us of the identity of conception between Aristotle's and the Mishnah's authors' ideas on true value:

> Aristotle . . . sought for a canon of justice in pricing, and he found it in the "equivalence" of what a man gives and receives. Since both parties to an act of barter or sale must necessarily gain by it in the sense that they must prefer their economic situations after the act to the economic situations in which they found themselves before the act—or else they would not have any motive to perform it—there can be no equivalence between the "subjective" or utility values of the goods exchanged or between the good and the money paid or received for it.[16]

Given the idiom in which they made their statement, the framers of the Mishnah found an acutely concrete way of saying the same thing, first, the notion of a just price, second, the emphasis upon barter; and they said both ideas in juxtaposition, for precisely the same reason Aristotle had to. Let me give the reason with emphasis: *the logic of the one demanded the complementary logic of the other.* Once we impute a true value to an object or commodity, we shall also dismiss from consideration all matters of worth extrinsic to the object or commodity; hence money is not an abstract symbol of worth but is itself a commodity, and, further, objects bear true value. The two are really different ways of saying the same thing. And what that is, from our perspective, is the negative message that the market is not the medium of rationing, because another medium is in play. But we do not, here, know what that other medium is. Only in our progress through the definition of wealth, on the one side (chapter 6), and the vast panoply of rules expressing the workings of the Mishnah's distributive economics, on the other (chapter 7), shall we grasp the entire picture.

We proceed to a still more stunning reiteration of the same, now in the notion of the perfect equivalence of both parties to a transaction. Not only must the seller not make "too much" money, the buyer also must not receive "too much" value.

A. All the same are the buyer and the seller: both are subject to the law of fraud.
B. Just as fraud applies to an ordinary person, so it applies to a merchant.
C. R. Judah says, "Fraud does not apply to a merchant."
D. He who has been subjected [to fraud]—his hand is on top.
E. [If] he wanted, he says to him, "Return my money."

F. [Or, if he wanted, he says to him,] "Give me back the amount of the fraud."

(M. B.M. 4:4)

The statement at A is bald and unadorned. It cannot be embellished; the perfect complementarity of exchange is simply announced in the simplest possible way. At B–C we turn to the merchant, who forms the counterpart to what we should call a wholesaler, who collects commodities in small volume and forms a large volume for transportation and sale in distant markets. B–C in fact repeat and dispute A. D is clarified by E–F. The buyer has the power to nullify the sale or merely to collect the amount of the overcharge. In our context, fraud pertains to counterfeiting, and the same notion is introduced here. But the difference should not be missed. What is fraudulent in the counterfeit is the representation of value that is not present; that is to say, a defective coin is defective because it lacks that intrinsic value that it is supposed to contain. It is subject to fraud for the same reason that a keg of wine may be subject to fraud. That is to say, in a barter exchange for a keg of wine, one may receive "too much" value, and so too, in a barter exchange for a sela coin, one also may receive "too much" value.

A. How much may a sela be defective and [still] not fall under the rule of fraud?
B. R. Meir says, "Four issars, at an issar to a denar."
C. R. Judah says, "Four pondions, at a pondion to a denar."
D. R. Simeon says, "Eight pondions, at two pondions to a denar."

(M. B.M. 4:5)

If a sela is short-weight, it is not to be paid out. A sela = four denars; a denar = twelve pondions; a pondion = two issars, so Meir permits a short weight of one-twenty-fourth, Judah one-twelfth, and Simeon one-sixth, in line with M. B.M. 4:3A–B. The point then is clear. "Fraud" in commodities is the measure, also, of fraud in coinage. The upshot is to treat the exchange of money as barter, just as we noted at M. B.M. 4:1.

A. How long is it permitted to return [a defective sela]?
B. In large towns, for the length of time it takes to show a money changer.
C. And in villages, up to the eve of the Sabbath.
D. [If the one who gave it] recognizes it, even after twelve months he is to accept it from him.
E. But [if the one who gave the coin refuses to take it back], he has no valid claim against the other except resentment.
F. He may give it for produce in the status of second tithe [for easy transportaton to Jerusalem],
G. and need not scruple,
H. for it is only churlishness [to refuse a slightly depreciated coin].

(M. B.M. 4:6)

A. Defrauding involves [an overcharge of] four pieces of silver [for what one has bought for a sela].

(M. B.M. 4:7)

We go back over the issue of M. B.M. 4:3, now with reference to M. B.M. 4:5. The defective coin may be returned, within the specified time limits, A–C. The one who handed it over has to take it back, D–E, if he recognizes the coin. But if he does not, E, the one who has been given the bad coin has no recourse. The defective coin may be exchanged for second-tithe produce and taken to Jerusalem.

This brings us to the complementary question: what sorts of things *lack* a true or intrinsic value? Given the logic that imposes upon all transactions the fiction that a barter of equal value has taken place, we should anticipate that things that are not subject to barter will lack, also, an intrinsic value. Commodities are bartered, because we can measure (so it is imagined) the intrinsic worth of things. But what has no intrinsic worth, such as a piece of paper; or what has no worth readily treated as standard for purposes of measuring equivalency, such as a person; or what is not a commodity at all, such as real estate, or what is not subject to a this-worldly evaluation as something accessible to human utilization at all, such as what has been sanctified to heaven— these will not be subject to barter and therefore also will not be given the status of commodities bearing intrinsic value for purposes of exchange. Here the really interesting item is real estate, which is removed from the scale of true value and deemed to have a value beyond all estimation. That (presently minor) exception later on will become the touchstone and key to the system as a whole, for it reflects the definition of wealth upon which everything else depends.

A. These are matters which are not subject to a claim of fraud [on account of overcharge]:
B. (1) slaves, (2) bills of indebtedness [which are discounted and sold], (3) real estate, and (4) that which has been consecrated.
C. They are not subject to twofold restitution.
D. Nor [in the case of a consecrated ox or sheep] to fourfold or fivefold restitution.
E. An unpaid bailee is not required to take an oath [on their account, that he has not inflicted damage].
F. And a paid bailee does not have to pay compensation [on their account, if they are stolen or lost].
G. R. Simeon says, "Holy Things for which one is liable for replacement [should they be lost] are subject to a claim of fraud on account of overcharge.
H. "Holy Things for which one is not liable for replacement [should they be lost] are not subject to a claim of fraud on account of overcharge" [compare M. B.Q. 7:4].

    I. R. Judah says, "Also: He who sells a scroll of the Torah, a beast, or a pearl—

    J. "they are not subject to a claim of fraud by reason of overcharge."

    K. They said to him, "They have specified only these [of B]."

(M. B.M. 4:9)

The items of B are exempt from the rules governing movables which are sold, A, stolen, C–D, or subjected to negligent bailees, E–F. B2 refers to writs of indebtedness, which are sold at a discount to a bill collector. Simeon qualifies B4. The conception of equivalency extends to transactions of a non-material character. But I see the following as essentially beside the point of the chapter in which they occur:

    A. Just as a claim of fraud applies to buying and selling

    B. so a claim of fraud applies to spoken words.

    C. One may not say to [a storekeeper], "How much is this object?" knowing that he does not want to buy it.

(M. B.M. 4:10)

The remainder of the pericope proceeds to other matters and hardly carries forward what is at stake in the foregoing. The transaction of exchange commences at the point at which the buyer and seller engage. Therefore the obligation of the buyer encompasses his or her integrity in entering into the barter. Asking about the value of an object when one does not sincerely intend to buy imposes upon the seller the courtesies of exchange that, in fact, he does not owe, and acquires for the putative purchaser the courtesies of exchange that the purchaser does not in fact deserve. That is what is at stake in preserving the integrity of the barter transaction not only in the exchange of goods but also in the exchange of what we now call politeness noises. The remainder proceeds to other matters entirely. But we should not miss the point of relevance. When the courtesies of exchange are not equivalent, then one party simply abuses the other, and the inappropriate examples make that simple point as to the alternatives—fair exchange, even in words, or mere abuse, in one form or another:

    D. If there was a penitent, one may not say to him, "Remember what you used to do!"

    E. If he was a child of proselytes, one may not say to him, "Remember what your folk used to do!"

    F. For it is said, *And a proselyte you shall not wrong nor oppress* [Ex. 22:20].

(M. B.M. 4:10)

C–E illustrate A–B. But D and E are cases not of fraud but of mere churlishness, so it is only C which is directly relevant.

We recall the emphasis, for the definition of the market, upon the standardization of items of exchange. In a barter economy, that standardization proves all the more required, since we have to make certain that each party to the exchange contributes a known and uniform value, something of entirely consistent character. If we mix diverse species, we have no exchange; but even if we mix diverse volumes of a single specie, e.g., old and new produce, we also cannot effect a fair barter. Accordingly, the provision of a transaction of barter will impose the requirement of a pure and unadulterated commodity exchange. What is in play in the matter of pure foods is not fraud or out-and-out misrepresentation. The concern is now that we keep separate and distinct commodities that are not wholly like one another. Mixing different things together disrupts the equal exchange that is in the center of all transactions. That principle is expressed in the following:

A. They do not commingle one sort of produce with another sort of produce,
B. even new and new [produce, plucked in the same growing season],
C. and it goes without saying, new with old.
D. To be sure, in the case of wine they have permitted commingling strong with weak.
E. because it improves it.
F. They do not commingle the lees of wine with wine.
G. But one may hand over [to the purchaser] the lees [of the wine he is buying].
H. He whose wine got mixed with water may not sell it in a store,
I. unless he informs [the purchaser],
J. nor to a merchant,
K. even though he informs him.
L. For [the latter buys it] only to deceive others thereby.
M. In a place in which it is the custom to put water in wine,
N. one may dilute it.

(M. B.M. 4:11)

A. A merchant purchases grain from five threshing floors and puts it [all] into one storage bin,
B. [wine] from five wine presses and puts it into a single storage-jar—
C. on condition that he not intend to commingle [wine of diverse quality for the purpose of fraud].
D. R. Judah says, "A storekeeper should not hand out parched corn and nuts to little children, because in that way he makes it their habit [to buy from] him."
E. But sages permit.
F. And he should not cut the prevailing price.
G. But sages say, "[If he does so], his memory will be blessed."
H. "He should not sift crushed beans," the words of Abba Saul.
I. And sages permit.

J.   But they concede that he should not sift them [solely] at the entry of the storage bin.

K.   For he would do so only to create a false picture [of the quality of what is in the bin].

L.   They do not beautify [what they sell]—either man, beast, or utensils.

(M. B.M. 4:12)

Despite certain formal inconsistencies, I am inclined to see M. B.M. 4:11 as a triplet: A, F–G, and H–I, with rich augmentation of A at B–E and of H–I at J–N. The point is consistent with what has already been said. One may not improve the appearance of his goods (M. B.M. 4:12L). Produce from one field should not be mixed with (better-looking) produce from some other. Certainly one who buys seasoned produce does not want new produce, or vice versa. D–E then qualify the foregoing. One may not sell the lees of a jug of wine with the wine. H–N simply make the point that small stores may sell diluted wine, so long as purchasers are informed. But wholesale merchants are not to be allowed to buy diluted wine. M. B.M. 4:12A–C continue this same matter. A wholesale merchant is allowed to collect merchandise from diverse sources and store it in a single bin. The triplet of disputes at the end (D–E, F–G, and H–I, J–K) is clear as given. One must not place at the top of a bin produce of a better quality than what is on the bottom, and L restates the same point in general terms. In my judgment, the chapter we have reviewed has now completed its program and made its entire statement. While Aristotle might not have fully grasped the idiom, because of its specificity, contrary to his power at generalization and abstract statement of principles, I am confident he would have grasped and accorded with the principles at hand.

Let us now turn to yet another statement that the function of trade and commerce is to assure the equivalency of exchange, so that no party emerges from the market richer, none poorer. In this case we move from the market to transactions between craftsmen and householders. It involves several distinct matters. First, what happens if one gets back from an artisan assigned the repair of an object something worth less than he has presented to the artisan? Second comes the just disposition of the detritus of the artisan's shop. If one brings commodities for manufacture, e.g., wool to be washed and carded, who gets the remnants? The basic principle of a perfect equivalency of exchange takes a somewhat different turn. In the first instance, if the craftsman has ruined the object brought for repair, he must restore full (intrinsic) value. The transaction thus cannot leave one party poorer than he was when he entered it. Not surprisingly, the advantage lies with the householder, and the craftsman's liability reaches the full value of the object he has ruined.

A.   [If] one gave [something] to craftsmen to repair, and they spoiled [the object], they are liable to pay compensation.

B.   [If] he gave to a joiner a box, chest, or cupboard to repair, and he spoiled it, he is liable to pay compensation.

C. A builder who took upon himself to destroy a wall, and who smashed the rocks or did damage is liable to pay compensation.
D. [If] he was tearing down the wall on one side, and it fell down on the other side, he is exempt.
E. But if it is because of the blow [which he gave it], he is liable.

(M. B.M. 9:3)

B illustrates A. C–E carry the matter a step further. If the damage is part of the normal course of events, D, the contractor is not liable. If it is because of his incompetence, he is. In the next statement, we find a still more explicit expression of the notion of equivalency of exchange, which is to say, the counterpart, in the present context, of barter.

A. He who hands over wool to a dyer, and the [dye in the] cauldron burned it, [the dyer] pays the value of the wool.
B. [If] he dyed it in a bad color,
C. if [the wool] increased in value more than the outlay [of the dyer],
D. [the owner of the wool] pays him the money he has laid out in the process of dyeing.
E. But if the outlay of the dyer is greater than the increase in value of the wool,
F. [the owner] pays him back only the value of the improvement.
G. [If he gave wool to a dyer] to dye it red, and he dyed it black,
H. [or] to dye it black, and he dyed it red—
I. R. Meir says, "[The dyer] pays him back the value of his wool."
J. R. Judah says, "If the increase in value is greater than the outlay for the process of dyeing, [the owner] pays him back the outlay for the process of dyeing.
K. "And if the outlay for the process of dyeing is greater than the increase in the value of the wool, [the dyer] pays him only the increase in value of the wool."

(M. B.M. 9:4)

A sets the stage for two further developments of the theory of M. B.M. 9:3B–F,G–K. In the former the owner of the wool is given an advantage when the work is done poorly. In the latter, the dyer's liability for error is unlimited, in Meir's view, for the dyer pays the cost of the wool. In Judah's, the owner pays only the specified amount. The dyer loses less. The point of the assessment (C–F, J) is that if the wool was worth ten denars, and when dyed (improperly, to be sure), it is worth fifteen, and it cost the dyer three denars, the owner of the wool pays the dyer what he spent, which is three denars. But if the expense of the dyer was seven denars, and the wool increased in value by only five, the owner of the wool pays out five denars and takes his wool.

We come to the second of the two matters, the division of the detritus of the manufacturing process, e.g., shreds of wool, threads, sherds of the carpenter's plane or adze. They derive from the raw materials supplied by the householder (and the usage here retains that precision to which I earlier called attention). He should surely own them. But then the carpenter or woolcomber or laundryman will be obliged to spend time and energy, which also have value, in preserving matters of no account. How are we to sort out matters?

A. Shreds of wool which the laundryman pulls out—lo, these belong to him.
B. And those which the woolcomber pulls out—lo, they belong to the householder.
C. The laundryman pulls out three threads, and they are his.
D. But more than this—lo, they belong to the householder.
E. If they were black [threads] on a white [surface], he takes all, and they are his.
F. A tailor who left over a thread sufficient for sewing,
G. or a piece of cloth three by three fingerbreadths—
H. lo, these belong to the householder,
I. What the carpenter takes off the plane—lo, these are his.
J. But [what he takes off] with a hatchet belongs to the householder.
K. And if he was working in the household of the householder, even the sawdust belongs to the householder.

(M. B.M. 10:10)

The contrast of A and B, and of C and D, is to stress that what is paltry in the view of the householder may be kept by the craftsman, and no scruple about thievery is invoked. E refers to threads which surely are unwanted. The second triplet, F–H, I–J, K, makes the same points. The upshot is that the householder who has handed over raw materials retains ownership of all the raw materials, hence their value, unless the remnant is null. In this way we preserve the true value that the householder possessed when he entered the transaction. The costs, to the artisan, of keeping the sherds for the householder do not register, because the householder remains owner of the entire value of the commodity he has handed over for manufacture and cannot be permitted to lose any of the value of that material.

This leads us to repeat the observation with which we concluded our survey of the category of the householder. The economics expressed in these rules clearly is one of barter, and the transactions are exchanges of commodities of equal intrinsic worth. But the actual market, we realize full well, is made up not of householders alone, but also of traders, shopkeepers, and other holders of capital. The arena of exchange—hardly a market—conceived by the framers of our document, by contrast, is one in which the proprietors of the means of production exchange on a perennially equal basis the things they have produced: this for that, this worth that. It is one thing to insist that barter characterize trade in potatoes, so that the crop of one year is not to be mingled with the crop of another. But what sort of barter will permit the exchange of potatoes and, let us say, a physician's services, or a clay pot? And, more to the point, what of the role of capital? The Mishnah's economics takes a remarkably unsympathetic view of the holder of liquid capital or even of trading goods of any kind. The householder appears in the market as principal of exchange because he is in command of the goods of exchange. Moreover, as we shall see in the next chapter, the householder plays his central role in the economics of the Mishnah as borrower, not lender. The lender is treated as outsider, watched and regulated.[17] The purpose of the market (now using the word in an inexact sense, that is, merely for the arena for exchange) is to secure for the economy precisely the opposite result of markets as ooccasions for the rationing of scarce goods (and services).

In all, in the Mishnah, we have a statement of a thoroughgoing Aristotelian economics, with the indicative conceptions of true value, money as commodity, and barter paramount. Where we uncover a difference between Plato and Aristotle, as in the matter of the definition of money, Aristotle's, and not Plato's, definition applies. And connections between topics, natural in the logic of Aristotle's system, are drawn in the Mishnah as well. But in one important way, the authors of the Mishnah differed from Aristotle's disposition of economics. To those authors economic questions, worked out in detail but expressive of clearly accessible theoretical principles, played a central role in the system as a whole. In the Mishnah issues of economics take a more considerable role in sustained discourse than the—on the whole paltry—role accorded to them in the writings of Aristotle, all the more so of Plato. We may judge very simply that the authors of the Mishnah gave more sustained attention to the economic component of political economy, and invested in that matter more rigorous and far more detailed reflection than did Aristotle, Plato, and the Christian counterparts among the system builders of antiquity.

Why so heavy an emphasis upon such matters as barter of commodities of equivalent, and true, value? And why such sustained attention to the specification of how society is to preserve stationary worth and wealth? In due course, I shall explain these facts and show that they carry us deep into the fundamental affirmations, as to this world and the supernatural as well, of the system builders of the Mishnah. That the Mishnah forms a *Staatsroman,* a utopian statement of how things ought to be (but, therefore, also a recognition of widespread violation of norms in the practice of the day), not how they actually were, as much as Plato's *Republic* and Aristotle's *Politics,* in light of conceptions of true value and of "fraud" as divergence from that mystic imputed worth, no longer can be subject to doubt. The real questions are why those details of distributive economics played so central a role in the economic doctrine of the system, and, still more urgent, why this system of world construction found so vital a concern in economics at all. But before we can answer the ultimate, and the critical, issue of why the system accorded centrality to economics at all, we have first of all to turn to the matter of wealth: what it was, and what it was not. The answer to that question leads us deep into the heart of matters.

6

Wealth

There are two sorts of wealth-getting: . . . one is a part of household management, the other is retail trade. The former is necessary and honorable, while that which consists in exchange is justly censured; for it is unnatural, and a mode by which men gain from one another. The most hated sort, and with the greatest reason, is usury, which makes a gain out of money itself, and not from the natural object of it. For money was intended to be used in exchange, but not to increase at interest.

Aristotle, Politics, 1258a–b, trans. W. D. Ross[1]

The key to the importance imputed by the authors of the Mishnah to economics lies in the definition of wealth. For economics addresses questions of value defined in material terms, the disposition of scarce resources in accord with a defined rationality concerning, as it does, things accorded palpable and concrete value. Now, as a matter of fact, I cannot find a sentence in the Mishnah and in its continuations that calls into question the worth of wealth. The contrast between that self-evident trait of the system and the recurrent leitmotif that material wealth is evil or merely irrelevant to the important matters of life characteristic of schools of Greco-Roman philosophy and Christianity alike alerts us to the generative question of description, analysis, and interpretation. It is why this system accords an important place to the disposition of wealth, the definition of right action in the market, and the delineation of the traits of the householder, designated as one who controls one of the available means of production, in a circumstance in which other system builders, including, after all, Plato, do not do so. And the issue having drawn us to the center of the system, we have to know, first, what the system understands by wealth, and, second, why the system defines wealth in that way and not in some other. The former question finds its answer in the present chapter, the latter, in the one to follow. The two answers together form the account of the economics of the Mishnah as I am able to present it.

Part of the answer to the question before us must appeal to the state of thought of the age, though, of course, that answer begs the question. Still, we do well to remember that a document so profoundly shaped by Greco-Roman conceptions and values will certainly have conformed to the simple notion stated by Finley, "The judgment of antiquity about wealth was fundamentally unequivocal and uncomplicated. Wealth was necessary and it was good."[2] Defining wealth, too, the authors of the Mishnah fit well into the conceptions of their age. For them, as much as for Aristotle half a millennium earlier, wealth meant not money but real estate.[3] The basic wealth of the upper strata of Rome was in land, with consequent chronic shortages of cash.[4] That fact will help us to understand the prevailing bias against capital and in favor of the land-poor householder that characterizes the Mishnah's treatment of wealth, money-making, and the definition and uses of money and of capital. But that bias stated, in its context, a conception integral to the Mishnaic system as a whole. Money represented something of worth, was a kind of commodity, no different in its way from land itself. Wealth was tangible and material, best embodied in real property.[5] For, as we shall see, the framers took for granted that money formed a commodity for barter, and that all forms of profit—all forms!—constituted nothing other than that "usury" that Scripture had condemned.[6] It follows that the economics of the system forms a cogent and wholly coherent chapter in the system's larger and encompassing statement. But these familiar facts do beg the question, since they merely repeat the simple allegation that the framers of the Mishnah valued wealth and assigned to economics an important systemic task. They do not tell us why, rather explaining only the context in which the system made its choices. Others in the same setting made different choices, so we have not yet explained why this, not that.

The answer to the question of the reason for the importance of wealth, together with consequent issues of the economic definition of the householder, on the one side, and the correct conduct of the market in accord with the conception of true value, on the other, derives from one simple fact. In the system of the Mishnah, as we shall see, wealth to the householder is (ownership of) land, and the concerns of householders are in transactions in land. We have first fully to appreciate the unique status, as wealth, accorded to real property, and only then, in the chapter beyond this one, spell out the fundamental systemic message that is borne by that fact. We begin from the beginning, the absolute value imputed to ownership of land, without regard to the size or productivity of that land. Any ownership of a piece of land, however small, constitutes "wealth," and so, for one example, is liable for the designation of God's portion in the crop. This conception is expressed in terms of being liable to the laws of leaving the corner of the field to the poor (*peah*), as follows:

    A. R. Eliezer says, "An area of land within which is planted a quarter-qab of seed is subject to the laws of *peah*."

B. R. Joshua says, "An area of land that produces at least two seahs of grain is subject to the laws of *peah*."
C. R. Tarfon says, "An area of land measuring six by six handbreadths is subject to the laws of *peah*."
D. R. Judah b. Beterah says, "An area of land that produces sufficient grain that the farmer must cut twice, that is, with two strokes of a sickle, is subject to the laws of *peah*."
E. And the law accords with his opinion.
F. R. Aqiba says, "Land of any size at all is subject to the laws of *peah* and to the laws of first fruits . . ." [Dt. 26:1].

(M. Peah 3:6)

A. A dying man who wrote over his property to others as a gift but left himself a piece of land of any size whatever—his gift is valid.
B. If he did not leave himself a piece of land of any size whatever, his gift is not valid.

(M. B.B. 9:6A–D)

The context of the opening pericope, gifts to the poor, introduces a fundamental qualification.

This brings us to the centerpiece of the system's definition of wealth. When we speak of (ownership of) "land," it is, self-evidently, land that produces a crop liable to the requirements of the sacerdotal taxes (a matter on which we shall spend ample time in the coming chapter). It follows, therefore, that ownership of land speaks of a very particular acreage, specifically, the territory known to the framers of the Mishnah as the land of Israel, that alone. Land not subject to the sacerdotal taxes is not land to which the legal status and traits before us are imputed.

But there is a second equally critical qualification. Land in the land of Israel that is liable to sacerdotal taxes must be owned by an Israelite. Gentiles are not expected to designate portions of their crop as holy, and if they do so, those portions of the crop that they designate as holy nonetheless are deemed secular. So we have an exceedingly specific set of conditions in hand. Wealth for the system of the Mishnah is not ownership of land in general, for example, land held by Jews in Babylonia, Egypt, Italy, or Spain. It is ownership of land located in a very particular place. And wealth for that same system is not wealth in the hands of an undifferentiated owner. It is wealth in the domain of an Israelite owner in particular. Wealth therefore is ownership of *land of Israel* in two senses, both of them contained within the italicized words. It is ownership of land located in the land *of Israel*. It is ownership of land located in the land of Israel that is *of Israel,* belonging to an Israelite. "Israel" then forms the key to the meaning of wealth, because it modifies persons and land alike: only an Israel[ite] can possess the domain that signifies wealth; only a domain within the land called by the name of "Israel" can constitute wealth. It is in the enchanted intersection of the two Israels, (ownership of) the land, (ownership by) the people, that wealth in the system of the Mishnah finds realization.

It must follow that the position of Greco-Roman economics on the ultimate value and status of real estate is vastly modified here. The distributive economics of the Mishnah is not simply an adaptation of temple economics to the needs of the Israelite Temple. The theology of the Mishnah *utilizes* the principles of distributive economics in order to make a statement of not economics but theology. In the case of the economics of Judaism, only real estate in a particular, designated area enjoys that standing as source of status (defining the householder) and value (beyond price, however miniscule the property) that the passages at hand impute. Everything that follows derives its full meaning from that fact: ownership of land means land of Israel, that alone, and land of Israel means not land possessed by Jews wherever they are located, but land of Israel in the possession of Israelites (male housholders) within the designated boundaries (whatever they were) of the Jewish part of what was then called Palestine. These, we rapidly realize, are not definitions of an economic character at all, bearing no relationship to the productivity of land or its value in producing goods and services of a material character. The system's peculiar definition of ownership of land forms the first bit of evidence toward our understanding of how the economics of Judaism adapted for the purposes of Judaism principles of distributive economics. It was in that way— through the applied principles of distributive economics as defined herein— that the system of the Mishnah was permitted to make a fundamental and acutely detailed statement of its ultimate principle in the terms and idiom in which the framers wished to speak: the humble and obscure detail of the sale of grain or beets in the marketplace. But in stating the main lines of the conclusion, I have moved ahead of my story. Let us go back to the simple question: how did the innate value of land express itself in the system of the Mishnah's definition of wealth and the exchange of wealth?

Through ownership of real estate critical social transactions are worked out. The marriage settlement depends upon real property. Compensation for torts and damages is paid out of land of the highest quality (M. B.Q. 1:2H). The householder's measurement of value is expressed in quality of acreage, top, middle, and bottom grade.[7] Civil penalties, meant to restore the social balance upset by an act of aggression against the person or property of another, thus are exacted through restoration accomplished in payment of real property.[8] The principal transactions to be taken up are those of the householder who owns beasts which do damage or suffer it; who harvests his crops and must set aside and by his own word and deed sanctify them for use by the scheduled castes; who uses or sells his crops and feeds his household; and who, if fortunate, will acquire still more land. At M. Ket. 6:1ff., for example, the wife's dowry is assumed to be in land, or to be convertible into land, which is the only valid investment. If ready cash came to the wife in an inheritance, land is purchased with it, and the husband has the usufruct (M. Ket. 8:3). Land is the

only valid investment. So too M. Ket. 10:3 treats only real property as value
to be taken into account. As we saw in chapter 4, the household exists—finds
validity and definition as a unit of economic productivity—because of ownership of land, not only *upon* land, for the sharecropper is not classified as a
householder. A householder without real estate, that is, real wealth, is inconceivable. It is to householders that the Mishnah addresses its conception of the
social order. It is the householder who is the pivot of society and its bulwark.
It is the household that makes up the village; the corporate component of the
society of Israel is measured in land, which, therefore, also forms the measure
of wealth.

Once, moreover, we take full account of the structural components of the
Mishnah's economy (the household, defined in terms of command or ownership of landed domain, however small, composing, with other households, the
village; the village constituting the market in which all things hold together in
an equal exchange of a stable population in a steady-state economy), we revert
to the consequent question: then what is wealth? And the answer to that question must accommodate the fact that wealth is conceived as unchanging and
not subject to increase or decrease; hence, by the way, the notion of true value
imputed to commodities. For if we imagine a world in which, ideally, no one
rises and no one falls, and in which wealth is essentially stable, then we want
to know what people understand by money, on the one hand, and how they
identify riches, on the other. The answer is very simple. For the system of the
Mishnah, wealth constitutes that which is of lasting value, and what lasts is
real property (in the land of Israel), that alone.[9] Real estate (in the land of
Israel) does not increase in volume; it is not subject to the fluctuation of the
market (so it was imagined); it is permanent, reliable, and, however small,
always useful for something. It was perceived to form the medium of enduring
value for a society made up of households engaged in agriculture. Accordingly, the definition of wealth as real and not movable, as real estate (in the
land of Israel) and nowhere else, as real estate and not as other kinds of goods,
conformed to the larger systemic givens. A social system composed of units
of production, households, engaged in particular in agricultural production,
made a decision entirely coherent with its larger conception and character
in identifying real estate as the sole measure of wealth. And, as we recall,
Aristotle would not have been surprised.

True enough, we find more spiritual definitions of wealth, for example,
M. Avot 4:2: "Who is rich? He who is happy in what he has." One can become rich through keeping or studying the Torah, e.g., "He who keeps the
Torah when poor will in the end keep it in wealth" (M. Avot 4:9). So too we
find the following, "Keep your business to a minimum and make your business Torah" (M. Avot 4:10). But these sayings have no bearing upon a single
passage of the Mishnah in which a concrete transaction in exchanges of material goods take place, nor does anyone invoke the notion of being satisfied
with what one has when it comes to settling scores. None of them to begin

with occurs in the Mishnah, but only in its later apologetic, produced about a half century after the closure of the document. No decision in the exegetical literature generated by the Mishnah (e.g., the Tosefta, the two Talmuds) ever appealed as grounds for the practical disposition of a case of conflicting interests to the notion that, e.g., both parties should forfeit the case and go off and get rich, instead, by studying the Torah. I think we may dismiss as systemically irrelevant, indeed inconsequential, all definitions of wealth outside of the context of how actualities of conflict and exchange are sorted out, and in every such concrete and material setting, ownership of land is the medium of adjudication.

Ownership of a landed domain (by a Jew in Palestine, that is, by an Israelite in the land of Israel; from this point, I need not continue to insert the required systemic qualification) therefore provides the key to much else. Transfer of land ownership through proper deeds is subject to very careful scrutiny and detailed legislation. A piece of land, however small, was the unit of the economy deemed sufficient to support a person; if someone thought he was dying but held onto a bit of land, all his gifts in contemplation of death remained valid in the event of recovery. The small bit of property kept in reserve showed that the gifts were not on the mental stipulation that the donor die. Land served as the medium of exchange in marriage settlements and in paying compensation for torts and damages. Money bears no interest for the system of the Mishnah. As we shall see, when money comes under discussion, it is only to distinguish what functions as specie from what does not function as specie. As we fully realize, money has no intrinsic meaning; it is a commodity that, because of its universal utility and acceptability, may serve as a more convenient instrument of barter than any other commodity, that alone. Wealth is not money in volume; it is real estate, however small.

Given the range of objects, animate and inanimate, that, being valued, fall into the classification of wealth, we must find remarkable the limited definition of wealth framed by the authors of the Mishnah. Wealth meant land, and the entire economics focused upon real property. To be rich meant to own land; to make a secure investment, along the lines of U.S. government bonds for instance, meant purchasing land, however fragmentary, however limited the yield by reason of size. Judicial civil penalties were exacted by transfers of land. Women's dowries were collected in real property. Not only so, but individuals could hold and transfer wealth in the form of land. For these facts presuppose private ownership of land.[10] Otherwise, transfers from person to person cannot have formed the premise of both civil penalties, e.g., recompense for torts and damages, and dowries, and, in both instances, what was transferred, through the land, was wealth. For, as we noted, the purpose of penalties was to restore the situation prior to the commission of the tort (for example), so that, so far as possible, each party retained the wealth he or she had possessed prior to the transaction that had made one poorer, the other richer. The same conception of a steady-state economy governed in the mar-

ket. Accordingly, individuals owned wealth. It follows that, alongside the notion of land as wealth, the authors understood that individuals, householders,
owned and disposed of wealth.

The Mishnah's writers, accordingly, took for granted the concept of private
property.[11] People controlled and might dispose of resources of their own,
whether time, money, chattels, or land.[12] Some public property is shared by
all concerned in a village, such as well, bathhouse, town square, synagogue,
ark, and scrolls (M. Ned. 5:5), but there is no passage in which a property
that is farmed is held by the village in common. Not only so, but the Mishnah
took for granted that some authority, not specified in concrete terms but assumed to be the government of the Mishnah's "Israel," would accord to owners their legal rights, for example, restoring lost or stolen goods.[13] It follows
that the authors of the Mishnah understood by wealth not only such spiritual
matters as contentment with what one has, or vast mastery of Torah teachings,
but also "crass," material things. In that same context of the notion of private
property, of course, the framers recognized the existence of rights of private
ownership, also of chattels and movables. But money as such bore slight permanent value and constituted no measure, or form, of wealth. The operation
of the market has already shown us the stipulative, indeed nearly adventitious,
status accorded to a mere transfer of coins. That fact derives from the suspi-
cion in which transactions in money, for profit, were held.

Let us proceed to the obvious by dismissing the notion of wealth as equivalent to money. In the Greco-Roman context, MacMullen states, "urban wealth
lay chiefly in rural holdings."[14] As Schumpeter presents the matter of money
as wealth, Aristotle's theory of money regards money as principally a medium
of exchange. In order to serve as a medium of exchange in markets of commodities, money itself must be one of those commodities: "it must be a thing
that is useful and has exchange value independently of its monetary function,
. . . a value that can be compared with other values."[15] None of this would
have surprised the framers of the Mishnah, as we saw in the preceding chapter. Money is contingent, serves a function, bears no intrinsic worth, constitutes a mere medium of exchange, like any other commodity. It cannot form a
definition of wealth. The authors of the Mishnah of course concurred, seeing
silver and gold as fundamentally commodities, subject to redefinition, under
specified circumstances, also as specie—in that order.

To understand still more clearly the conception of wealth as land, we return
for a brief moment to the conception of barter as natural exchange, trade as
unnatural, characteristic of Aristotle's thought. Aristotle defines wealth as "a
means, necessary for the maintenance of the household and the *polis* (with
self-sufficiency a principle in the background), and, like all means, it is limited by its end."[16] Barter involves not the increase of wealth, which is contrary to nature, but only exchanges to accommodate the needs of households,
which, by nature, cannot be wholly self-sufficient. Money serves as a substitute for items of barter. But money also is something people wish to accu-

mulate on its own, and that is unnatural. Household management satisfies the needs of the household; wealth beyond those needs is meaningless, unnatural. Retail trade aims at the accumulation of coins through exchanges; there is no natural limit to the desire for money, corresponding to the natural limit to the desire for commodities. Money serves all sorts of purposes and can be hoarded. Money is not the same thing as wealth. People confuse the two, however; as Davisson and Harper summarize Aristotle's view: [17]

> The cause of this confusion is that wrong-headed men believe that the purposes of household management may be served by seeking and increasing bodily pleasures. Since the enjoyment of bodily pleasures depends upon property, their aims becomes the unlimited acquisition of property, including money. When this occurs, men try to change every art into the art of getting riches, and consequently they transform the art of household management into the art of retail trade. But this is an unnatural perversion and the two should be distinguished. The profit motive attaches not to wealth but to the accumulation of riches or coin which is accomplished in a market distinct from the state and the household.

Along these same lines, as we have already noticed, the authors of the Mishnah take a remarkably unsympathetic view of the holder of liquid capital. The system builders know much about factors, who provide to a householder capital in the form of animals, to be tended, raised, and sold, with both parties sharing the profits. The Mishnah's deepest interest in factoring contracts was that the farmer not work for nothing or for less than he put into the arrangement; that would smack of "usury," which, in context, stands only for making money on one's investment of liquid capital or its equivalent in livestock. The position encompassed true value not only in the now familiar notion that a sixth of deviation from true value involved fraud, but in the conception that the value of seed and crops may vary, but capital will not. Lending money for investment is not permitted to yield a profit for the capitalist. True value (in our sense) lies in the land and produce, not in liquid capital. Seed in the ground yields a crop. Money invested in maintaining the agricultural community from season to season does not. The bias is against not only usury but interest, in favor of not only regulating fraud but restricting honest traders.

While for the Mishnah, as I said, material wealth was land, here I must introduce an important qualification. By "wealth" the framers of the Mishnah in general did not mean enormous land holdings, e.g., large estates worked by sizable numbers of slaves. Theirs was not the notion that large landed estates were required for one to be a householder; however miniscule the property owned by an Israelite in the land of Israel, that property stood for wealth, that is, a domain. [18] In general, like Xenophon in his *Economics,* the framers of the Mishnah had in mind small or medium estates, in which a few slaves worked together with the householder. The notion of the *latifundia,* with gangs of slaves, makes no appearance, directly or by implication, in the world of small-holding householders conceived by the Mishnah's authors. [19] For example, the industrial enterprise in agriculture involved housing for slaves,

dormitories for men and women; it involved the housekeeper, who supervised
the women slaves, and the overseer, who directed the men in the field. The
Mishnah knows nothing of dormitories, assumes the wife of the householder
supervises the female slaves, and has the householder himself working in the
field alongside the slaves. When the Mishnah's authors referred to ownership
of a beast, it was assumed to be plural, hence shared; whether that is merely a
linguistic convention or stands for the notion of multiple partnership in a
single cow, I do not know. In general, however, we form the impression, in
the pages of the Mishnah, of a modest imagination, one that cannot conceive
of vast estates under absentee ownership and professional management, and I
doubt that in the land of Israel at that time many Jews held such estates in any
event. We deal with the modest conceptions of a society of limited aspira-
tions. Accordingly, the fundamental givens for the large estate lay beyond the
imagination of our authors. Nonetheless, those authors recognized wealth in a
single form: land, however constricted its borders.

The conception of wealth as land owned by an Israelite in the land of Israel
just now outlined comes to concrete expression in Mishnah-tractate Baba
Mesia 5, which defines usury, applying and expanding the scriptural prohibition against it.[20] The reason that discourse on usury defines the arena for
thought about wealth is simple. The chapter at hand discusses the matters of
interest and increase, in line with Lev. 25:35–36. And it is that prohibition
that forms the arena in which the framers of the Mishnah define their conception of wealth, its identification with land and the produce of land; the exclusion, from the notion of wealth, of (mere) money; the indifference to
capital and investment; and the other aspects of the profoundly Aristotelian
economics characteristic of their system. For land is limited and does not increase, e.g., in volume, and hence wealth also will stand stationary and in a
steady state. But matters are not quite so simple.

For before us is a long and subtle discussion. The reader may fairly ask why
I point, as systemically indicative of the character of the economics of the
Judaism of the Mishnah, to the treatment of the prohibition of usury, a commonplace for all Judaic systems, deriving as it does from the Scripture shared
among them all. There are two reasons for that view of mine, one that applies
generally, the other particular to the case at hand.

What makes the chapter systemically indicative in a general way is the
simple fact that the framers have chosen to expound this topic as they do—this
and not some other, this one here and not elsewhere. Were we to ask for systemically active data, deriving from Scripture, in the Judaism of the Essenes
of Qumran, we should look in vain for attention to the matter at hand, even
though, self-evidently, the Judaism of the Essenes at Qumran rejected usury,
and that by definition. To understand why I consider materials commonplace
in any other Judaism critical to the economics of the Judaism of the Mishnah,
I revert to the statement of Schumpeter with which this book commences: "In
economics as elsewhere, most statements of fundamental facts acquire impor-

tance only by the superstructures they are made to bear and are commonplace in the absence of such superstructures."[21] In the present context, the fact at hand, the prohibition of usury, scarcely prepares us for the importance accorded to that fact by the framers of the Mishnah, an importance indicated by the exegesis and development of the fact into an encompassing principle of economic transactions of exchange. Whatever the possibilities or potentialities of the scriptural prohibition of interest, the actualities at hand testify to the larger systemic bias and traits of the system makers before us.

But there is a second consideration, particular to the case at hand. We shall now see that the words translated "usury" really refer to a variety of ordinary market procedures, and "usury" really means "profit."[22] For in the end what is prohibited is not merely interest on a loan, in cash or in kind, but any transaction which leaves one party materially richer than he was when he entered the transaction, even though the other party is no poorer. So the bias is against interest per se. Not only so, but even the appearance of usury, or profit, must be avoided, as in the following:

> He who sells a house among the houses in walled cities, lo, this person redeems the house forthwith. And he redeems it at any time in twelve months. Lo, this is a kind of usury which is not usury.
>
> (M. Ar. 9:3A–C)

The point is that the one who redeems the house during the year does not deduct from what he repays to the purchaser the rent for the use of the house during the period between the sale and the redemption. It therefore appears that the purchaser has had the use of the house in exchange for the use of his money from the time of the sale to the time of redemption. But this is not usury, since usury applies only to a loan, not to a purchase.[23]

Another, more important, case in point is the absolute prohibition of factoring. Here there is no consideration that the shopkeeper, selling goods on consignment, or the farmer, raising animals for a share in the profit, is going to be poorer than he was before he undertook the contract.[24] Yet factoring is so organized as to prohibit the capitalist, who supplies the goods on consignment or the capital in the form of the young beasts, from making money on the (mere) labor of the trader or farmer. That is profit on investment, not usury in any sense in which the word is used today. Since the same prohibition is invoked for a variety of modes of the increase of capital, we have to take to heart what really is at stake for our system. And that is Aristotle's conception that profit, including, by the way, usury, is unnatural, but barter, encompassing all manner of goods (theoretically including coins, viewed as commodities), is natural. Only within that framework do we grasp the full testimony to the systemic economics that the exegesis of usury presents to us.

Let us turn to the exposition of the remarkable chapter on the subject, containing, as it does, whatever theory of wealth, expressed in concrete detail, our authors propose to impose upon the actualities of everyday trade and commerce. The chapter opens with a distinction between interest (*neshekh*) and increase (*tarbit*). The former is defined simply as repayment of five denars for a loan of a sela, which consists of four denars, or repayment of three seahs of what for a loan of two. The going rate of interest appears to have been 25 percent for a loan in cash, and 50 percent for a loan in kind. We do not know the length of time of the loan. Increase is a somewhat more subtle question. It involves payment for delivery, later on, of a commodity valued at the market price prevailing at the time of the agreement. The one who pays the money in advance thus profits, since prices are much lower at harvest time than in advance. Trading in futures occupies much attention. The prohibition of interest is expanded with great care at M. B.M. 5:2–6. The concern not to trade in futures or to gain increase through commodities is at M. B.M. 5:7–10. The main point is to treat as prohibited interest diverse sorts of payments in kind in consideration of a loan. M. B.M. 5:2 prohibits the debtor from renting out to the creditor a courtyard at no cost or at less than the prevailing rate. It does allow a deduction for payment of rent in advance—a very different matter. M. B.M. 5:3 takes into account the possibility of a subterfuge in which, in exchange for what is in fact a loan, the creditor enjoys the usufruct of a field. This matter will require close attention.

This brings us to what is an essentially unrelated matter, but one joined to the rest because of the overriding consideration of the prohibition of interest. For interest really stands for nothing less than profit, that is, getting money not through barter. M. B.M. 5:4 goes on to prohibit interest in the form of what it deems to be uncompensated labor. But what is at stake is return on capital, and that is not interest in any sense of usury, but (merely) profit of a different species from the profit that a farmer makes by planting seeds and raising crops and selling them. Specifically, we have in hand the prohibition of factoring in all forms. If a capitalist assigns goods or capital to a storekeeper in exchange for half the profit, the storekeeper in addition must be paid a salary for his attention to that half of the goods, the profit of which accrues to the capitalist. But, (M. B.M. 5:5) if one hands over cattle to a rancher to raise, in exchange for half the profits, the cattle are deemed to work for their keep, so that rancher need not be paid an additional fee for his labor. One may make an advance agreement on the value of the herd, when the herd yields labor for the benefit of the rancher (M. B.M. 5:6). M. B.M. 5:7, finally, prohibits the arrangement of a farmer's tending a block on "iron terms," that is to say, on such terms that the owner of the flock is guaranteed a return of all his capital, specified at the outset, and in addition a fixed yield, while the rancher will receive the increase of the flock over and above these two fixed items. Thus the rancher, bearing the entire risk for the upkeep of the flock, shares only part of the profits thereof. Israelites may pay or exact interest from gentiles. The notion of risk capital as risk is rejected. In all, we must concur that Aristotle would have found himself entirely at home in the premises of these rules.

M. B.M. 5:7–10 go on to deal with agreements on futures and other aspects of increase. One may not agree to pay in advance a fixed sum for a certain amount of produce, if a market price is not yet available. That sort of speculation, again, has no bearing upon the conception of usury or interest, but it does form a critical component of the use of capital, further evidence that for the system at hand usury and interest are simply the same thing as profit on liquid capital. In any case, we have the opposite of market economics, for the premise of discourse here is that the market price is administered, not set by the market itself; rather, it is announced and adhered to, as the produce of a given sort reaches the market. No one is supposed to speculate on that matter, and that is the mark of a distributive, not a market, conception of the economy. What follows from speculation? It is that something other than an agreed-upon price is determinative. All of this is translated downward into the (mere) prohibition of usury, but, we realize, now "usury" simply stands for market economics. If the produce should prove to be more expensive, then the one who receives the money will lose out and turn out to have paid interest on the advance money. Once there is a market price, one may pay in advance for delivery later on; but then one enjoys an unfair advantage in exchange for his payment in advance. M. B.M. 5:8−9 deal with a loan to be repaid in kind. Once more barter imposes its conceptions upon the market, which means a kor of wheat stands for a kor of wheat, without regard to market conditions, which are inadmissible in evidence. In general if one borrows a kor of wheat, he cannot pledge to repay a kor of wheat. It may turn out that he will have to pay much more for the kor than it cost at the time of the loan. This is interest. One may lend his tenant-farmers a kor of wheat for seed, however, and receive at the end a kor of wheat. That is deemed an investment by the landlord in his own property. If one presently owns a kor of wheat but has not got access to it, on the other hand, he may agree to return a kor later on for one he now receives, without scruple as to violating the laws of interest.

M. B.M. 5:10 has three kinds of prohibited interest of a nonmaterial character. If one party works for another party in exchange for the other's equivalent labor, the equivalence must be exact. One may not give a gift to a lender, either before or after the loan. He also may not provide him with valuable information in consideration of the loan. M. B.M. 5:11, finally, completes the ambitious and successful essay with an appropriate homily. These concluding passages lead us far beyond the antecedent conceptions, just as we noted in our earlier encounter with the composition of a Mishnah chapter, and have no more to do with usury in any sense than reminding one's fellow of his (prior) sin has to do with market exchanges.

A. What is interest, and what is increase [which is tantamount to taking interest]?
B. What is interest?
C. He who lends a sela [which is four denars] for [a return of] five denars,

D. two seahs of wheat for [a return of] three—
E. because he bites [off too much (N'SK)].
F. And what is increase (TRBYT)?
G. He who increases (HMRBH) [profits] [in commerce] in kind.
H. How so?
I. [If] one purchases from another wheat at a price of a golden denar [25 denars] for a kor, which [was then] the prevailing price, and [then wheat] went up to thirty denars.
J. [If] he said to him, "Give me my wheat, for I want to sell it and buy wine with the proceeds"—
K. [and] he said to him, "Lo, your wheat is reckoned against me for thirty denars, and lo, you have [a claim of] wine on me"—
L. but he has no wine.

(M. B.M. 5:1)

A formal structure is clear, with its prologue, A, then a systematic commentary on A at B and C–E, F and G–L. The Mishnah clearly has Lev. 25:35–36 in mind, since it alludes to the biblical word choices, N'SK and TRBYT. But the remainder of the chapter is satisfied to refer solely to interest, or usury, as RBYT, which is translated "interest" or "usury" as the case requires. So M. B.M. 5:1 is essentially secondary to the linguistic and conceptual core of the chapter as a whole, which hardly refers to the distinction announced at the outset. The meaning of interest is clear as given. It involves a repayment of 25 percent over what is lent in cash, or 50 percent over what is lent in kind. Increase is less clear. We deal with a case of trading in futures. The purchaser agrees to pay at the current price of 25 denars for a kor; delivery is postponed until the harvest. M. B.M. 5:7 permits this procedure. When the purchaser calls his contract, the vendor concurs in revising the price of the contract. But he also revises the cost of wine upward to its then prevailing price. In point of fact, the seller has no wine for sale. This would appear, in contemporary terms, to be trading in "naked," or uncovered, futures. If that is at issue, the prohibition would be based upon the highly speculative character of the vendor's trading practices. But the "increase" is that the vendor now has to pay for the wine at a higher price than is coming to the purchaser.

A. He who lends money to his fellow should not live in his courtyard for free.
B. Nor should he rent [a place] from him for less [than the prevailing rate],
C. for that is [tantamount to] usury.
D. One may effect an increase in the rent charge [not paid in advance], but not the purchase price [not paid in advance].
E. How so?
F. [If] one rented his courtyard to him and said to him, "If you pay me now [in advance], lo, it's yours for ten selas a year,

G. 'But if [you pay me] by the month, it's a sela a month'—
H. it is permitted.
I. [But if] he sold his field to him and said to him, 'If you pay me the entire sum now, lo, it's yours for a thousand zuz.
J. 'But if you pay me at the time of the harvest, it's twelve maneh [twelve hundred zuz],'—
K. it is forbidden.

(M. B.M. 5:2)

A–C prohibit interest in kind. D is neatly explained by F–H and I–K. In F–H the rent falls due month by month, so there is no fee for waiting on the payment, while at I–K there is a 20 percent surcharge for postponing payment, tantamount to mortgage interest. Since the rent falls due only month by month, it is not as if the tenant is gaining an undue advantage. The landlord is handing over two selas in exchange for the tenant's paying money which has not yet fallen due. But in the latter case, the seller of the field is owed the money as soon as the sale has been effected. By collecting 20 percent extra some time later, he is receiving interest on money which, in fact, already is owing to him. This is not permitted.

A. [If] one sold him a field, and [the other] paid him part of the price,
B. and [the vendor] said to him, 'Whenever you want, bring me the rest of the money, and [then] take yours [the field]'—
C. it is forbidden.
D. [If] one lent him money on the security of his field and said to him, 'If you do not pay me by this date three years hence, lo, it is mine'—
E. lo, it is his.
F. And thus did Boethus b. Zonin do, on instruction of sages.

(M. B.M. 5:3)

At issue here, in the contrast of A–C and D–E, is a subterfuge for the payment of interest. A–C indicate the possibility, for, as we shall see, either the vendor or the purchaser may prove to be the lender at interest. In this case the interest is usufruct of the field. All depends upon whether the sale is actually consummated through the payment of the whole of the stipulated price. The case of A–C involves partial payment for a field. Transfer of ownership is postponed until full payment is made. The transfer is dated from the time of the sale. What of the usufruct? The vendor, by the terms of B, will enjoy the usufruct of the field in the meantime. If, then, the sale *is* completed, the vendor will retrospectively have made use of what in fact turns out to belong to the purchaser from the date of sale. That usufruct is a form of interest on the outstanding balance of the debt. But what if we assign the usufruct of the field to the purchaser? Then, if the sale is *not* completed, the purchaser will turn out to have enjoyed the usufruct of a field from the time of the deposit. The deposit will be returned to him. The usufruct thus will appear to be interest on it. So the terms hide a usurious loan, whether of purchaser-lender to owner-borrower or vice versa.

The second, and contrasting case, simply permits a loan to security, with the proviso that the security or pledge is transferred to the lender only in the event of default at the end. That is not conceived to be interest. The case at D differs from that at B because the status of the field is not left in doubt. It remains the property of the borrower, who is not represented as a purchaser, just as the lender is not a vendor. So there is no unclarity as to the status of the usufruct, which remains fully in the domain of the borrower. That is why the stated precedent, F, is acceptable.

A. They do not set up a storekeeper for half the profit,
B. nor may one give him money to purchase merchandise [for sale] at [the return of the capital plus] half the profit,
C. unless one [in addition] pay him a wage as a worker.
D. They do not set the hens [of another person to hatch one's own eggs] in exchange for half the profit.
E. and they do not assess [and commission another person to rear calves or foals] for half the profit,
F. unless one pay him a salary for his labor and his upkeep.
G. But [without fixed assessment] they accept calves or foals [for rearing] for half the profits,
H. and they raise them until they are a third grown—
I. and as to an ass, until it can carry [a burden] [at which point profits are shared].

(M. B.M. 5:4)

The conception before us involves interest in the form of personal service, which also is prohibited. The case has a man commission a tradesman to sell goods in his shop and take half of the profits. But the condition is that, if the goods are lost or destroyed, the tradesman has to bear responsibility for half of the loss. Even if the stock depreciates, the tradesman makes it up at full value. Half of the commission, therefore, is in fact nothing but a loan in kind, for which the tradesman bears full responsibility. It follows that his personal service in selling the owner's half of the stock, if not compensated, in fact is a kind of interest in labor on that loan.

D, E, and G restate this matter in the context of a factor, who commissions a farmer to raise his cattle. At D the man gives eggs to a fowl keeper, who is to have them hatched. The keeper receives half the profits. He also bears full responsibility for half the loss. It follows that he must be paid a salary. At E, we make an assessment of the value of the calves or foals. Half of this sum becomes the fixed responsibility of the cattle rancher. If the calves or foals die or depreciate, the rancher has to pay back that sum. So it is a loan in kind. If in addition he is not compensated for time spent taking care of the cattle factor's share of the herd, once more his work will constitute interest. If, G–H, there is no assessment in advance of the fixed value for which the rancher bears full responsibility, however, then there is a genuine partnership. The rancher receives half the value of the profit. He acknowledges no responsibility for their loss, so there is no loan here. The conditions of the contract are such that the man's labor is amply compensated by his participation in the potential profits on half the herd.

A. They assess [and put out for reading] a cow, an ass, or anything which works for its keep,
B. for half the profits.
C. In a locale in which they are accustomed to divide up the offspring forthwith, they divide it forthwith.
D. In a place in which they are accustomed to raise the offspring, they raise it.
E. Rabban Simeon B. Gamaliel says, "They assess [and put out] a calf with its dam, a foal with its dam."
F. (And) one may pay increased rent [in exchange for a loan for the improvement of] one's field,
G. and one need not scruple by reason of interest.

(M. B.M. 5:5)

The one who supplies the capital, in the form of the cow or ass, benefits from the work of the rancher in raising the animal. But, unlike the case of M. B.M. 5:4D–F, since the animal works for its keep, the rancher gains the usufruct of the animal and so cannot be thought to pay "interest" to the capitalist in exchange for his share in the capital, namely, in the profits on the animals when they are sold. The rancher gets the work of the beast in return both for what he feeds it and his own work with it, so that the considerations of M. B.M. 5:4 are not invoked. C–D provide a minor qualification. Simeon even goes so far, E, as to permit the offspring of a dam to be assessed and raised, even though it is only the dam which will work. F–G, which are separate, complete the list of permissible investments. The point of F–G is that the increased capital investment in the land may yield an increased fee to the landowner for use of the land, without scruple as to usury.

A. They do not accept from an Israelite a flock on "iron terms" [that the one who tends the flock shares the proceeds of the flock but restores the full value of the flock as it was when it was handed over to him],
B. because this is interest.
C. But they do accept a flock on "iron terms" from gentiles.
D. And they borrow from them and lend to them on terms of interest.
E. And so is the rule for the resident alien.
F. An Israelite may lend out the capital of a gentile on the say-so of the gentile,
G. but not on the say-so of an Israelite. [If the gentile had borrowed

money from an Israelite, one may not lend it out on interest with the
Israelite's knowledge and consent.]

(M. B.M. 5:6)

We continue the interest of the foregoing. "Iron terms" are such as to guar-
antee to the investor both full restitution of capital and a fixed return on the
capital. Unlike the conditions at M. B.M. 5:4–5, the rancher undertakes to
share in the profit but to bear the full burden of loss. This arrangement involves "interest" in the form of unequal risk. There must be a full participation in both profit and loss in any shared undertaking involving the investment
of capital—the animals—on one party's part and of labor and grazing land on
the other party's part. (It goes without saying that the perspective of the Mishnah is that of the rancher.)

C–D are linked to the foregoing in detail only, but in theme they proceed to
conclude the entire discussion of interest. Their point is that the stated prohibition of M. B.M. 5:1–5 applies solely to transactions among Israelites.
Gentiles may receive or pay interest. Israelites may work for gentiles in this
context. G's language is obscure. It may mean that gentiles may not borrow
funds from Israelites and then, through the medium of an Israelite factor, lend
them to other Israelites. Or G may wish to say that on his own initiative an
Israelite may not lend at interest money belonging to a gentile. The main point
is clear.

A. They do not strike a bargain for the price of produce before the mar-
   ket price is announced.
B. [Once] the market price is announced, they strike a bargain,
C. for even though this one does not have [the produce for delivery],
   another one will have it.
D. [If] one was the first among the reapers [of the given crop], he may
   strike a bargain with him
E. for (1) grain [already] stacked [on the threshing floor],
F. or for (2) a basket of grapes,
G. or for (3) a vat of olives,
H. or for (4) the clay balls of a potter.
I. or for (5) lime as soon as the limestone has sunk in the kiln.
J. And one strikes a bargain for the price of manure every day of the
   year.
K. R. Yosé says, "They do not strike a bargain for manure before the
   manure is on the dung heap."
L. And sages permit.
M. And one may strike a price at the height [of the market, the cheapest
   rate prevailing at the time of delivery].
N. R. Judah says, "Even though one has not made a bargain at the
   cheapest rate [prevailing at the time of delivery], one may say to him,
   'Give it to me at such-and-such a rate, or give me back my money.'"

(M. B.M. 5:7)

To begin with, let us see how Maimonides, who restates the rules with great perspicacity and so clarifies matters, spells out the law just now given (*Civil Laws: Creditor and Debtor* 9.1):

> No agreement may be made with respect to produce until the market price has been published; but once the market price has been published, such an agreement may be made, for even if the seller does not have the produce, another man has it. How is this to be understood? If the market price has become fixed at four *seah* to the *sela,* one may make an agreement with a vendor for the purchase of 100 *seah,* giving him 25 *sela,* and if the vendor delivers 100 *seah* of wheat after the lapse of some time, when wheat at a *sela* per *seah,* there is no usury at all in the transaction, even though the vendor had no wheat at the time when he made the agreement. This applies only if the vendor, at the time when the agreement is made, has none of the kind which he agrees to sell. But if he has some of that kind, although it has not been completely processed, it is permissible to make an agreement with respect thereto, even if the market price has not yet been published.

We take up the second general theme of M. B.M. 5:1, increase. The case before us involves a prepayment for merchandise, e.g., produce. If the merchandise or produce is not yet on the market, one may not strike a price for delivery and accept prepayment on the contract. For this smacks of increase, in line with M.5:1—trading in naked contracts for futures. When a market price is available, then prepayment may be accepted for later delivery, B–C. As we shall see, Judah, N, maintains that that price must be assumed to be the lowest available, that is to say, either the price at the time of the agreement or the price at the time of the delivery, whichever is lower. The Mishnah will spell this matter out in a principal generalization, A–C, a secondary and gray area, D–I, a special problem, J–L, and then a concluding qualification, M–N, the whole a most interesting exposition.

The main objection to trading in futures in the form of "naked calls" is that it smacks of usury. Why? First, the seller of the contract has the use of the money without clear knowledge of what his ultimate costs will be. Second, the buyer of the contract has no protection from the seller's default, should the produce not be available to the seller of the call, all in line with M. B.M. 5:1. That is why one cannot undertake to deliver a quantity of produce at a given price, unless there is some indication of the prevailing market price for the produce. B–C complete the thought of A. Even though a given farmer has not harvested his crop, he may sell what he is going to harvest, since now there is clear evidence as to what he will receive and what the purchaser should have to pay. In the case of crop failure, the farmer can make it up, C.

D–I present a secondary qualification of the foregoing rule. The prohibition of A pertains to crops which have not been harvested, and also have not been subjected to a prevailing market price. If crops have been harvested, even though there is no prevailing market, one may strike a bargain. Why? Because the crops are now in hand and nearly ready for delivery. There is no possibility of trading in futures as naked calls. D bears five illustrations. The items are not fully manufactured. So there is an agreement to make delivery later on. The market price may go up. The prepayment, however, is not deemed to fall into the category of interest, in line with M. B.M. 5:1's conception, because it is lower. So what D–I treat is a gray area between crops which are still in the field (M. B.M. 5:1) and those which are fully harvested and ready for delivery (M. B.M. 5:7M–N). There is no market for the former. The market price is set for the latter. There will be a lower price, when prepayment is involved, for partially completed produce, and, as we see, this is all right.

J–K go on to deal with what is always in production. J's view is that the market price is perpetual. Yosé regards the manure as subject to a process of preparation, and L repeats the theory of J. M–N are important. M allows striking a price at the height of the market, when the produce is cheap. The vendor then agrees to supply the produce through the year at the lowest prevailing price for each delivery. This is an important qualification of A, since the market price is now set as a maximum, not a minimum—the theory of D–I all over again. Judah fundamentally concurs and carries the conception still further. Even though we have assumed that we speak of an advance payment at a fixed rate, Judah holds that that fact is always implied, even when it is not stipulated. The purchaser has the right to retract the sale if the lowest prevailing price is not allowed.

A. A man may lend his tenant farmers wheat [to be repaid in] wheat, [if] it is for seed,

B. but not [if it is] for food.

C. For Rabban Gamaliel would lend his tenant farmers wheat [to be repaid in] wheat [when it was used] for seed.

D. [If one lent the wheat when the price was] high and [wheat] became cheap,

E. [or if he lent the wheat when the price was] cheap and [wheat] became expensive,

F. he collects from them at the cheapest price,

G. not because that is what the law requires,

H. but because he wished to impose a strict rule upon himself.

(M. B.M. 5:8)

A. A man should not say to his fellow, "Lend me a kor of wheat, and I'll pay you back [a kor of wheat] at threshing time."

B. But he says to him, "Lend it to me until my son comes [bringing me wheat],"

C. or, ". . . until I find the key."

D. Hillel prohibits [even this procedure].

E. And so does Hillel say, "A woman should not lend a loaf of bread to her girlfriend unless she states its value in money.

F. "For the price of wheat may go up, and the two women will turn out to be involved in a transaction of usury."

(M. B.M. 5:9)

Once more our concern is to avoid setting a price so long in advance that there is the possibility of usurious profit. If someone lends a kor of wheat and is to be repaid a kor of wheat six months later, then there is the variable that the kor of wheat may now be much less, or more, expensive than the kor of wheat later on. Consequently we have to make provision for what is, and is not, permissible, in line with the basic theory of M. B.M. The passages at 5:1, 5:7, 5:8 and 5:9 go over this ground. M. B.M. 5:8A–B make a fundamental distinction between a kor of wheat which is invested in the land owned by the lender; it may be lent with the proviso that it will be returned, in like kind and quantity, at the harvest. Even though it may increase in value, the lender is deemed not to lend but to invest in his own property (= M. B.M. 5:3F–G), since, after all, he recovers a share in the profit. But if the loan of the wheat is solely for the benefit of the tenant, then it cannot be repaid in kind, for the stated reason. C–H then provide an illustration of this matter. Gamaliel's procedure, C, is worked out at D–F and glossed at G–H. F means to speak separately to D and to E. If wheat was high when he lent it to his tenants for seed, at the harvest, when it is cheaper, he simply collects the same volume of wheat as he had lent. This then is to their advantage. So it is volume for volume. If wheat was cheap when he lent it for seed, and then, in consequence of a poor harvest, the price went up, he collects in return not the same volume of wheat, but the same value as he had lent, thus collecting less wheat than he had lent but wheat worth the same amount of money as he had handed over. This benign procedure must be in mind, even though F is rather succinct and hardly explicit, for otherwise G–H would be meaningless.

M. B.M. 5:9A–C provide for a mode by which the loan may be effected. In line with M. B.M. 5:8A–B, one cannot promise to give back the same volume of wheat. However, if he owns that amount of wheat at this time, but, e.g., his son is bringing it, or he does not have the key to the granary, he may effect a loan to be repaid in the exact volume, without reference to the variation in price which may take place in the meantime. Hillel prohibits even this procedure, for the reasons stated at F. We now revert to a still more encompassing definition of "usury" or "interest," a definition so lacking in concrete action, let alone potential sanction, as to indicate the end of actualities and the entry of mere morality.

A. A man [may] say to his fellow, "Weed with me, and I'll weed with you,"
B. "Hoe with me, and I'll hoe with you."
C. But he [may] not say to him, "Weed with me, and I'll hoe with you."
D. "Hoe with me, and I'll weed with you."
E. All the days of the dry season are deemed equivalent to one another.
F. All the days of the rainy season are deemed equivalent to one another.
G. One should not say to him, "Plough with me in the dry season, and I'll plough with you in the rainy season."

H. Rabban Gamaliel says, "There is usury paid in advance, and there is usury paid at the end."

I. "How so?"

J. "[If] one wanted to take a loan from someone and so sent him [a present] and said, "This is so that you'll make a loan to me,"—

K. "this is a usury paid in advance.

L. "[If] one took a loan from someone and paid him back the money and [then] sent [a gift] to him and said, "This is for your money, which was useless [to you] when it was in my hands,"—

M. "this is usury paid afterward."

N. R. Simeon says, "There is usury paid in words."

O. "One may not say to him, "You should know that so-and-so from such-and-such a place is on his way."

(M. B.M. 5:10)

The passage covers three final matters, usury exacted through labor in excess of what one has coming, A–G, usury paid through a voluntary gift, H–M, and usury paid through inside information, N–O. The point of the first group is that an exchange of labor must be absolutely equal in all details. That of the second is that gifts either prior to the making of a loan or after the repayment of the loan are prohibited. Finally, as is clear, one must not provide inside information in exchange for a loan.

A. These [who participate in a loan on interest] violate a negative commandment:

B. (1) the lender, (2) borrower, (3) guarantor, and (4) witnesses.

C. Sages say, "Also (5) the scribe."

D. (1) They violate the negative commandment, *You will not give [him] your money upon usury* [Lev. 25:37].

F. (3) And [they violate the negative command], *You shall not be a creditor to him* [Ex. 22:25].

G. (4) And [they violate the negative command], *Nor shall you lay upon him usury* [Ex. 22:25].

H. (5) And they violate the negative command, *You shall not put a stumbling block before the blind, but you shall fear your God. I am the Lord* [Lev. 19:14].

(M. B.M. 5:11)

M. B.M. 5 concludes with a striking homily, with the apodosis laid out in accord with sages' enumeration.

To this point we have concentrated on Aristotle's conception of economics and in the (somewhat uneven) workings of the market economy within that conception.[25] But distributive economics, that historically prior and independent source of economic theory, worked out only in detail and not made explicit in general terms, predominated and vastly contributed to the economics of Judaism, yielding a mixed theory, partly a market, partly a distributive, economics. For our survey of Judaism's economics of the householder, the market, and wealth has repeatedly shown us a puzzling fact. As we shall now see, market economics persistently has appeared not to compete with but to be subordinated to a theory of distributive economics, in which a political authority, in the present case the temple, intervenes in the control of production and distribution. Distributive economics in the Mishnah's theory in fact sets aside the market mechanism by according consideration to the status of individual participants in the transaction of distributing goods and services. The priests got goods and services for which they did not have to work or compete in the marketplace; the rules of the Temple imposed taboos on the processes of production; the definition and evaluation of wealth bore no close relationship to market realities.

In these principal components of its economics, concerning the definition of ownership of the means of production, the market, and wealth, the Judaism of the Mishnah restated, in its odd and particular idiom, the distributive economics of the paramount, three-thousand year old system of the Near East, going back to Sumerian times, to the details of which, for the Mishnah's theoretical economics of the householder, market, and wealth, we now turn. For when we understand the details of the Mishnah's theory of distributive economics, we can explain with little difficulty the reason that the authors of the Mishnah have appealed to economics for the exposition of their systemic message. But, predictably, God lives in the details, a statement peculiarly congruent to the facts we shall now survey. At the heart of matters is who owns what, when, why, for what purpose, and with what outcome. And these are questions essentially beside the point of market economics, which deal, after all, with other forces than those that (adventitiously) define ownership, and which care little for the character and definition of what is traded in the market.

7

The Mishnah's Distributive Economics

Householder, Market, Wealth

> The market mechanism of exchange must determine the use of resources
> regardless of the status of the individual participants to the transaction. . . .
> Davisson and Harper[1]

The economic data with which the Mishnah's framers made their statement
came to them from the Priestly Code. On the face of matters, therefore, the
authors of the document appealed to an economic theory that derived from an
ancient age (we would say it was seven hundred years old, back to ca. 500 B.C.,
but they would say it was fourteen hundred years old, back to Sinai, which
would bear a date of ca. 1200 B.C.).[2] The truly anachronistic character of the
Mishnah's distributive economics becomes clear, however, when we realize
that by the fourth century B.C., the Middle East received and used the legacy
of Greece, brought by Alexander, in which a type of private property, prereq-
uisite to the development of the market and available for the free use of the
holder of that property independent of the priesthood or other government intervention, had developed.[3] For the theory of the Mishnah both the market and
the distributive systems form one system and represent two components
of one system. So we deal with a single theory, holding together two distinct economics. What we shall now see is how the distributive component of
the Mishnah's economic theory reshapes the three principal categories that
have occupied our attention, the household, the market, and wealth. But we
ask, first of all, why the system of the Mishnah appealed to economics to begin with, and the answer to that question comes to us from theology, not economics. What the Mishnah's authors wished to say, we shall now see, they
could express only by utilizing the principal categories of economics under
study here.

At the center of the Mishnah's economics is the disposition of resources
with unremitting regard to the status of participants in the transaction. In no
way does the economics of Judaism in its initial statement conform to the definition of market economics just now cited. Our task therefore is now to under-

stand in detail the foundation of the principles of distribution that define the theory of economics within the larger system of the Mishnah. In this way we grasp how profoundly the economics of the system has been shaped by the larger systemic statement and message.[4] The Mishnah's distributive economics derives from the theory that the Temple and its scheduled castes on earth exercise God's claim to the ownership by the holy land. It is, in fact, a theology that comes to expression in the details of material transactions. The theology derives from the conviction expressed in the psalm, "The earth is the Lord's." That conviction is a statement of ownership in a literal sense. God owns the earth. But the particular earth that God owns is the land of Israel, and, within that land, the particular earth is land in the land of Israel that is owned by an Israelite. With that Israelite, a landowner in the land of Israel, God is co-owner.[5]

From that theological principle, spun out of the notion that when Israelites occupy the land that God has given to the Israelites, namely, the land of Israel, that land is transformed, and so too are the principles of ownership and distribution of the land, all else flows. The economics of the Judaism rests upon the theory of the ownership of a designated piece of real estate, ownership that is shared between God and partners of a certain part of humanity whose occupancy of that designated piece of real estate, but no other, affects the character of the dirt in question. The theology consists in an account of what happens when ground of a certain locale is subject to the residency and ownership of persons of a certain segment of humanity. The generative conception of the theology involves a theory of the effect—the enchantment and transformation—that results from the intersection of "being Israel": land, people, individual person alike. But let us turn directly to the economics of it all.

Since God owns the land of Israel, God—represented by, or embodied in, the Temple and the priesthood and other scheduled castes—joins each householder who also owns land in the land of Israel as an active partner, indeed, as senior partner, in possession of the landed domain. God not only demands a share of the crop, hence comprises a householder. God also dictates rules and conditions concerning production, therefore controls the householder's utilization of the means of production. Furthermore, it goes without saying, God additionally has provided as a lasting inheritance to Israel (the people) the enduring wealth of the country, which is to remain stable and stationary and not to change hands in such wise that one grows richer, the other poorer. Every detail of the distributive economics therefore restates that single point: *the earth is the Lord's*. That explains why the householder is partner of the Lord in ownership of the land, so that the Lord takes his share of the crop at the exact moment at which the householder asserts his ownership of his portion.[6]

But the ongoing partnership between God and Israel in the sanctification and possession of the land is not a narrowly secular arrangement. Both parties share in the process of the sanctification of the land, which accounts for, and justifies, Israel's very possession of the land. The Israelite landowner has a particular role in effecting the sanctification of the land, in that land is holy and subject to the rules of God only when the Israelite landowner owns land in the land of Israel. Once more, land located elsewhere owned by Israelites, and land located in the land of Israel but not owned by Israelites, have no material relationship to the processes of sanctification, in utilization and in the disposition of the products of the land, but are at the heart of the distributive economics at hand. That fact is demonstrated by the conception about the character of the land, and of God's relationship to it, that the longer Israel has lived in the land of Israel, the holier that part of the land. Israel's dwelling in the land makes it holy. "Areas in which Israelites have lived for longer periods of time are holier and are subject to more rigorous restrictions" than those in which Israel has lived for a shorter period.[7] The laws of the sabbatical year apply more strictly to the territories in which Israel lived before and after 586. Areas occupied only before but not after, or vice versa, are subject to fewer restrictions. This has an important implication for the nature of God's ownership of the land. Newman comments, "In Leviticus that land is sanctified by God alone, who dwells in it and who has given it to Israel, his people. The Mishnah's framers, by contrast, claim that Israelites also play an active part in sanctifying the land."[8] Accordingly, in the Mishnah's system, the partnership of Israel, represented by the householder, with God in ownership of the land affects the very character of the land itself, making it different from other land, imparting to it the status of sanctification through the presence of two sources of sanctification, God and the Israelite, the Israelite householder in particular, as we shall presently see.

   To understand the full impact of that one conception, we must recall that the Mishnah's utopian vision is realized in the exquisite detail of rules. Hence before proceeding to the secondary exposition of the implications for the distributive theory of economics of God's ownershp of the land, we turn to a particular statement of the rules to see what it means, in rich exegesis, to conceive that God and the householder have formed a partnership in joint tenancy of the land that the householder owns. The tractate on tithing, Maaserot, gives expression to the definition of the householder's relationship to his partner and joint tenant in possession of the land, God, meaning the priesthood.[9] The basic point is that produce may be tithed as soon as it ripens, for, as Jaffee says, "at this point the crop becomes valuable as property"; but one is required to pay the tithes only when the householder "actually claims his harvested produce as personal property."[10] That moment arrives when the householder brings untithed produce from the field to the house, or when he prepares untithed produce for sale in the market.[11] The reason is that that is the point at which the householder claims the produce for his own benefit and gain, at which point the partner, God, is to receive the portions that belong to him. The author of the tractate develop a quite subordinate issue, as Jaffee defines it:

The framers of the tractate, however, are troubled by their own notion that produce need be tithed only after it has been claimed as property. What disturbs them is that now there normally will be a lengthy period of time—beginning with the ripening of the crop and extending until well after the harvest—during which the produce will remain untithed. It is precisely during this indeterminate period prior to tithing, however, that some of the produce is likely to be eaten by those who harvest it or who are otherwise involved in its processing or transport. This is what concerns Tractate Maaserot, for untithed produce presents a taxonomical problem. On the one hand, such produce is not sacred food, restricted for the use of priests, for the dues have not yet been designated within the produce and set aside from it for their meals. On the other hand, the produce cannot be used as profane or common food, for it is capable of yielding offerings which stand under the claim of God. Untithed produce, it follows, is subject to a special set of rules which take account of its ambiguous character[,] . . . produce which is neither sacred nor profane, neither wholly God's nor wholly man's.[12]

The upshot is that untithed produce may not be eaten in meals, but it may be used for a snack or in some other informal way. Again Jaffee: "The point is that the anomalous character of untithed food prevents it from serving the normal purpose of food which is sanctified to priests or of tithed food which is available for the use of commoners."[13] A variety of rules then govern the use of untithed produce from time of its ripening in the field, through the harvest field, until the point at which it is taken into the courtyard of the householder or sold in the market, at which the produce must be tithed.

At that moment before the householder exercises his property rights, he must give the partner's share to Him. Jaffee formulates this matter as follows:

God's claim to the tithes of the produce . . . is made only when the produce itself becomes of value to the farmer. Only after produce has ripened may we expect the farmer to use it in his own meals or sell it to others for use in theirs. Thus God's claim to it is first provoked and must therefore be protected from that point onward. . . . The produce is permitted as food only if the farmer acknowledges God's prior claim, e.g., by refraining from eating it as he would his own produce. . . . Once God's claim against the produce is satisfied by the removal of the tithes, the produce is released for use in all daily meals. It is now common food.[14]

The process is precipitated by the householder's evaluation of the state of the crop. Priests have a claim, as God's surrogates, not whenever they wish, but only when the householder determines that the crop is of value to him; so Jaffee: "God's claims against the Land's produce . . . are only reflexes of those very claims on the part of Israelite farmers. God's interest in his share of the harvest is first provoked by the desire of the farmer for the ripened fruit of his labor. . . . God acts and wills in response to human intentions."[15] The centrality of the householder to the entire system of the Mishnah cannot be stated with greater force than this.

In the conception of the author of the Mishnah, therefore, all land was held in joint tenancy, with the householder as one partner, God as the other. That mixed ownership then placed side by side two economic systems, one distributive, resting on control of property by the Temple acting in behalf of the owner of the land, who was God, the other the market system in which private persons owned property and with legal sanction could use it and transfer title without intervention from any other power. As Davisson and Harper state, "for an economic system to be a market system, exchanges of private property must be accompanied by simultaneous exchanges of legally recognized rights in property and its use."[16] To the degree that the private person, the householder in our system's instance, shared those rights with another and functioned within limits imposed by that other, the consequent economy was not wholly a market economy at all. That is the case, particularly, when other-than-market considerations affected the use of land or other goods and when the other-defined limits bore no congruence to the policies and plans of the (secular) partner, the householder.

Before proceeding, let me catalogue what is at stake in the claim that God makes against the householder's crops and herds. The disposition of God's designated share of the crop is laid out, all together, as follows:

> [The Mishnah] requires the separation of four gifts from all edible and cultivated agriculture produce before that produce may be eaten. [1] Heave-offering is the first gift to be separated. It is given to the priest, who eats it in conditions of cleanness. No fixed amount is set for this gift, but one-fiftieth is deemed an average quantity. . . . [2] First tithe, one-tenth, is given to the Levite, who separates from it [3] a further tenth [i.e., one-hundredth of the whole] as heave-offering of the tithe and gives it to the priest. . . . [4a] Second tithe, one-tenth, then is separated from the remainder of the produce [for consumption in Jerusalem]. [4b] During the third and sixth years of the sabbatical cycle poorman's tithe is separated instead of second tithe. In the case of bread [5] a further dough-offering is separated after the other tithe. This consists of one twenty-fourth part of the whole . . . and is given to the priest. Produce from which all tithes have been separated is called . . . "set right" or "fully tithed," "unconsecrated." The faithful separation of all of the Mishnah's tithes means that slightly less than 22 percent (or, in the case of bread made by an individual, slightly less than 26 percent) of one's produce is set aside. . . . This is a considerable amount of produce which the owners cedes (over and above the amount paid in taxes to the Roman authorities from 64 B.C.E. onwards).[17]

The priests have a claim upon parts of both the animal slaughtered for the cult and the one slaughtered for secular purposes. Specifically, the shoulder, two cheeks, and the maw of a beast slaughtered for secular purposes are to be given to the priest. The priests have a claim on the first of the fleece (Dt. 18:4, M. Hull. 11:1 ff.). The firstborn male offspring of cattle must be given to the priest. The firstborn of man and of an ass must be redeemed, and the money goes to the priest. The firstborn of clean cattle must be slaughtered in the Temple. If it was blemished, the priest gets it and may do with it as he likes. Clearly, we deal with a formidable claim. Let me now spell out its rationale.

In the case of the conception of ownership of wealth set forth by the authors of the Mishnah, a conception informed by the rules of Leviticus, God's joint ownership and tenancy with the farmer imposed a dual economics, the one a distributive economic order, the other a market system. The one partner, God, had no strong interest in the market system; the other partner, the householder, was assumed to have such an interest only in the rational utilization and increase of scarce resources, land and crops, herds and chattels. God's share was to be distributed in accord with God's rules, the farmer keeping the rest. That is what I mean by a mixed system, one partner framing policy in line with a system of distributive economics, the other in line with market economics. The author of the Mishnah thus effected and realized in a systematic way rules governing land use, placement of diverse types of crops, rights of ownership, and provision of part of the crop to those whom God had designated as recipients of his share of the produce. That explains why those authors could not imagine a market economy at all, and why the administered market (which, as we noted, is no market at all), in which government— priests' government—supposedly distributed status and sustained economic relationships of barter, took the place of the market.

The householder is represented by the Mishnah's authors as a tenant farmer, a sharecropper on land owned by God. Brooks spells this out as follows:

> As a tenant-farmer [the householder] works God's Land and enjoys its yield, with the result that a portion of all that he produces belongs to God. In order to pay this obligation Israelites render to the priests grain as heave-offering, tithes, and other priestly rations. Similarly, a specific portion of the Land's yield is set aside, by chance alone, for the poor. So underlying the designation of both priestly rations and poor-offerings is a single theory: God owns the entire Land of Israel and, because of this ownership, a portion of each crop must be paid to him as a sort of sacred tax. According to the Mishnah's framers, God claims that which is owed him and then gives it to those under his special care, the poor and the priests.[18]

The task of the householder, therefore, is to give over to God, through the representatives designated by him in his discourses with Moses, God's share of the crop.

We have now to ask, precisely how does God assert his claim to his portion of the crop? The way in which we know God's portion of the crop is through some sort of accident that separates grain from the normal crop. This is taken to represent God's intervention in matters, in line with the way in which the casting of lots, e.g., with the Urim and Thummim, or in the story of Esther, constitutes the way of finding out God's preference. Designating God's portion by the workings of chance is illustrated by the category of the forgotten sheaf, an offering separated when the farmer has completed reaping the field and binds the grain into sheaves. A sheaf forgotten by all involved in the processing then becomes the forgotten sheaf that is the property of the poor (M. Pe. 5:7). Single grapes that fall due to no identifiable cause during the harvest fall into the category of the separated grape. Clusters that grow without shoulders or pendants are defective and go to the poor (M. Pe. 7:4). When the farmer thins the vineyard, the law of the defective cluster begins to apply; that is the point at which the householder asserts his right of ownership (M. Pe. 7:5).

Produce that is designated without any intention of the householder and not by identifiable cause has been chosen by God. That portion of the crop is what goes to the poor, or, under other circumstances, to the priest (hence: offering that is raised up for priestly rations). As Brooks explains, "whether it is the grain that happens to grow in the rear corner of the field (and that the farmer himself will later designate as *peah*) or the stalks that by chance fall aside from the edge of the farmer's sickle (gleanings), all this food apportioned seemingly by accident must be left for the poor. So the framers of the Mishnah believe that God alone determines what produce falls into the category of poor-offerings."[19] The same consideration affects the designation of produce for the priests' rations. The procedure for designating those rations at the threshing floor is for the priest to declare that the priestly ration (heave-offering) is isolated in one part of the pile of grain. Whatever the householder then grabs from the pile falls into the status of sanctified grain, and there can be no measuring nor designing specific grain. Again Brooks: "It is through chance alone that God determines which particular grain in which quantity will fall into the category of priestly rations."[20] The householder's partner can be relied upon, therefore, to make his selection of the shared crop.

When God does so forms yet another detail in which the system as a whole restates its prevailing and single principle of joint ownership. The point at which the joint holder of the land, God, asserts his rights of ownership and so also demands his share of the crop is when the householder asserts his ownership of the crop. When the field is reaped, the laws of providing for the caste of the poor come into effect (M. Pe. 4:6–7). When the grain pile at the threshing floor is smoothed over, then produce becomes subject to the separation of tithes (M. Pe. 4:8). There are two such points in the process of reaping the grain. First, when the householder harvests the grain, claiming it for himself, a bit of food left at random goes for the poor. Then, when the farmer collects the grain at the threshing floor, God asserts ownership of his share, and that is what goes to the priests.[21] The sole difference in procedure is that while the poor persons' share is designated by the accident of leaving a corner of the field unharvested, dropping a few stalks accidentally, forgetting sheaves, and the like, the householder is the one who designates what is to serve as the priestly ration. Here he takes an active role, since he is the one to set aside produce for the priests. In this latter act the householder serves as God's partner, in sharing the crop, but also as God's agent, in designating and delivering the share of God to the priest. But the householder in no way may intervene in the process. "Householders must not in any way interfere as God apportions the grain."[22]

Since the Mishnah's framers regard the land as God's property, when Israelite farmers claim it as their own, and grow food on it, they must pay for using God's earth. The householder therefore must leave a portion of the field unharvested as *peah* and give this food over to God's chosen representatives, the poor. The underlying theory is that householders are tenant farmers who pay taxes to their landlord, God.[23] The point at which the divine taxes become valid is, Jaffee says, "the critical moment when he takes possession of the food. Before smoothing over the grain pile he may dispose of the food freely; he has not yet claimed full ownership of it and so need not separate tithes (cf. M. Maaserot 1 : 1)." Once the farmer has processed the grain, he has claimed ownership. This arouses the intense interest of God, the farmer's agricultural partner: "The householder must pay to God a part of the profits."[24]

The cattle, moreover, are to be tithed three times a year (M. Bekh. 9: 1–8), with the priests given the tithed beasts for use in the temple. Tithing cattle derives from Lev. 27:32–33: "And all the tithe of herds and flocks, every tenth animal of all that pass under the herdsman's staff, shall be holy to the Lord (and given to the temple). The beast is brought to Jerusalem, the blood and fat are offered up, and the owner gets the meat, to eat in the city."

Disposition of the crop also involves presenting to the Temple priesthood the first fruits of the crops. But only householders are liable to present first fruits of their produce. Others are exempt. This negative rule bears in its way the same message as the positive one. Those who do not own the land are not liable to bring first fruits, even though they own them as sharecroppers. Those who own land but are proselytes, or who do not fully own the land, may not make the recitation. Only full ownership of the land permits one to carry out the rite. God's claim is limited to what God has made and distributed, the land. This is a mark that the householder occupies a distinctive place in the scheme of things.[25] First fruits are thereby distinguished from other agricultural gifts, obligation to provide which apply to all. The relationship between ownership of land and the obligation to bring first fruits and make the recitation that acompanies their offering constitutes the critical issue of much of the tractate on the subject of first fruits, Bikkurim.

The effect of distributive economics upon the station of the householder should not be missed. The system at hand, after all, distributed more than scarce material resources; it also parcelled out equally valued, if nonmaterial, goods such as status and standing. Owning land conferred a place in Israel's history that owning mere money did not. For what is interesting here is that the owner arrogates to himself a first-person narrative that, in fact, in its original scriptural context refers to all Israelites. But when the text, Dt. 26: 1–11, that the householder must recite says, "Behold, now I bring the first fruit of the ground which you, O Lord, have given me," the authors of the Mishnah understand that reference is made, in particular, to the householder, who alone can say, "which *you* have given *me.*" That fundamental theory of what it means to be a householder may be expressed in a single sentence: the householder is normative Israel. All others take up positions, within Israel, in relationship to him. For, in his monopoly of the right to make the required recitation, the householder *is* Israel, when the sacred history of Israel is recited with the presentation of the first fruits. The householder's own personal history then conforms to the statements made in the text, but then that personal history becomes Israel in the here and now. The picture of land ownership in Deuteronomy (Dt. 26:1–11) emphasizes that God has kept his promise to give the people the land of Israel. The Priestly Code speaks of the offerings of first fruits, now identified with the sheaf of grain known as the *omer* (Lev. 23: 9–21). It sets the presentation of the sheaf of the first fruits of the harvest into the sabbatical system, now the concluding sabbath of the feast of unleavened bread; this is then waved for seven full weeks, counting fifty days to the morrow after the seventh Sabbath. This forms one of the many significations of the relationship between the Sabbath, the land, and the Lord, who owns the land and sanctifies the Sabbath.[26]

Let us take a simple fact as an example of the Mishnah's authors' indifference to the commercial economy and its participants. It is that the sabbatical year does not cancel payments which would prevent Israelite merchants from conducting their business. The *prozbul,* a legal fiction, allows for normal transactions. Commercial credit, fines, assessments for damages, and the like, are not released by the sabbatical year. Secured loans remain collectable. Newman explains, "This is because the Mishnah's authorities regard the collateral as a temporary repayment of the loan until the borrower actually repays the money he owes. Since these loans are deemed not to be outstanding, they cannot be cancelled by the sabbatical year. Loans turned over to a court for collection are not cancelled."[27] The net effect of this remission of the full effects of the law is to exclude from the sabbatical system the entire commercial economy.

No wonder then that the householder stands alone in sharing with God ownership of the land, and, it follows, it is the householder alone, among all Israelites, who can effect an act of intention and designation that transforms the status of produce from secular or neutral to sacred. That power of consecration matches the control over Israel's history that is assigned, through the law of first fruits, to the householder. How so? The householder's produce becomes consecrated as heave-offering only through the intention or thought and the deed of the Israelite householder. The householder is the one—the only one—who has the power to cause produce to be deemed holy. This he does by (in Avery-Peck's words) "formulating the intention to consecrate produce as the priestly gift. Then he pronounces a formula by which he orally designates a portion of his produce to be heave-offering. Finally, he effects his intention by physically separating that portion from the rest of the batch. Through these thoughts and actions the householder determines what produce, and how much of it, is to be deemed holy."[28] While human intention in general plays a central role, because of the arena defined by the law, namely, the disposition of the crop by its mortal owner, it is the intention of the householder in particular that is determinative. That intention is what changes the substance at hand from secular to holy, for holiness does not inhere in it but is only imputed by the householder.[29] Avery-Peck makes this matter clear in his summary of the main interests of the tractate, Terumot, on the designation and disposition of the priestly rations (commonly, but incorrectly, translated "heave-offerings"):

> The topics of the tractate reveal the point which its framers wish to make . . . , first, the role of the Israelite in the designation and separation of heave-offering; second, his responsibility to protect the priestly due for the priest; and, third, the part he plays in the ultimate disposition of the offering. The tractate as a whole thus speaks about common Israelites. It proposes to delineate their responsibility as regards all aspects of the designation and disposition of the priestly gift. Its particular rules, moreover, make clear the centrality of the Israelite's own intentions and perceptions. At each point these determine the status of sanctification of produce which the Israelite sets aside as the priest's share. Through the Israelite's powers of intention, produce first comes to be deemed holy. Later, the holiness of the priest's gift may be encroached upon only through actions which the Israelite performs purposely. Finally, the offering no longer is considered holy when the Israelite himself does not deem it to be edible.[30]

When we take into account that the particular Israelite with the power to designate produce as heave-offering is only the householder, and it is the produce of the farm that is at stake, we understand how central, indeed, unique and crucial, a role is reserved for the householder in the processes of sanctification, that is, in this context, the disposition of scarce resources outside of normal market transactions and relationships.

The householder, for the system of the Mishnah, therefore occupies an exalted position as God's partner. Consequently, the opinions, attitudes, plans, and intentions of the householder form the centerpiece of the system. Indeed, the will and intention of the householder, in matters of the disposition of scarce resources in particular, are what make the system work. For one example among many, at M. Kil. 7:6, we find that the action and attitude of the householder set aside the violation of the taboo which, had the householder deliberately done the deed, would have rendered forfeit the entire vineyard. If a usurper sows a vineyard with mixed seeds and the vineyard leaves his possession, the rightful owner must cut down the sown crop immediately. If he does so, however, there is no consequence to the prior presence of what should have been prohibited. The decision and action of the landowner make all the difference; e.g., if a wind hurled vines on top of grain, the householder cuts the vines at once and there is no further penalty, since the householder bears no responsibility for the violation.

In respect to the taboos against mixed species, not only the householder, but any other person, is subject to the law. We can see the consequence, in that the owner of a garment made of mixed fibers, wool and linen, bears responsibility for the violation of law. Here the owner of the garment is the responsible party; e.g., "Clothes dealers and tailors may carry garments of diverse kinds in the course of their work, provided that they do not intend to use them as garments" (M. Kil. 9:5–6). This proves that the owner of the

garment is the one who bears responsibility for violating the law and underlines the fact that, as to mixed seeds, it is the householder who is wholly in
charge. That proves that the premise of all rules of mixed seeds and mixed
species, Kilayim, is that the householder's judgment is what is decisive. For
the householder is the archetypal owner, master of a domain; the craftsman or
manufacturer, tradesmen or merchant, is in his model.

Intervention of God—that is to say, the considerations of cult and taboo,
not solely those of market and trade and value—into land ownership is total
and complete. No householder can sell his land permanently, if he received it
by inheritance. Lev. 25:10 has land revert after fifty years, in the jubilee, to
the original owner. What does not revert? The portion of the firstborn, inheritance of one who inherits his wife's estate, inheritance of the one who enters
into Levirate marriage (M. Bekh. 8:10). Consequently, the householder cannot alienate his property and invest his capital in some other medium. The
cultic rule imposes a valuation on the real estate that otherwise it cannot have
enjoyed, and, at the same time, freezes in land the equity of the householder.
An other-than-market consideration overrides the market's valuation of the
land. This consideration affects not only the householder's land, but also his
residence. Specifically, a house in a walled city cannot be permanently sold
but reverts to the original owner, so Lev. 25:25–34. Tractate Arakhin in chapters 7 and 8 goes over this rule. When someone dedicates a field, and another
person then buys it (redeems it) from the Temple, he may not do so permanently. The field or the house reverts at the jubilee. At issue is only the field of
possession, which is one that is received by inheritance, so Lev. 27:16–25/
M. Ar. 7:1–8:3. The field received as an inheritance and the dwelling house
in a walled city, which are to revert to the "original" owner, are treated at
Lev. 25:25–34/M. Ar. 9:1–8. The sale here is assumed to be brought about
because of need: "if your brother becomes poor and sells part of his property . . ." (Lev. 25:25). The intervention of the law into the disposition of the
capital of the household that is in the form of the herds and the flocks derives
from Ex. 13:2 and Num. 18:15–18. Invalidated holy things are sold in the
marketplace, but the blemished firstling may not be sold in the marketplace
(M. Bekh. 5:1). Here too the Mishnah's framers invent nothing but integrate
into their larger statement rules of Scripture deemed systemically urgent.

The Mishnah's economics of the householder conforms to the theory of the
market. As we now realize, the Mishnah's economics knows the market, but it
is not a market economics. Distributive economics, that is, the distribution of
scarce goods and services not through the market mechanism, involves designation of recipients who do not form normal participants or undifferentiated
constituents of the market. These scheduled castes[31] lay an enormous claim,
therefore, upon the resources of the economy, that is, the harvest of the household, for reasons other than their providing a quid pro quo.[31]

One such designated group is the poor, who do not own a share of the land.
They are comparable to the priests and Levites, likewise not given a share of

the land (Dt. 18:1–5), and, like the sacerdotal castes, the poor therefore receive a share of the crop.[32] The rationale always is the same: God is the partner, in ownership of the land, with the householder. Consequently, God's share of the crop is apportioned to the castes or classes who form the surrogate for God in the division of the crops among the rightful owners. The rules governing the poor's share occur in tractate Peah, that is, "the corner-offering for the poor," which asserts that the poor have a claim on the produce of the land.[33] In point of fact there are several such portions of the crop reserved for the caste of the poor. The first is the rear corner of the field, *peah* (Lev. 19:9, 23:22); then come gleanings (Lev. 19:9, 23:22), the forgotten sheaf (Dt. 24:19), the separated grape (Lev. 19:10), the defective cluster (Lev. 19:10, Dt. 24:21), and poorman's tithe (Dt. 26:12), a tenth of the crop separated in the third and sixth years of the sabbatical cycle and handed over to the poor. Some of these offerings therefore involve leftovers or rejected portions of the crop, others quite marketable produce.

To understand the true character of this support for the poor, we must take account of the simple fact that it is not support accorded out of sympathy or social concern. The system of the Mishnah knows a quite distinct source of eleemosynary support for the poor, in addition to the provision of God's share of the crop to them. It was a system of soup kitchens. Through them transient poor are supported (M. Pe. 8:7), and the community maintains a soup kitchen as well. We should not therefore confuse the holy, Godly rights of the scheduled castes, on the one side, with the social benefits of supporting the poor, on the other. The former constitute a chapter in distributive economics, the latter do not. The difference is in the rights of ownership. In the case of the scheduled castes, the poor stand in for the "other Householder," who is God, and the disposition of the crop follows rules of distribution decreed by God, that is to say, by the priesthood that comprises the authors of parts of the Pentateuch and the editors of the whole of the Pentateuch as the framers of the Mishnah among all Israel possessed the document.

The rationale for poor relief, in its several forms, differs in Scripture. The priestly authors of Leviticus identify God as the cause: "You shall leave them for the poor and for the sojourner: I am the Lord your God" (Lev. 19:9–10; 23:22). The deuteronomist promises that God will reward those who do the same, but does not invoke God's name and ownership. Rather, he gives an essentially eleemosynary reason: "When you reap your harvest in your field and have forgotten a sheaf in the field, you shall not go back to get it. It shall be for the sojourner, the fatherless and the widow, that the Lord your God may bless you in all the work of your hands. . . . You shall remember that you were a slave in the land of Egypt, therefore I command you to do this" (Dt. 24:19–22). The reason then has nothing to do with God's ownership of the whole land. It is, rather, that the Israelites too were once members of the scheduled caste of slaves, and that is why they must now act generously. Here too we discern two distinct forms of poor relief, the one an expression of the land-theology of the priestly writings, the other of the social concern of the deuteronomic code. These produce the same kind of action, to be sure, but appeal to different motives.

Distributive economics accords an ample share in the scarce resources of the economy not only to the scheduled castes, but also to a particular location, namely, Jerusalem. Indeed, assigning a share of the crop to Jerusalem, without a corresponding outlay by participants in the Jerusalem market, corresponds explicitly to assigning a share of the crop to the scheduled castes. This is accomplished by treating as comparable the tithe of the crop given to the poor and the tithe of the crop delivered for consumption in Jerusalem. Specifically, in the first, second, fourth, and fifth years of the sabbatical cycle, the tithe that the householder separates from his crop is devoted not to the needs of the poor but to the maintenance of Jerusalem (in the third and sixth years, the tithe goes to the poor). This is accomplished by requiring the householder to bring to Jerusalem and consume there a tenth of his crop or the monetary equivalent thereof (Dt. 14:22–26). The result is to provide for Jerusalem an artificially inflated supply of food, and so to keep under control the cost of food in the Jerusalem market on the occasion of pilgrim festivals, when large numbers of tourists will have come to the city. Compensating for the inflated demand, the sizable supply will have lowered food costs in Jerusalem, but only at the expense of removing from the supply available in the rest of the country approximately 10 percent of the crop. The farmer, that is, the householder, is responsible for designating the portion of the crop and transporting it.[34]

The impact of the produce's having been in Jerusalem upon the status of the produce is considerable. Food that has been designated as second tithe, that is, consecrated, must be used only in the way in which produce of its type is normally used. Before the produce has been in Jerusalem, it is sold at local market prices, it may be sold at the lowest prevailing price, and so on (M. M.S. 3:5–4:8). Then the money received is brought to Jerusalem. But once the produce itself has entered Jerusalem, it acquires a different status altogether. At that point, the produce is holy and may no longer be sold. Then, in Jerusalem itself, it must be eaten by the householder or those to whom he gives the food.

We have now to identify that component of the goods and services of the market that is subjected to distributive, rather than market, economics, within the mixed economics at hand. It is, in particular, food that is subjected to the distributive system at hand—food and, in point of fact, nothing else, certainly not capital, or even money. Manufactured goods and services, that is, shoes on the last, medical and educational services, the services of clerks and scribes, goods in trade, commercial ventures of all kinds—none of these is subjected to the tithes and other sacerdotal offerings. The possibility of the mixed economics, market and distributive alike, rests upon the upshot of the claim that God owns the holy land. It is the land that God owns, and not the factory or shop, stall or store, ship or wagon, and other instruments and means of production. Indeed, the sole unit of production for which the Mishnah legislates in rich and profound exegetical detail is the agricultural one. The distributive component of the economy, therefore, is the one responsible for the production of food, inclusive of the raising of sheep, goats, and cattle. Again, the centerpiece is ownership of land. What does not derive from the earth owned jointly by God and the Israelite householder falls outside the economics of Judaism in its initial statement.

The agricultural produce of which God owns a share is explicitly what is marketable: it is that which is edible, tended, grown in the land of Israel, and harvested as a crop, and which can be stored (M. Pe. 1:4–5). These traits, of course, characterize the produce that a householder will cultivate. Edibility guarantees use; tending defines an indicative trait of the household and further guarantees that the produce is valued by the householder; the land of Israel is God's land; harvesting involves the taking of possession; and storage, like edibility, is a mark of valuing the crop. But produce that is not owned, e.g., what grows wild, what is used as feed for beasts or seed, all is exempt; God's claim extends only to what the householder will use for his own needs and his family's and dependents'. There is no divine share in what is not owned to begin with, and that accounts also for the suspension of the designation of God's share of crops in the seventh year in the sabbatical cycle, when the householder, for his part, exercises no rights of cultivation or ownership of the land.

The distributive economics of the Mishnah affects not only the distribution, but also the production and utilization for the market, of agricultural goods. The supply of produce on the market, therefore, responds not only to market considerations, but also to extrinsic ones imposed by the Temple and its taboos. The intervention of rules of proper slaughter into the disposition of the capital represented by beasts prepared for meat certainly imposes extramarket considerations. Tractate Hullin declares invalid for Israelite use beasts that are improperly slaughtered, or that produce certain marks of invalidity of another sort, and this vastly lowered the return on the beast. The market for meat fit for Israelite consumption was prepared to pay a premium for such meat. Among the prohibitions affecting the suitability of animals is the removal of the sinew of the hip, or sciatic nerve. Gentiles of course may purchase such meat (e.g., M. Hul. 7:2). Israelites may slaughter a beast in behalf of a gentile (M. Hul. 2:7). Here the concern is the intention for which the beast is slaughtered. Gentiles are assumed to slaughter the beast in honor of an idol (M. Hul. 2:7E), and that would render the meat unacceptable to the Israelite market, just as is the case with wine in the whole of tractate Abodah Zarah, on idolatry. It follows that nonmarket considerations as to the disposition of scarce resources intervene here as well, to the detriment not only of the gentile, who loses the Israelite market for his meat, but also the Jews. For the supply of meat in their market is diminished by the consideration at hand, even though, in all other respects, the meat may be suitable for Israelite consumption and, of course, also nourishing. Both supply and demand therefore are affected by extramarket considerations. One fundamental rule for non-market economics introduces the consideration of Israel's not worshipping idols, and this affects the disposition of a variety of goods that, in all other respects, are entirely valid for sale and use in the Jews' market.

The intervention of cultic considerations in the market affects the supply of meat in a positive way. Farmers or butchers are required to slaughter beasts even against their will on the eve of the last festival day of the Festival of Sukkot, on the eve of the first festival day of Passover, on the eve of Pentecost, and on the eve of the New Year (M. Hul. 5:3). However slight the demand, butchers are forced to slaughter beasts to supply meat for the market for the festival celebration. It is taken for granted that on that occasion people will eat meat, and, in consequence, the Mishnah's framers wish to assure a large supply to meet the demand, intervening in the normal working of the market, which should set the price in such a way that supply will routinely meet demand. This is stated explicitly: "Even if the beast was worth a thousand denars, and the puchaser has only one denar, they force the butcher to slaughter the beast" (M. Hul. 5:4).[35] It follows that the supply of goods to the market is affected both negatively and positively by nonmarket considerations imposed in the system of distribution at hand.

Taboos affecting production of produce were not inconsiderable. Let us take, for example, the application to production of scriptural taboos as to commingling different categories of plants, animals, or fibers (Lv. 19:19, Dt. 22:9–11). That taboo certainly represents an intervention into the free conduct of the means of production for the market. In that aspect, also, the Temple intervened in the economy and introduced considerations not pertinent to the market. The Mishnah tractate devoted to these taboos, Kilayim, established criteria for distinguishing among different classes, defined what constitutes the commingling of such classes, and determined how to keep each category separate and distinct from others. Mandelbaum defines the interest of the tractate as follows: "Although the Mishnah's regulations clearly depend upon their scriptural antecedents, the conception of the law which they express is distinctive to the Mishnah. . . . It is man, using his powers of observation, who determines what is orderly and what lies in confusion. Unlike Scripture, which takes for granted the existence of an established and immutable order, the Mishnah calls upon man to create order based upon his own perception of the world around him."[36] Man defines what constitutes a class and determines how to keep the different classes distinct from one another; man thus imposes upon an otherwise disorderly world limits and boundaries which accord with human perception of order and regularity.[37] The priestly conception of this matter, in Leviticus, is set forth by Mandelbaum as follows:

> In the view of the priestly circles which stand behind P, order is a precondition of holiness. This notion is clearly reflected in P's account of the creation. . . . P describes the making of a well-ordered, hierarchical world. Each type of creation is brought forth in order of ascending importance. . . . All living things furthermore

were created each according to its kind. . . . Creation is thus an act of ordering, the purpose of which is to make the world perfect and thus prepare it to be made holy. The actual act of the sanctification of the world then takes place on the Sabbath. The point of P's laws in Leviticus. . . . is to prevent the confusion of those classes and categories which were established at the creation. P thus commands man to restore the world from its present condition of chaos to its original orderly state and so to make the world ready once again for sanctification. . . . The Mishnah claims that it is man who decides what is orderly and what is confused.[38]

The "man" whose judgment is decisive in these matters of course is the farmer, that is to say, the householder, and, it is no exaggeration to frame matters, a human being becomes fully human through ownership of land: land "of Israel" in the ownership of a human being "of Israel," in partnership with God.

An important dimension of distributive economics encompasses production, not solely distribution, of goods and services. In this matter, rules not dictated by the need to achieve maximum productivity on the farm yet governing the conduct of the household farm take first place. Among those rules dictating means and conditions of production, without regard to maximum utility of the farm, the single most important is the one that prohibits all agricultural activity in the seventh year of a seven-year cycle. We may now recognize that that rule, which requires fields to lie fallow, in fact fructifies the soil by renewing nutrients in it. But the reason for that prohibition derives solely from theological myth, and the system at hand imposes the law solely to realize that myth.

> The land shall observe a sabbath of the Lord. Six years you may sow your field, and six years you may prune your vineyard and gather in the yield. But in the seventh year the land shall have a sabbath of complete rest, a sabbath of the Lord; you shall not sow your field or prune your vineyard. You shall not reap the aftergrowth of your harvest or gather the grapes of your untrimmed vines; it shall be a year of complete rest for the land. But you may eat whatever the land during its sabbath will produce, you, your male and female slaves, the hired and bound laborers who live with you, and your cattle and the beasts in your land may eat all its yield. (Lev. 25:1–7)

Now the notion of the land's observing the Sabbath carries not a trace of recognition that the land gains from lying fallow. The priestly conception is not made explicit, except in the opening phrase, "the land that I give you, the land shall observe a sabbath of the Lord." Here again the priestly authors underline God's ownership of the land, God's giving to Israel[ite householders in particular] their share of what is God's. That is why, as a matter of fact, God may also dictate the conditions under which the land is used, when and how it will be productive. The point here is that just as God rested from the work of creation on the seventh day and sanctified it as a day of rest (Gen. 2:3), so God has given the seventh year to the land as its Sabbath. The land of Israel "is enchanged, for it enjoys a unique relationship to God and to the people of Israel. . . . God sanctified this land by giving it to his chosen people as an exclusive possession. Israelites, in turn, are obligated to work the land and to

handle its produce in accordance with God's wishes."[39] In the seventh year,
therefore the householder cannot do those things that in other years constitute
their mode of asserting and exercising ownership over the land. That is how
the householders acknowledge that God is the owner of the land alone, and
they enjoy the usufruct as a gift from God.[40]

God intervenes into the market in yet another way, namely, by requiring the
remission of debts every seventh year, an extraordinary intervention in the
normal working of the market, by which money becomes wealth that can be
accumulated. Here, we see, wealth in the form of money cannot be accumulated but must be relinquished.

> Every seventh year you shall practice remission of debts. This shall be the nature of
> the remission. Every creditor shall remit the due that he claims from his neighbor.
> He shall not dun his neighbor or kinsman, for the remission proclaimed is of the
> Lord. You may dun the foreigner, but you must remit whatever is due you from
> your kinsmen.
>
> (Dt. 15:1–3)

The upshot is, the poor do not grow poorer through accumulated debts. But,
as a matter of fact, it also means that the rich cannot become richer. "Israelites restore equilibrium to their commercial transactions."[41]

Mishnah-tractate Shebiit develops the prohibition against working the land
during the seventh year. The authors of the tractate extend the prohibition
against sowing and reaping grain and grapes to all agricultural activities, including fertilizing and irrigating. Produce that grows of itself in the seventh
year may not be sold or otherwise used for benefit. God owns that produce,
and it is treated as having no other owner, hence, as ownerless property that
may not be sold or exchanged for personal gain. The one point introduced by
the authors to the repertoire of facts of Scripture, similar to the shift in regard
to mixed seeds, is that the housholder through his actions and perceptions
plays a role in determining how the agricultural restrictions of the sabbatical
year apply. So Newman: "Israelite . . . householders have the power within
specified limits to decide when, how, and where the laws of the sabbatical
year take effect. This is realized in a fundamental rule that the householder
may not do anything that appears to others to transgress the law, even though
the action does not actually benefit the land. Removing stones from the field
for use in construction may also appear to constitute clearing the land for
planting. Stockpiling manure in the field looks like fertilizing the field. Accordingly, the householder may not so act as to appear to violate the law (M.
Sheb. 3:1–4:10)."[42] The observance of the sabbatical year serves to sanctify
the land and express its sanctification, and that depends upon the actions and
will of the people, Israel. But among the people, the ones who count are the
householders.

Ceasing all productive labor on the farms in the seventh year of the sabbatical cycle dictated the conditions for supply, cutting the crop to what grew
on its own without human intervention, and, further, governed what might or

might not be sold in the market. For example, in the sabbatical year a crafts-man may not sell a plow and its accessories, but he may sell a sickle (M. Sheb. 5:6). The general rule is as follows: as regards any tool the use of which during the sabbatical year is limited exclusive to the performance of an act which is a transgression, it is forbidden to sell such a tool during the sab-batical year. But as for any tool which may be used both for work which is forbidden and for work which is permitted according to the laws of the sab-batical year, it is permissible to sell such a tool during the sabbatical year (M. Sheb. 5:6).[43] Along these same lines the potter may sell to an individual only so many pots as one usually needs to store produce gathered in accordance with the law (M. Sheb. 5:7).

Essentially the markets are supposed to close, in that the prevailing assump-tion is that everything is free. That seems to me a considerable intervention. In the eighth year, that is, the year following the sabbatical year, people may assume that vegetables in the market no longer derive from the crop of the seventh year (M. Sheb. 6:4). All rights of ownership of crops are suspended by the advent of the sabbatical year. Produce in that year is held to be owner-less property. That food belongs equally to all Israelites, so it is not a common commodity, like produce grown in other years. People may not use it for their own financial gain, and if they sell it or process it, it must be done in an un-usual manner. They may not hoard it but must remove it from the house if it has been stored there, at exactly the same time at which the produce is no longer found in the fields. The householder places the produce outside his house and makes it accessible to all.[44] Accordingly, what people have to do with their crops is remove from their house and declare ownerless whatever has grown in the sabbatical year. When a given crop disappears from the fields, it also may not longer be stored in the household. Whatever is fit for human or animal consumption or use and is an annual is subject to the require-ment of removal, that is, to the declaration of being ownerless (M. Sheb. 7:1-2).

The sanctified produce of the sabbatical year is also subject to important restrictions. First, of course, it may not be sold in the usual manner, e.g., by volume, weight, or in fixed quantity. Second, what is ordinarily used as food may only be used for food. Nothing may be wasted. The produce is always deemed consecrated. People must use it for the correct purposes (M. Sheb. 8:1-9:1). What grows wild may be bought from anyone during the sab-batical year, on the assumption that it has not been cultivated. The main point is that people may not stockpile edible produce and deprive others of access to that same (ownerless) produce. That is the purpose of removing stockpiled produce from the household.[45]

Other taboos governing the supply of produce to the market were hardly of so drastic a character as those concerning the production and disposition of crops in the sabbatical year. Mishnah-tractate Orlah works out the rule gov-erning fouth-year fruit, in line with Lev. 19:23, "When you come to the land

and plant any kind of tree for food, you shall treat it as forbidden. For three years it shall be forbidden, it will not be eaten." In the fourth year, the fruit is placed into the status of second tithe, which is to say, it is to be brought to Jerusalem and consumed there.[46] That rule, like the one governing produce designated as second tithe, removes from the market a share of the produce that would ordinarily be available for sale, consequently raising the price for other produce not subject to the same restrictions.

Disposition of a small portion—approximately 2 percent—of the crop to the priests intervened in the normal working of the market in two ways.[47] First, the supply of produce for the market was correspondingly diminished, with the result that prices will have been affected. This seems to me not a negligible consideration. Second, a part of the population, namely, priests and their families and dependents, received support without corresponding investment in production of goods and services. That is a considerable matter. Produce in the status of heave-offering, or priestly rations, commanded a much lower price, there being a limited demand. Produce available for "secular" use, that is to say, produce not subject to taboos limiting its market and utilization, commanded a substantially higher price. Heave-offering derived only from the householder, constituting a portion of the yield of the vineyards and fields, and could be given only by the householder or his agent, not by any third party. Accordingly, only the householder participated in the process.[48] The householder designated a portion of his produce to be heave-offering and bore responsibility to protect it from common use until it was handed over to the priest. The theory of the matter is expressed at Num. 18:8–13. Heave-offering was to support the priest and formed part of the provision for maintaining the sacerdotal caste. The produce was eaten in a state of cultic cleanness, only by the priest and his household.

The rules of tithing impose upon market transactions certain considerations of a nonmarket character, e.g., whether or not one must tithe produce that one purchases (M. Ma. 2:5–6). One who purchases five figs for a coin may not eat them without tithing, since they are regarded as distinct and random, so Meir. Judah maintains that one may eat them one by one without tithing, but if he takes the purchase together as a batch, he must tithe them. Now the net effect on the price of the figs cannot be reckoned, since one may avoid tithing the purchased figs by conducting himself in one way, rather than in another. But to use the figs for one's family, one surely will have to gather the purchase together as a batch and take it home. Accordingly, untithed produce will command a correspondingly lower price at the market than tithed produce, again a consideration in the setting of the price for food in the marketplace. The effect upon price, therefore, is going to be more than negligible, since 10 percent of the volume of what one purchases may, in fact, go for some other purpose than the purchaser's needs.

Distributive economics not only dictated supply (and, it follows, also, demand) but also governed who might, and might not, participate in the market at all. Penalties for violating the law include exclusion from trading, for ex ample: "He who is suspected of breaking the law of firstlings—they do not purchase from him meat of gazelles or untanned hides, bleached wool or dirty wool, but they do purchase from him spun wool or wool made into garments. If he is suspected of violating the restrictions of the seventh year, they do not purchase flax from him" (M. Bekh. 4:7–8). So too the following:

A. "He who is suspected of selling food in the status of heave-offering as if it were unconsecrated food—they do not purchase from him even water or salt," the words of R. Judah.
B. R. Simeon says, "Whatever is subject to the rules of heave-offerings and tithes they do not purchase from him."

(M. Bekh. 4:9)

These rules intervene into the market available to such a person and affect the normal demand for food, restricting it, just as much as the rules that are reinforced here limit the supply of food as well.

A further intrusion of the market, one that causes no surprise, is the system's clear policy of favoring the Temple as against the market and assigning all advantage to the temple. For example:

A. All invalidated Holy Things once redeemed may be sold in the marketplace and slaughtered in the marketplace and weighed by exact volume, except for the blemished firstling and tithe of cattle.
B. For the advantage of selling them in the market [where demand is higher] belongs to the owner. Invalidated Holy Things are so disposed of that the advantage falls to the sanctuary.

(M. Bekh. 5:1A–F)

The laws against idolatry represent an enormous intrusion into the working of the market. For example, for three days before gentile festivals one may not do business with gentiles in the market (M. A.Z. 1:1ff.). There are things one may not sell to gentiles, for example, small cattle, which are used for sacrifices to idols, or bears, lions, or anything which is a public danger (M. A.Z. 1:50–57). One may not sell gentiles ornaments for an idol, produce not yet harvested, land in the Holy Land (M. A.Z. 1:8–9). One may not lend to gentiles or borrow from them, borrow money or repay a loan, prior to a festival (M. A.Z. 1:1A–D). The marketplace in which there is an idol is subjected to prohibitions, e.g.:

A. A town in which there is an idol, and in which there were shops that were adorned and shops that were not—this was a case in Beth Shean.
B. And sages ruled, "Those which are adorned are prohibited, but those which are not adorned are permitted."

(M. A.Z. 1:4)

One may sell to a gentile nothing that may be used for idolatrous purposes (M. A.Z. 1:5). Israelite craftsmen may not make ornaments for an idol, nor may farmers sell produce as yet unplucked. One may not rent to gentiles houses or fields in the land of Israel, but one may do so abroad (M. A.Z. 1:8G–M). These rules and stipulations have concrete bearing upon the market, in a way in which other laws do not; e.g., "They accept from gentiles dealing for property but not for a person" (M. A.Z. 2:2); "They do not leave cattle in gentiles' inns because they are suspect in regard to bestiality" (M. A.Z. 2:1).

Trade in wine is subject to special prohibitions. Wine on which gentiles have worked is assumed to have been devoted to idolatry, and Israelites therefore may derive no benefit whatsoever from the remaining wine in the same bottle (M. A.Z. 2:3). These rules are concrete and have nothing to do with the general prohibition against idolatry (M. A.Z. 3:1–4:7). The principal consideration is the prohibition against libation wine, which is fully worked out at M. A.Z. 4:8–12, 5:1–7. The prohibition as to libation wine greatly intruded into relationships of all sorts, but the point at which economic action and policy were affected had to do with the production of, and trade in, wine. Gentile workers could not be employed unless constantly watched; if a jar of wine was opened by a gentile, it was assumed to have been used for a libation, and the rest of the wine thereby to have been spoiled. This led to various complications, e.g., "Israelite craftsmen to whom a gentile sent a jar of libation wine as their salary are permitted to say to him, 'Give us its value'" (M. A.Z. 5:7).

The definition of wealth forms a component of the rationale for the system as a whole. As we now recognize full well, the object of concern, in connection with tithing, is land and its produce. That conception is expressed in the following statement:

A. A general principle they stated concerning tithes:
B. Anything that is food, cultivated, and which grows from the earth, is subject to the law of tithes.
C. And yet another general principle:
D. Anything which at its first stage of development is food and which at its ultimate stage of development is food, even though the farmer maintains its growth in order to increase the food it will yield, is subject to the law of tithes, whether it is small or large, that is, at all points in its development.
E. But anything which at its first stage of development is not food, yet which at its ultimate stage of development is food, is not subject to the laws of tithes until it becomes edible.

(M. Ma. 1:1)[49]

The point is that all plants cultivated by man as food are subject to the law of tithes. When the householder harvests the crop, he must designate a fixed percentage of it as heave-offering or tithes; these are sanctified and set aside from the rest of the harvested crop and handed over to the priests and other scheduled castes. Only then is the rest of the produce available to the owner. What therefore falls into the system of sanctification is what grows from the land through the householder's own labor ("cultivated") and is useful to the householder for sustaining life ("food"). God owns the land, the householder is the sharecropper, and the wealth of the householder therefore is the land that God allows for the householder's share and use.

Wealth consists of land and what land produces, crops and cattle, as well as a large labor force, comprising the children of a growing population. The link of fertility to tithing occurs at Dt. 14:22–29, in connection with the separation of the tithe and the delivery of the tithe to Jerusalem, where it is to be eaten by the householder: "that the Lord your God may bless you in all the work of your hands that you do." "Proper disposition of the tithe . . . will result in God's blessing of the soil and its increased productivity."[50] The conception that wealth is solely land is expressed not only in rules for the householder but also in silence: tithe derives only from herds and agricultural produce. The artisan and craftsman, the personnel of the service economy, merchants and traders and other commercial persons—none of these has anything to tithe. While they may have possessed wealth in the form of goods and even money, the distributive economics of the Mishnah had no rules governing the disposition of that wealth, which was left without recognition. And yet, as we have seen, the market economics of the Mishnah made ample provision for the governance of wealth in other forms than real estate. On that basis—the inconsistent theory of wealth—I maintain the Mishnah presents, side by side, two distinct theories of economics, the one a market economics, the other a more familiar distributive economics. But once more we enter the caveat: the Mishnah's economics is distributive, but it makes provision for an economics of a market enclave as well. So the theories are distinct but not dual, not correlative.

At the end we have to listen not only to what the Mishnah says, but also to what it does not treat. In fact, the economics of the system expresses in tacit omissions a judgment concerning the dimensions of the economy that to begin with falls subject to the enchantment of sanctification expressed in glorious triviality by our author. For matching the explicit rules are the authors' ominous silences. The Mishnah's land-centeredness permits its economics to have no bearing not only upon Jews who were not householders, but also Jews who lived overseas. The Mishnah's distributive economics is for the "Israel" of "the land of Israel" to which the Mishnah speaks. There is no address to the economics of "Israel" outside of the land. For distributive economics governs only agricultural produce of the land of Israel, and, it follows, market economics is tacitly assigned as the mode of distribution for everything else, and operative everywhere else (and that conception is consistent with the Temple-centeredness of the holiness system worked out by the Mishnah). No wonder, then, that the framers of the Talmud of Babylonia, addressing, as they did, Jews who did not live on holy or sanctified ground, took no interest whatsoever in the Mishnah tractates upon which we have focused here, the ones that state in rich detail the theory of a distributive economics of God as owner, scheduled caste as surrogate, Temple as focus, and enlandisement as rationale for an utterly fictive system.

8

Theology, Class Ideology, and Distributive Economics

Cui Bono?

The distributive economics presented, at least in a statement of details that stand for a structural theory, by the authors of the Mishnah joins two distinct viewpoints. First, of course, the caste interest of the priests forms the criterion for the distribution of scarce resources, and, not only so, but the passages of Scripture important to the priesthood dictate the conditions of production. Second, the central actor in the system, quite naturally defined as the one who controls the means of production, finds in this same caste interest a legitimation for his class interests.[1] The Mishnah's economics derives from the interests of the undercapitalized and overextended farmer, who does not appreciate the interests of those with liquid capital or understand the role of trading, e.g., in commodity futures. The landed proprietor of the estate sees a bushel of grain as a measure of value, but does not concede that, in the provision of supplies from year to year, from harvest to harvest, also lies a kind of increase no less productive than the increase of the fields and the herd. The Mishnah's economics conceives of the unit of production as the household, identified with the landholding and proprietary class of farmers; the Mishnah's problems are those of the landowner, the householder, the basic and recurrent subject of nearly all pertinent predicates. The Mishnah's sense of what is just and fair expresses his sense of rightness of the present condition and equilibrium of society. Earth matches heaven. The Mishnah's hope for heaven and its claim on earth, to earth, corresponding to the supernatural basis for the natural world, speaks for the householder.

Shall we now conclude that the economics of the Mishnah represents an alliance of two groups, the class of landowners and the caste of priests? A Marxist-Talmudist, Yulii Aronovich Solodukho (1877–1963) reached the second of these two conclusions in his lifelong effort to hold together the traditions of talmudic learning and the new sciences of Marxism that took command of the U.S.S.R. after the Bolshevik revolution of 1917.[2] Solodukho's fundamental premise is stated in his 1938 dissertation: "The exploiting classes of the Hebrew population used Talmudic literature for their own interests over many centuries; to this end, they tried to veil the Talmudic literature with religion. Proclaiming the whole Talmudic material sacrosanct and untouchable, they thus preserved it as a charter of class jurisdiction and class attitude."[3] The important application of that thesis, for our purpose, is in Solodukho's "On the Question of the Social Structure of Iraq in the Third to the Fifth Centuries A.D."[4]

Beginning his description of the social structure with the Mishnah, Solodukho concentrates on the Talmud of Babylonia (Bavli). But his theses, the reader will rapidly observe, pertain as directly to the Mishnah as to the Bavli. His basic thesis is as follows:

> The overwhelming majority of people who figure in the Babylonian Gemara represent a new type of landowner, that is, new in origin, who had moved up out of the milieu of craftsmen and tradespeople and had become rich. Sometimes they were even from the milieu of small landowners. Simultaneously, they continued to be occupied in crafts or trade, or to fulfill state and social duties. In such social-economic relationships these landowners, in the period under discussion, can be related to the large feudal landholders, which grew up together with the ruling class of not very numerous representatives of the landed gentry. These people were heirs of lands worked for the most part by slaves.[5]

Solodukho identifies various important figures in the Bavli as "affluent landowners":

> The large feudalizing landholders stood for a new, more progressive means of production. They struggled against the gentry, landed by inheritance, who exploited slave labor, and against other large landholders from the milieu of the aristocracy of high rank and of the leaseholders from the government. They therefore represented a more progressive layer of the ruling class. They were, however, especially interested in strengthening the exploitation of the direct producers in agriculture. They sought to institute serfdom and actually to bind to the land the many tenant farmers and sharecroppers, people of their own faith, who belonged to the laboring part of the Hebrew population. To this number also belonged day laborers, day agricultural workers, and slaves.[6]

In these citations of Solodukho's reading of materials we gain ample perspective on a potential interpretation, also, of the role and place of the householder in the system of the Mishnah. Solodukho's mode of interpretation is entirely explicit:

> The material they included in the Germara was subjected to filtration, selection from the point of view of class interest. We may . . . follow both the dynamics of the process of the birth and the gradual establishment of early feudal relationships, and also the phenomena accompanying this process: taking the land and enslavement of the small landholders, turning them into tenants and increasing the exploitation of the direct agricultural producers.[7]

That reading derives from the position of Marxism-Leninism. From Solodukho's viewpoint, the "bourgeois nationalist historians" fail to "concentrate on materials which plainly reveal the class character of the Iraqi-Hebrew [=Babylonian Jewish] society and point up the contradictions of this society."

These Solodukho describes as "riches and luxury, on the one hand, immeasurably heavy labor, material need and half-starved existence, on the other; above all the cruel exploitation of the broad mass of laborers, especially of the direct producers in agriculture." The class interests of the "bourgeois nationalist historians" guide them to ignore materials "which mercilessly expose their antihistorical conclusions about the special course of development of Hebrew society, the absence of class distinctions within it, the absence, consequently, of premises for class contradictions productive of class struggle."[8]

Were Solodukho to read the first seven chapters of this book, it seems to me obvious that he would identify as an early stage in the unfolding of the class struggle the economics of the Mishnah. For he would surely find in the union of sacerdotal and landholding interests the conditions for the rise to prominence and power of the landholding or proprietary class, first allied with, then predominant over, the priesthood. Then, in his reading of the Bavli, he would find the second stage in the same unfolding class struggle, the rise to power of the large landholders over the small, the elimination of the priesthood as a contending force in the class struggle (evidenced by the utter rejection of the Priestly Code's and Mishnah's agricultural taboos concerning conditions of production and rules for disposition of the crops), and the consequent account of the class struggle that he gives in the principal statement just now cited. Working backward from the story that he does tell, we may reasonably anticipate chapters along these very lines. The absence of evidence on the everyday state of affairs—the Mishnah containing very little material that alleges a picture of how things actually were—Solodukho surely would find little reason for reluctance to provide his own account.[9]

But I think a criticism of a Marxist view merely because evidence is lacking to sustain it is, while in the present case devastating, still, trivial. For, when we deal with a systemic construction of a social world, such as the Mishnah's authors have made for themselves, the more interesting question is one of interpretation, not of fact. The structure and composition of the system are fully factual matters, portrayed for us by the document that constitutes the statement of the system. So there is no issue of historical knowledge. The correct point at which to take issue with Solodukho, as representing a Marxist interpretation, is rather the *interpretation* of a system that, in its initial statement, proposes not to reflect, but to impose shape and structure upon, the (historical) society to come. The class interests expressed in the document therefore form a question not of historical fact but of systemic analysis, and the issue of whether the system in fact aims at effecting those class interests forms part of that same analysis. So we revert to some fundamental facts and simple questions.

Let us start with the observation that the authors of the Mishnah placed limitations upon ownership of private property, maintaining that every householder held his real property in joint tenancy with God and therefore had to dispose of the scarce resources of land and crops in response to the requirements of that partnership. The result is to aggrandize the social position of the landholder, however modest his holding, by setting him into a direct relationship with God. But it also calls into question the conception of ownership that surely will have confronted the householder. For the aggrandizement of the social position of the small householder was attained at the cost of introducing into the conduct of agricultural production the concerns of the priesthood, e.g., for not mixing seeds of two species, for faithfully observing the sabbatical year not as a means of restoring the nutrients of the soil but of utterly disrupting the agricultural economy.[10] Not only so, but a further cost to the householder lay in the restriction against fully maximizing return on investment, e.g., through holding back produce until the best price, based on scarcity, could be gained. Accordingly, considerations other than those of economic gain had to compensate the householder, and the rise in class status was gained only at a considerable compromise of class interest. Distributive economics furthermore directed investment into agriculture, to the detriment of commerce, trade, and manufacturing. But beyond these observations lurks a question that has, until now, managed to hold its peace.

Several times I have observed that the economics of the Mishnah addresses only one sector of the economy, and the distributive economics that prevailed clearly ignores important arenas of economic action, e.g., trade, commerce, manufacturing, as well as labor. So I must wonder, have I then established that the Judaism of the Mishnah has an economics at all? If we take up the definitions current in the first half of the nineteenth century, we regard economics as an investigation into "the nature and causes of the wealth of nations," "the laws which regulate the distribution of the produce of the earth," and "the laws of motion of capitalism."[11] I of course have taken at face value the contemporary view of the science as a "science that analyzed 'human behavior as a relationship between given ends and scarce means which have alternative uses.' "[12] In that setting, while distributive economics may well form a truly economic theory of economics, the Mishnah's adaptation of that economic theory does not. Quite to the contrary, an economics that speaks of one component of the economy and utterly ignores others, that treats value as something inhering in land but not in merchandise, that exacts taxes only from the things it deems of worth and so imputes value to one activity and denigrates all others—such an economics is a theory of politics in society, expressed in economic terms. But it is not a political economics, it is an economics within a politics. And the distinction makes a difference, if we claim to make judgments about the economics of a system. For what we begin to understand is that a system may make its statement through economics, indeed, may be constrained to do so and find no other suitable way of saying what it wishes to say, without, in point of fact, setting forth a theory of the economy of the society that that system proposes to design.

The following definition, for instance, surely would have puzzled the authors of the Mishnah:

> The problem that gave rise to economics in the first place . . . is that of market exchange: there is a sense of order in the economic universe, and this order is not imposed from above but is somehow the outcome of the exchange transactions between individuals, each seeking to maximize his own gain. The history of economic thought . . . is nothing but the history of our efforts to understand the workings of an economy based on market transactions.[13]

At this point the authors at hand would have concurred that there is an order in exchange transactions but would have found puzzling the conception that such an order is not in some manner or other an extension of heaven's plan and program for earth. In this regard, Aristotle's antimarket theory about what is natural and what is unnatural addressed questions economists can grasp, for Aristotle aimed at an economy of balance, order, and stasis and appealed to secular facts in order to justify that goal. But the Mishnah's sages in reaching the same conclusions as Aristotle invoked other than an ideal of a social system and structure. Theirs was a supernatural (one might want to say, metaphysical) *Staatsroman,* drawing down from heaven illumination for the affairs of humanity here on earth. In that context, the fact that economic questions emerged is purely adventitious, while, in Aristotle's setting, it was, by contrast, a deliberate and logical initiative. And who ever heard of an economics that pertained only to certain persons living in a certain place? Aristotle could not imagine such an economics; his theory pertained everywhere. The Mishnah's framers' economics, by contrast, explained the rules governing not an economy but a holy society, abstracted from economics, made up only of certain persons, owners of land who were Israelites, located only in a certain place, the land called the land of Israel. That, once again, is hardly a counterpart, even, to Aristotle's economics, even though both the Mishnah's and Aristotle's economics spoke of the same subjects and made the same points about those subjects.

For the framers of the Mishnah maintained that scarcity represented heaven's judgment upon the condition of the nation, and, therefore, to prevent scarcity one had to secure the favor of heaven. The things that became scarce when heaven was displeased had properly to be arrayed before and transported to heaven through the heavens. And these things were the product of the earth, the fields and farms, the herds and vineyards and orchards. Heaven governed these things, and so, in order to avoid scarcity, heaven's rules had to be observed, a conception brought down to this morning's labor by appeal to God as joint holder and joint owner of the land along with the Israelite owner of the land in the land of Israel in particular. Not only so, but when scarcity affected the nation, or classes within the nation, that same mode of arraying goods and transporting them dictated what was to be done rationally to deal with scarcity. So faced with a set of choices about the disposition of scarce goods, the authors of the Mishnah made entirely rational decisions on how to make use of the goods and services of the economy in such a way as to prevent scarcity by removing its cause, on the one side, and to deal with scarcity when it arose, on the other.

A full account, therefore, of the economics of the Mishnah as a rational program of dealing with scarcity requires us to enter into the rationality of the system as a whole, for, we now realize, the parts of the system that concern economics form an integral component of the statement of that large, whole world view and way of life that, all together, constituted the Judaism of the formative document under study. Through the system of the Mishnah at each of its principal constituents, sages say pretty much the same things about the world of nature and supernature which they express in the other divisions of the Mishnah. What is that point of emphasis? At point after point in their system, the framers of the Mishnah declare one conviction. It is that the Israelite world—Jews in Palestine / Israelites in the land of Israel—forms a world unto itself, a world order of enduring stasis, in which no significant change will disturb the stable society. This world order, down below, attains that enduring, indeed eternal, stasis because it serves to complement and complete the other world order, the one in heaven. In the complementarity and wholeness attained through the union of two opposites—heaven and earth—on the sacred time of the Sabbath and in festivals, creation is renewed, and, on that account, creation in all its completeness and perfection once more provokes in God the benediction and sanctification of the creator such as the original excellence of creation had elicited.

This absolutely fundamental conviction comes to concrete expression in diverse ways. The one, within economics, that has time and again drawn our attention emphasizes the true, intrinsic worth and value of things, the perfect balance in transactions, so that each party to an exchange, conceived as equal barter, gets worth equivalent to what he gives, and both parties emerge precisely at the same level of worth as at the outset. But that conception of the perfection of the steady-state economy is only one way in which the systemic principle is expressed in the details of everyday exchange. To give one example of how in other ways the conception of the basically stationary character of the world order reaches concrete expression, we turn to politics. Specifically, the Israelite government is supposed to preserve that state of perfection that society everywhere attains and expresses in economic and other material transactions as well. People are to follow and maintain the prevailing practice of their locale. The purpose of civil penalties is to restore the injured party to his prior condition, so far as this is possible, rather than merely to penalize the aggressor. So there is no surprise that the system invoked economic theory in order to make its statement. In a perfect society (as perfection is understood by our mishnaic philosophers) true value means that a given object has an intrinsic worth, which in the course of a transaction must be paid. And, for that same reason, we introduce the topic of usury, which, we noted, sages treated as integral to the conception of fraud as the violation of true value. There can be no such thing as usury, which means essentially profit. Any pretense that money increases or has become more than what it was violates the conception of true value. When real estate is divided, it must be done with full attention to the rights of all concerned, so that one party does not gain at the expense of the other. In these and many other aspects the law of the Mishnah expresses its obsession with the perfect stasis and endur-ing order of Israelite society. Its paramount purpose is to preserve and insure that that perfection of the division and order of this world is kept inviolate or restored to its true status when violated. And that systemic message required attention to economics, not because the subject matter was necessary to a full and encompassing statement of the social order, for other world constructions made their statements of the right construction and composition of the social order without addressing economics at all. It was because only by addressing the *theory* of economics, the received distributive theory adapted to the Mish-nah's purposes and subjected to exquisite amplification and extension in the exegesis of the Mishnah's authors, could the systemic program reach full real-ization. That is why the Mishnah presents an economics.

But the economics of the Mishnah is not an economics at all. The reason is that, as I have explained, in the Mishnah's system, economics is embedded in an encompassing structure, to which economic considerations are subordi-nated, forming merely instrumental components of a statement made not in response to, but merely through, economics. And economics can emerge as an autonomous and governing theory only when disembedded from politics and society. Economic institutions, such as the market, the wage system, a theory of private ownership, and the like, in no way can have served the sys-tem of the Mishnah, not because in their moral or ethical value they proved less, or more, suitable than competing institutions, such as the sacerdotal sys-tem of production and distribution, a theory of divine-human joint tenancy, and a system made up of both wages for labor and also fees for correct gene-alogy, that the Mishnah's framers adopted. Economics viewed in its own terms cannot have served the system of the Mishnah because the system builders viewed nothing in its own terms, but all things in the framework of the social system they proposed to construct. I earlier observed that Christian theologians for the first seven centuries simply ignored economics, having no theory to contribute to economic thought and no sustained interest in the sub-ject. But when we realize the character and function of economics in the sys-tem of the Mishnah, we realize that the same reason accounts for the presence of an economics as for its absence.

The way forward leads us to Max Weber's insistence that the correct point of analysis of a system, and then for comparison and contrast of system to system, is the description, analysis, and interpretation of the rationality of the system, then the comparison of rationality to rationality. I argue for Weber not because a Marxist reading in the case at hand, as Solodukho has presented it to us, is not sustained by the facts, whether literary or archaeological in venue.[14] That reading is simply beside the point. For if we cannot explain the economic theory of a system by reference only to class interest and class struggle, then what makes the system work is some other generative component than class interest and class struggle. In the case of the Mishnah, class status seems to me to compete with class interest and therefore to form a negative force in the working out of what the Marxists, as Solodukho represents them, must conceive to be the class struggle. True, class status, the comparison of the householder in particular to God in particular, can have valued economic consequences. But in the system before us, the opposite is the fact. The economic interests of the householder contradict the requirements of class status, for reasons I have specified time and again. That is why I find the rationality of the system elsewhere than in those considerations of class structure and class struggle that to Solodukho appeared prominent and even determinative. To the forces of class structure and class struggle, my analysis has taught me to counterpose the considerations of systemic rationality.

Economics, nonetheless, defines an important component of the rationality of a social system aiming at the construction of a society. And that is why, if we are to compare the rationality of one system to the rationality of some other, we have to learn, also, how to compare economics to economics, political economy to political economy. This mode of analysis—comparison and contrast—demands us even to know *which* component of a given system serves as the counterpart and corresponding component to the economics of another system, beginning, of course, with our own. And that explains the larger program of the inquiry now concluded. For I have addressed—in a very particular framework, to be sure—the question of translating from one culture to another the theory of economics, that is, rational action in regard to scarcity, and, in a subsidiary sense, also to the increase and disposition of wealth. Describing the economics of a world different from our own, I have meant ultimately to penetrate into the meaning of rationality, encompassing rational action in matters of scarcity and also wealth, its increase and disposition, in a universe other than the familiar one of the secular West. To do so, we have found, we cannot simply adopt and apply to an alien world that contemporary and commonplace theory of economics that for us describes and accounts for the rationality of economic action. We quickly realized that that would tell us nothing about rational economic action in a world in which rationality bears different rules from the ones we know.

Rather, we have had to identify within that other world, different from our own, the things that to them fell into the category we know as economic. Specifically, we have asked, what are the things they regarded as rational actions in regard to scarcity, and also to matters of wealth, its increase and disposition? And how did they uncover hypotheses of rationality in economic action, test them, and translate them into rules of intelligent economic action? In this way we have not merely adopted but have adapted the issues of economics by allowing for economic action to follow rules different from the ones we know, yet to accord with conceptions we nonetheless can claim to understand. In asking our questions about economics—theory of rational action in the face of scarcity and in the increase and disposition of wealth—we have discerned and, I think, in context understood alien answers to those same questions. Our rationality has constructed a program of inquiry into the rationality concerning common issues, differently sorted out, by different people, in a different world from our own. In that way we have aimed at entering into, and understanding, someone else's economic rationality, and so, too, someone else: an other.

Toward the Analysis of Systems and the Comparison of Rationalities

There is a still more interesting reason for engaging in the study of the economics, politics, and modes of thought we know as the philosophy of a given Judaism. In the interpretation of any religious system, such as the Judaism of the dual Torah, we have to compare what one system sets forth with what other systems present. If we are to interpret the Judaism of the dual Torah consequently, we have to undertake comparison with other modes—competing modes indeed!—of the formation of (a) civilization. These are not only or, today, mainly religious. So far, therefore, as we wish to make sense of one system, we require occasions for comparison with other systems, such as are presented by economics, politics, and modes of thought.[1] This modest book therefore addresses a small part of a large task, one to which many scholars may contribute. The work of making sense of things requires not only description and analysis of one thing, but also, in diverse contexts, the interpretation of one thing through comparison with other things. That accounts for the shape and program of this book and its companions.

One mode of comparison, which I have not explored here, is to reverse the definition of economics. We recall the reason for my claim that the Judaism of the Mishnah presents a theory of economics. I show that important components of the mishnaic system address the definition of rational action with regard both to the allocation of scarce resources, on the one side, and to the increase and disposition of wealth, on the other.[2] But comparison of system to system, rationality to rationality, also requires that the received definition of economics be read in two directions, first forward, then backward. That is to say any theory of rational action with regard to scarcity is economics. In this book, our recognition of distributive economics was such that we did not have to argue through such a reversal that taboos concerning production and distribution of crops constituted chapters of an economics. That these formed components of the economics of the Mishnah was shown very simply by my appeal to the general theory of distributive economics.

But there are systems, as I have pointed out, in which we have no economics at all; that is, topics concerning production, distribution, work and wage, ownership and conduct of economic entities, economic action in all its forms, simply are lacking. To account for that fact in the comparison and contrast of systems, I propose the notion that, as I said, any theory of rational action with regard to scarcity is economics. The reverse reading yields this sentence: *economics is a (any) theory of rational action with regard to scarcity.* Matters then that hardly fall into the category of economic theory at all may yield points of congruency and so validate systemic comparisons and contrasts. The result of reading both *economics is . . .* and also *. . . is economics* may serve to validate systemic comparison even among systems that are not point by point, component by component, congruent. And that leaves us at the point at which I concluded the final chapter: the comparison of rationalities.

Let me now spell out why I think this two-directional reading—first, "*economics is* [or encompasses] the theory of rational action with regard to scarcity," second, "a theory of rational action with regard to scarcity *is encompassed by economics,*"—yields important insight. What is at stake? In my view, it is the comparison of one rationality to another, made possible by the dual and reciprocal definition of [1] economics as the theory of rational action with regard to scarcity and [2] the theory of rational action with regard to scarcity as economics. When we understand the particular rationality of the economics of—to take the case at hand—the Judaism of the Mishnah, we find the way to translate that Judaism's alien and odd rationality, covering as it does matters we do not conceive of under the rubric of economics, into categories of rationality that we can grasp. That is to say, when we see that a category of an alien system and its rationality constitutes *its* economics and therefore forms a counterpart to economics as we understand that subject within our rationality, we learn how in a critical component to translate system to system. We may then make the statement: in that system, within their rationality, that category of activity forms a component of economic theory, while in our system, within our rationality, we do not think of that category of activity as a component of economic theory at all. And this we do without assuming a posture of relativism, for example claiming that their economics, and with it their rationality, is pretty much the same, or is at least as valid, as ours. That is not pertinent to my exercise in translation and comparison.

Their economics *is* economics by our definition. But in its range of concerns, not solely in its (in any event outdated and primitive) theorems, it is profoundly different from ours. Their economics, moreover, is equally different from the economics of a Greek or Roman treatise on economics. Any Judaism also bears comparison with a Christianity, and in the present instance, comparing the initial document of the Judaism of the dual Torah with the initial statement of all Christianities, namely, the Gospels, is entirely in order. What we learn is that while the Mishnah encompasses economics for its own systemic message, the Gospels do not. So the Mishnah's economics, that is, the economics of the initial statement of Judaism, is different, both in context and out of context. I propose to understand the difference. For, as a matter of fact, we may read a Greek treatise on economics as something very like economics as we know the subject, for such a treatise covers subjects as we may anticipate they are to be treated. But important portions of the Mishnah that we perceive as economics within their rationality in no way compare to economics as we know the subject. And when we know the difference, we shall propose to explain why this, not that, for both their economics and ours.[3]

In asking about rationality—the Mishnah's program of economics understood as rational action in regard to scarcity—I therefore point to other systems' rationalities in comparison to this one. I see the need to turn back to the economics of Greco-Roman antiquity, on the one side, and outward to the economics of Christianity in its initial statement, on the other. I should read the Gospels for pertinent thought on issues deemed consequential in the economic rationality of the Mishnah and attempt to set side by side the two economic rationalities, in the sense just now defined, the Judaic in the initial document of Judaism, the Christian in the initial statement of Christianity. That seems to me always a comparison of interest in the Western world.

These future areas of systemic study, the one of description, the other of comparison, seem to me to warrant further attention. But, to conclude appropriately with a saying of Tarfon, a sage whom we met earlier, "Yours is not to complete the task, yours also is not to walk away from it." We have gotten this far.

The Mishnah in Canonical Context and the Next Stages in Study of the Economics of Judaism

Let me now spell out further research on the economics of Judaism, beyond the initial statement given by the Mishnah. Now, it is clear, counterpart studies will have to describe the economics of authors who received the Mishnah and reworked its materials. Second, other studies will have to analyze the economics of the successive Judaic thinkers through comparison and contrast with writings of other system builders altogether.

A brief account of the writings between the Mishnah and the Bavli will place into context that authoritative and conclusive statement of the whole. Then the dimensions of the study of the economics of successor documents will become clear and emerge in context. For the Mishnah is only the initial statement in an unfolding system. Much work—description of the economics of those other systemic documents that present an economics, then the analytical comparison of the successive systems or theories (if that is what they were), and, finally, interpretation of the result for the study of social history— is to be done. Only after a considerable account of the writings shall we revert to our interest in the economics of Judaism.

The writings of the sages between the Mishnah and the Bavli, ca. A.D. 200 and 600, fall into two distinct groups, one beginning with the Mishnah and ending about two centuries later, in A.D. 400, with the Tosefta and close associates of the Mishnah; the other beginning with the Yerushalmi ca. A.D. 400 and ending about two centuries later, with the Bavli. The Mishnah, as we know, drew in its wake tractate Abot, a statement concluded a generation after the Mishnah on the standing of the authorities of the Mishnah. Attached to the Mishnah also is the Tosefta, ca. A.D. 300–400, a compilation of supplements of various kinds to the statements in the Mishnah. There were also three systematic exegeses of books of Scripture or the written Torah, tied to the Mishnah because, in passages, they may cite the Mishnah or the Tosefta verbatim and raise interesting questions about the relationship between the Mishnah or the Tosefta and Scripture. These works are the Sifra to Leviticus, the Sifré to Numbers, and the Sifré to Deuteronomy. These books overall form one stage in the unfolding of the Judaism of the dual Torah, oral and written, which stressed issues of sanctification of the life of Israel, the people, in the aftermath of the destruction of the Temple of Jerusalem in A.D. 70.

The second set of writings, A.D. 400–600, that culminated in the Bavli, stressed the dual issues of sanctification and salvation, presenting a doctrine of Israel's redemption by the Messiah in the model of the sage himself. The amplification of the Mishnah, which led to the first of the two sets of writings, defined the literary expression of the theological program at hand. It begins with the Yerushalmi, addressed to the Mishnah as oral Torah. Alongside, work on the written Torah was carried on through Genesis Rabbah, a reading of the book of Genesis to interpret the history and salvation of Israel today in light of the history and salvation of the patriarchs and matriarchs of old, deemed to form the founders of the family of Israel after the flesh. A second important work, assigned to about the next half century, Leviticus Rabbah, ca. A.D. 450, read for the lessons of Israel's salvation the book of Leviticus, which stresses issues of the sanctification in the here and now led to Israel's salvation at the end of time. Finally, the Bavli addressed both Torahs, oral and written, Mishnah and Scripture, within one and the same document—the first of the writings of the Judaism of the dual Torah to do so systematically and extensively. The difference between the Bavli and the earlier writings, therefore, is that while the authors of the Yerushalmi systematically interpreted passages of the Mishnah, and the other documents, as is clear, did the same for books of the written Torah, the authors of the Bavli did both. Alongside, there were some other treatments of biblical books important in synagogue liturgy, particularly the Five Scrolls, e.g., Lamentations Rabbati, Esther Rabbah, and the like. A remarkable compilation of scriptural lessons pertinent to the special occasions of the synagogue, Pesiqta deRab Kahana, reached closure at the same time—the fifth or sixth centuries—as well.

The difference in viewpiont between the documents from the Mishnah to the works on Leviticus, known as Sifra, and on Numbers and Deuteronomy, known as Sifré, is not merely technical. It is theological. The first of the two sets of writings, from the Mishnah to the Yerushalmi, exhibits no sign of interest in, or response to, the advent of Christianity. The second, from the Yerushalmi forward, lays points of stress and emphasis that, in retrospect, appear to respond to, and to counter, the challenge of Christianity. The point of difference, of course, is that from the beginning of the legalization of Christianity in the early fourth century, to the establishment of Christianity at the end of that same century, Jews in the land of Israel found themselves facing a challenge that, prior to Constantine, they had found no compelling reason to consider. The specific crisis came when the Christians pointed to the success of the church in the politics of the Roman state as evidence that Jesus Christ was king of the world, and that his claim to be Messiah and king of Israel had now found vindication. The Judaic documents that reached closure in the century after these events attended to questions of salvation, e.g., doctrine of history and of the Messiah, authority of the sages' reading of Scripture as against the

Christians' interpretation, and the like, that had earlier not enjoyed extensive consideration.

Sages worked out in the pages of the Yerushalmi and, later on, the Bavli, as well as in the exegetical compilations of the age, a Judaism intersecting with the Mishnah's but essentially asymmetrical with it. The Talmuds and associated writings presented a system of salvation, but one focused on the salvific power of the sanctification of the holy people. The first of the two Talmuds, the one closed at the end of the fourth century, set the compass and locked it into place. The second concluded matters. The Mishnah, in ca. A.D. 200, described an orderly world, in which Israelite society is neatly divided among its castes, arranged in priority around the center that is the temple, systematically engaged in a life of sanctification remote from the disorderly events of the day. The two Talmuds portrayed matters quite differently. While the Talmuds aim principally at the exegesis and amplification of the laws of the Mishnah, they also point toward a matrix beyond the Mishnah's text. Transcending the Mishnah's facts, the Talmuds' authors bring to the Mishnah a program defined outside of the Mishnah. Discourse encompasses a world of institutions, authorities, and effective power quite beyond the imagination of the Mishnah's framers. The Talmuds' picture of that world, furthermore, essentially ignores the specifications, for these same matters, of the Mishnah's law.

The Talmuds portrayed and coped with, rather than denying as did the Mishnah's writers, the chaos of Jews living among gentiles, governed by a diversity of authorities, lacking all order and arrangement, awaiting a time of salvation for which, through sanctification, they make themselves ready. That social fact of Israel's life did not change between 200 and 400 in the land of Israel, and between 200 and 600 in Babylonia. But the representation of the social realities did change. The sages of both Talmuds represented themselves—and we have no reason to doubt them—as fully in charge of the everyday life of the community, hence in constant touch with a real "Israel" consisting of a social group living a palpable everyday life. We may compare the Mishnah's authors to legal philosophers, thinking in abstract terms about logic and order. The Talmuds' authors included men deeply involved in the administration of the concrete social group, "Israel" as a real-life community. We may see them as analogous to judges, lawyers, bureaucrats, heads of local governments, not philosophers alone but men of affairs. When they represented "Israel," they drew upon concrete knowledge of, engagement in, a very real social world indeed. The facts portrayed by them draw upon experience entirely beyond the imagination of the framers of the Mishnah.

The Mishnah's Israel in imagination is governed by an Israelite king, high priest, and sanhedrin—a political world that for two centuries had existed, if at all, only in imagination or aspiration. The Talmuds' portrait of Israel represents Jews who lived under both rabbis near at hand, settling everyday disputes of streets and households, and also distant archons of a nameless state, to be manipulated and placated on earth as in heaven. The Mishnah's Judaism breathes the pure air of public piazza and stoa, the Talmuds', the ripe stench of private alleyway and courtyard. The image of the Mishnah's Judaism is evoked by the majestic Parthenon, perfect in all its proportions, conceived in a single moment of pure rationality. The Talmuds' Judaism is a scarcely choate cathedral in process, the labor of many generations, each of its parts the conception of diverse moments of devotion, all of them the culmination of an ongoing and evolving process of revelation in the here and now. As I have said in the body of the book, the Mishnah's system presents a counterpart to Plato's *Republic* and Aristotle's *Politics,* a noble theory of it all. When we study the Mishnah, we contemplate a fine conception of nowhere in particular, addressed to whom it may concern, a utopian vision in an exact sense of the word. When we turn to the Talmuds, we see a familiar world, as we have known it from the Talmuds' day to our own. It is a locative perspective upon the here and the now, so far as the Talmuds portray that concrete present. In literary terms, in the transition from the Mishnah to the Talmuds we leave behind the strict and formal classicism of the Mishnah, like Plato's *Republic* describing for no one in particular an ideal society never, in its day, to be seen. We come, rather, to focus upon the disorderly detail of the workaday world, taking the utopian Mishnah along with us.

How precisely was the Mishnah studied in the two Talmuds? The modes of study were mainly three. First, sages asked about the meanings of words and phrases, line by line, word by word. Then they worked on the comparison of one set of laws with another, finding the underlying principles of each and comparing, and harmonizing, those principles. So they formed of the rather episodic rules a tight and large fabric. Third, they moved beyond the narrow limits of the Mishnah into still broader and more speculative areas of thought. Once the work of reading the new code got under way, an important problem demanded attention. What is the relationship between the Mishnah and the established Scripture of Israel, the written Torah? The Mishnah only occasionally adduces texts of the Scriptures in support of its rules. Its framers worked out their own topical program, only part of which intersects with that of the laws of the Pentateuch. They followed their own principles of organization and development. They wrote in their own kind of Hebrew, which is quite different from biblical Hebrew. So the question naturally arose, can we through sheer logic discover the law? Or must we tease laws out of Scripture through commentary, through legal exegesis? The Mishnah represented an extreme in this debate, since, as I said, so many of its topics to begin with do not derive from Scripture, and, further, many of its laws ignore Scripture's pertinent texts in that these texts are simply not cited. The two Talmuds therefore paid attention, also, to the relationship of the Mishnah to Scripture.

This account of the topical program of the two Talmuds—which themselves share the same points of emphasis—tells us what the Talmuds did with the received statement of the Mishnah. But, on their own, they made their powerful and original statements as well. The most important point of those statements was to shift the focus upon the Temple and its supernatural principles to close attention to the people Israel and its natural, this-worldly history. Once Israel, holy Israel, had come to form the counterpart to the Temple and its supernatural life, that other history—Israel's—would stand at the center of things. Accordingly, a new sort of memorable event came to the fore in the Talmud of the Land of Israel. It was the story of Israel's suffering, remembrance of that suffering, on the one side, and an effort to explain events of such tragedy, on the other. The components of the historical theory of Israel's sufferings were manifold. First and foremost, history taught moral lessons. Historical events entered into the construction of a teleology for the Yerushalmi's system of Judaism as a whole. What the law demanded reflected the consequences of wrongful action on the part of Israel. So, again, Israel's own deeds defined the events of history. But the paradox of the Talmuds' system lies in the fact that Israel can free itself of control by other nations only by humbly agreeing to accept God's rule. The nations—Rome, in the present instance—rest on one side of the balance, while God rests on the other. Israel must then choose between them. There is no such thing for Israel as freedom from both God and the nations, total autonomy and independence. There is only a choice of masters, a ruler on earth or a ruler in heaven. It is Israel's history that works out and expresses Israel's relationship with God. The critical dimension of Israel's life, therefore, is salvation, the definitive trait, a movement in time from now to then. It follows that the paramount and organizing category is history and its lessons. In the Talmuds we witness, among the Mishnah's heirs, a striking reversion to biblical convictions about the centrality of history in the definition of Israel's reality.

Now to answer that question of the historical development, after the Mishnah, of the topical program of economics as well as the generative taxonomy of economics set forth in the Mishnah. I think we must survey not those documents that carried forward the program of the Mishnah, in particular, the Tosefta, the Talmud of the Land of Israel, or Yerushalmi, and the Talmud of Babylonia, or Bavli, but those documents that did not. For exegetical documents of the Mishnah follow the program defined by the Mishnah and amplify and refine ideas of the Mishnah. But if we want to know what happened outside of Mishnah exegesis, we have to turn elsewhere. And what I want to know is whether and how authors not subject to the guidance of the Mishnah's program dealt with the economic classifications and categories that the Mishnah laid out.

Specifically, I have to deal with documents centered upon the exegesis of Scripture or organized around verses of scriptural books. Here we ask whether later authors, after those of the Mishnah and its continuators in the Tosefta, Yerushalmi, and Bavli, pursued those same questions we have identified as economic ones, or ignored them. In this way we ask how perspective changed among those authors not bound by the topical program of the Mishnah but addressing a different organizing principle altogether, the one deriving from books to Scripture. For the canon of the Judaism at hand coalesced around two generative documents, of which the Mishnah was only one. The other was Scripture, which we in the Christian West know as the Old Testament. Judaism beginning with the Mishnah identified the scriptures of ancient Israel as the written Torah, to which the Mishnah and related writings formed the counterpart as the oral Torah. The other pole besides the Mishnah, namely Scripture, then attracted to itself such writings as Sifra to Leviticus, Sifré to Numbers, Sifré to Deuteronomy, Genesis Rabbah, Leviticus Rabbah, Pesiqta deRab Kahana, and the like. The topical program of these writings, set as it was by Scripture, is to be examined for its interest in the same economic program as takes a significant role in the Mishnah. That historical analysis will then show us what happened to the economics of Judaism, as the Mishnah defined that economics. I shall account for the answer, which is, not very much, and so place the economics of Judaism into that diachronic context in which, from the closure of the Talmud to modern times, Judaic thinkers were left essentially dumb before issues of economic theory.[1] When Jewry reentered the realm of politics in the diaspora and of state building in the land, then state, of Israel, the Judaic religious tradition that extended from the Judaism of the dual Torah offered few useful answers to urgent questions of conduct and belief alike. Wise aphorisms, such as were assembled by some scholars who described themselves as social scientists on topics deemed economic, did not help at all.[2]

Notes

PREFACE

1. "Aristotle Discovers the Economy," in Karl Polanyi, Conrad M. Arensberg, and Harry W. Pearson, eds., *Trade and Market in the Early Empires: Economies in History and Theory* (Glencoe: The Free Press, 1957), p. 66.

2. Joseph A. Schumpeter, *History of Economic Analysis,* (New York: Oxford University Press, 1954), p. 54.

3. S. Todd Lowry, "The Greek Heritage in Economic Thought," in S. Todd Lowry, ed., *Pre-Classical Economic Thought: From the Greeks to the Scottish Enlightenment* (Boston, Dordrecht, Lancaster: Kluwer Academic Publishers, 1987), p. 12.

4. In a companion study I plan to define and explain the politics of (a) Judaism, namely, the theory of rational action with regard to the institutionalization of authority.

5. In this context Professor Eugene Genovese comments (personal letter): "This point should be developed beyond the Weberian frame in which it is cast. Marx would serve better. What is rational for the economy per se may be irrational for the society as a whole. In fact, even at the economic level, what is rational for the individual or firm may be irrational for the economy as a whole."

6. Professor Genovese (personal letter) comments, "A market economy is precisely an economy dominated by markets, not merely an enclave within a distributive economy. A market economy implies large-scale commodity production, which existed in the world of the Roman latifundia but not here. A market economy was the creation of modern commodity production." That accounts for my formulation here: "the germ of a market economy."

7. Yet that is not to be taken as odd. A. Leo Oppenheim in his debate with Polanyi's "over-emphasis on the palace [i.e., the distributive] system . . . has tended to concentrate his own researches on the non-redistributive elements in the economic life of cities and on the private activities of merchants as opposed to the 'administered trade' emphasized by Polanyi," so Sally C. Humphreys, "History, Economics, and Antropology: The Work of Karl Polanyi," *History & Theory* 8 (1969): 165–212, p. 181. Oppenheim and others "denied that any period or area attested in cuneiform documents could be fully or adequately characterized as redistributive." The same is to be said of the Mishnah's mixed economics, which is neither wholly distributive nor entirely market in orientation.

8. But it seems to me not productive to pursue as an issue or theoretical economics the notion of an exchange between heaven and earth, that is, between God and Israel. The conception leads us deep into territory beyond the substance of economics, into intangibles that we cannot grasp, measure, or weigh. Accordingly, I leave out of this account any notion of an economics of reciprocity and deal only with (re)distribution and market exchange. Compare Humphreys, p. 204, on Polanyi's classification of economics. I also omit reference to "householding" as too vague;

no one imagines that Israel's economy in its land was a subsistence economy, certainly not at any point, from the sixth century B.C. forward, covered by the pentateuchal law codes or their successors. So I see no point of interest in householding, because it is irrelevant, nor can I cope with "reciprocity," because it is a category covering economic relations between units that are not this-worldly (to put it mildly).

9. See for example Shalom Albeck, *Diné hammamonot battalmud* (Tel Aviv, 1976: Debir). English title: *The Law of Property and Contract in the Talmud.* Studies of jurisprudence on comparable subjects in the *Encyclopaedia Judaica* and in the *Encyclopaedia Talmudit* and equivalent publications are many, but none has broad bearing upon our problem. The confusion of the jurisprudence of commercial and property transactions with economic theory is shown in Nahum Rakover, *Osar hammishpat: Mapteah bibliographi lammishpat haibri* [Thesarus of Law: Bibliographical Key to Hebrew Jurisprudence] (Jerusalem, 1975), pp. 433–43, where we find as a single rubric, for items 10941–10970, "commercial law, economic thought [mahshabah kalkalit]."

10. That my generative question is owing to Max Weber hardly requires explicit statement. But nothing in Weber characterizes (a) Judaism in such a way that we can make use of his ideas, except for the study of his system and thought. Weber's continuators seem to me remarkably uninterested in doing the necessary monographic studies to make possible a renewal of comparative studies of civilizations in Weber's traditions. He did, after all, detailed work, but his success in setting forth interesting questions was hardly matched by his mastery of the details of the civilizations that he subjected to comparison. In any event it is utterly outdated.

11. For an account of the conceptions of "Israel" worked out in different Judaisms, with a clear indication of how a system's "Israel" is particular to that system and expresses its larger systemic message, see my *"Israel:" Judaism and its Social Metaphors* (Cambridge and New York: Cambridge University Press, 1988).

12. *A History of the Mishnaic Law of Purities* (Leiden, 1976: E. J. Brill, vol. 11), *Tohorot: Commentary,* and vol. 12, *Tohorot: Literary and Historical Problems.*

13. In future research I plan to place the Mishnah into the philosophical world of the Second Sophistic, where, in terms of time and place, it belongs. But that is a quite distinct set of problems.

CHAPTER ONE

1. Robert Lekachman, *History of Economic Ideas* (New York: Harper, 1959), p. 4.

2. For an introduction to the economic study of talmudic literature, see Roman A. Ohrenstein, "Economic Thought in Talmudic Literature in the Light of Modern Economics," *The American Journal of Economics and Sociology* 27 (1968): 185–96, who cites earlier writings on the subject (see p. 185, n. 3). Later in this chapter we shall deal with some of the work that has been done. Ohrenstein's "Economic Self-Interest and Social Progress in Talmudic Literature: A Further Study of Ancient Economic Thought and its Modern Significance," *American Journal of Economics and Sociology* 29 (1970): 59–70, typifies the level of the field.

3. When we look back on how the issue at hand has come to definition over time, we may trace the history not of theories of economics, but of how the Jews as a group have formed the subject of study in the humanities and social sciences. That history, moreover, comprises merely a chapter in the story of what has happened to the Jews in the modern and secular West. For accounts of the economics of Judaism form an important component in the history of the Jews in our modern times. While these accounts claim attention only as evidence of the intellectual climate in which they were composed, not as useful points of entry into the subject that they treat, we gain perspective from the errors of predecessors and so discern for ourselves the correct definition of the work.

4. The edition I consulted is Werner Sombart, *The Jews and Modern Capitalism,* introduction by Samuel Z. Klausner, trans. M. Epstein (New Brunswick and London: Transaction Books, 1982). The most recent paper known to me on Sombart is Paul Gottfried, "Sombart's The Jews and Modern Capitalism Revisited," *This World* 1986, 3:138–144. Gottfried notes, "Sombart

was recognizably hostile to Judaism and capitalism, and in associating one with the other was linking what he considered a distinctively materialist and emotionally sterile culture to what was allegedly organized greed." Sombart at the end found a place within Nazism. Gottfried calls attention to the early critic of Sombart, Moses Hoffman, *Judentum und Kapitalismus* (Berlin, 1912).

5. True, the simple fact that Jews have lived in a variety of political and economic settings has not escaped attention. The further fact that Jews' economies flourish within larger economies, on the one hand, and do not form a single continuum through time, on the other, also has found recognition. But these obstacles to describing "Jewish economic history" have not prevented the composition of pictures of Jews' economics and Judaism's economics. One solution is simple. People assemble pictures of traits held to have proved common to Jews in whatever circumstances in which they conduct their economic activities, and these are adduced in justification of the description not merely of diverse Jews' economic action, but of "*the* Jews' economic history." The appeal is to a principal distinctive trait, allegedly indicative of Jews and not of others and therefore demonstrative of Jews' forming an economic entity, namely, Jews' "marginality." Whether or not that characterization has received precise definition, the impressionistic character of the category, its relative and subjective applicability—these matters need not detain us. But let us grant for the moment that "economic marginality" forms a category subject to investigation and replication. Then we surely notice that other groups have taken a marginal place in society and economics as well. Accordingly, the possibility that Jews' economic action and thought exemplifies not their "Jewish" and so their ideological traits but their (allegedly) marginal character has not yet attracted attention. We may ignore the flip and indefensible racism in such odd comparisons as yield the statement, "the overseas Chinese are the Jews of the Orient," and the like. These form no exception to the judgment that the comparative study of supposedly marginal economic entities awaits systematic attention, at least in writing about the Jews. It follows that while some may claim to present the Jews as an example of an "marginal" economic unit, without differentiating the case from the law of marginal economic action in general, others (and they form the larger part of the literature) do not even take the trouble.

6. Polanyi, "Aristotle Discovers the Economy," p. 79. As to whether or not even Aristotle counts as an economic theorist, see chapter 4, below, the debate between Schumpeter and Polanyi.

7. Elizabeth Fox-Genovese, *The Origins of Physiocracy: Economic Revolution and Social Order in Eighteenth-Century France* (Ithaca and London: Cornell University Press, 1983), p. 9. See also Karl Polanyi, *The Livelihood of Man*, ed. Harry W. Pearson (San Francisco, and London: Academic Press, 1977), p. 7.

8. William I. Davisson and James E. Harper, *European Economic History*, vol. 1, *The Ancient World* (Appleton-Century-Crofts, 1972), p. 130.

9. Ibid., p. 130.

10. See Morris Silver, *Economic Structures of the Ancient Near East* (London and Sydney: Croom Helm, 1985) and J. Wansbrough's review of that book in *Bulletin of the London School of Oriental and African Studies* 50 (1987): 361–62. In this and prior studies Silver has successfully refuted the thesis of Polanyi that "there were not and could not be circumstances conducive to a market economy" (Wansbrough, p. 362). But the distinction between distributive and market economics has no bearing whatsoever upon whether or not, in remote antiquity, there was no such thing as a market in an economic sense, as Polanyi maintained. My argument focuses only upon economic theory. But, as is clear, I take for granted that Silver and those he represents have established as fact the coexistence of market and distributive economics, such as I claim to discern, also, in the system of the Mishnah.

11. In chapter 6 we shall note the integral relationship of a theory of ownership of property, specifically, a conception of property being private, and a theory of market economics. A mark of a distributive economics will be systemic intervention into not only the rationing (distribution) of resources but also the means of production.

12. Davisson and Harper, p. 125.

13. A. Leo Oppenheim, *Ancient Mesopotamia: Portrait of a Dead Civilization* (Chicago: University of Chicago Press, 1972), p. 87.

14. Davisson and Harper, p. 115.

15. Ibid., p. 123.

16. True, the ideology of the Priestly Code insisted that payment of the Temple taxes insured that God would "bless" the country with ample harvests, large herds, big families, and the like. But these factors in shaping of public opinion, therefore of considerations of demand, on their own do not—and cannot—fall into the classification of economic facts.

17. Ibid.

18. Ibid., pp. 124–25.

19. But as we shall observe in due course, God does not lay claim to joint ownership of other goods and services of the economy, apart from the land and its produce, with the result that private ownership of the commercial and manufacturing economy assuredly prevailed, one of the reasons I refer to the Mishnah's economic theory as a mixed one.

20. My ultimate goal is to encompass the sociology of economic life as the Mishnah's theory of the matter lays things out. In this regard I found very illuminating the compelling programmatic statements of Neil J. Smelser, *The Sociology of Economic Life* (Englewood Cliffs, N.J.: Prentice-Hall, 1976). But we stand at a considerable distance from the realization of such a goal.

21. Walter C. Neale, "The Market in Theory and History," in Karl Polanyi, Conrad M. Arensberg, and Harry W. Pearson, eds., *Trade and Market in the Early Empires: Economies in History and Theory* (Glencoe: The Free Press, 1957), p. 357.

22. Ibid., p. 358.   25. Ibid., pp. 370–71.

23. Ibid., p. 364.   26. Ibid., p. 371.

24. Ibid., p. 367.

27. Karl Polanyi, "Marketless Trading in Hammurabi's Time," in Polanyi et al., *Trade and Market in the Early Empires*, p. 14.

28. Ibid., p. 19.

29. Ibid., pp. 20–22.

30. A. Leo Oppenheim, "A Bird's-Eye View of Mesopotamian Economic History," in Polanyi et al., *Trade and Market in the Early Empires*, p. 33.

31. M. I. Finley, *The Ancient Economy* (Berkeley and Los Angeles: University of California Press, 1985), p. 28.

32. Compare for the simplest statement of the matter ibid., p. 31.

33. I am not sure that any modern or contemporary theologian of Judaism would require study by a scholar in the field of the history of economic theory or thought, though many have expressed opinions on topics pertinent to economic behavior and even belief. The reason is that theology of Judaism in modern and contemporary times has not addressed the large issues of society and nation that engaged the sustained attention of the framers of the Mishnah, the Jews not constituting, until just now, a nation or even a distinct society at all. Whether or not, in the setting of the state of Israel, an economics of Judaism will emerge is not a question that requires attention here.

34. That is why I conceive the more profound inquiry to address the politics of Judaism, as the Mishnah presents that politics: the city of God which is the city of humanity, unlike the distinct cities conceived by Augustine. The matter is neatly expressed in numerous specific rules. See for example Roger Brooks, *Support for the Poor in the Mishnaic Law of Agriculture: Tractate Peah* (Chico: Scholars Press for Brown Judaic Studies, 1983): "The Mishnah's framers regard the Land as the exclusive property of God. When Israelite farmers claim it as their own and grow food on it, they must pay for using God's earth. Householders thus must leave a portion of the yield unharvested as *peah* and give this food over to God's chosen representatives, the poor. The underlying theory is that householders are tenant farmers who pay taxes to their landlord, God" (p. 49 to Mishnah-tractate Peah 1:4–5). In this concrete way the interpenetration of the realms of God and humanity is expressed. That conception of the household and the village made up of households, the *oikos* and the *polis,* yields not only an economics, such as we treat here in chapters 4 through 6 and 7 (market and distributive economics, repsectively), but also a politics. And the politics is the foundation for the economics, as we shall repeatedly observe.

35. That routine observation of what characterizes any Judaic system should not be deemed banal, since we can identify other species of the genus, religious system, which do not present an economics along with their theology, and which frame a politics only with considerable difficulty. Christianity before medieval times is one such species of the genus, religious system, which does not utilize economics in the formation and presentation of is fundamental systemic statement. That is because in repeating the denigration of wealth and indifference to material matters found in the New Testament, the later theologians as well as saints found little in economics that afforded important occasion for expressing their basic statement. On the contrary, asceticism closed off any serious study of the means of production, the working of the market, and the definition of wealth, such as proved, for the Mishnah's authors, so fruitful an area of reflection and systemic development.

CHAPTER TWO

1. The document has no named author and contains no story of its own origins. As I shall presently point out, it starts in the middle of nowhere and ends in no determinate place. It represents a collectivity of authors, a consensus. I have demonstrated that the final formulation of all materials coincides with the penultimate processes of redaction, since a single system of forms and mnemonics is imposed on all passages uniformly. Not only so, but the document follows a carefully calibrated topical program, in which each given subject is spelled out in accord with a rigidly logical thematic program, with more important aspects of a topic treated first, less important ones later on, and, as is clear, all things treated within a single syntactic pattern. That makes unlikely the possibility that the document took shape in an incremental process, lasting over many generations, in which each generation left its deposit on the unfolding writing.

2. We have no evidence known to me of how Jews in other parts of the Roman and Iranian empires governed themselves. While ample comparative study of the Mishnah's law in relationship to that of Rome has gone forward for nearly a century, we have no study at all of the comparison of the Mishnah's and the Talmuds' law to that of the Sasanians, though the *Matigan-i hazar datastan* (Collection of a thousand decisions) has been available in English for a century and is now in hand in a critical edition as well. Nearly thirty years ago (for three years between 1960 and 1964) I studied Pahlavi with the intention of working on the comparison of talmudic and Iranian law codes and law, but at that time the definition of the task, if it were to involve anything more than the collecting and arranging of essentially uninterpreted "parallels," eluded me. I now know how the work is to be done, but without a systemic study of the counterparts on the Iranian side, it still seems to me not an entirely promising inquiry. Before we can compare, we have to know what we are comparing, and not only what we are encompassing but also omitting.

3. Because the Mishnah's authors reach their own judgments on the system they propose to state, no good is served by surveying, out of all systemic context, sayings in Scripture pertinent in a general way to economic topics. No Judaism simply opened Scripture and paraphrased or restated what it found there; all Judaisms made their own choices, as I shall explain for the Mishnah later in this chapter. That is why I do not survey biblical statements. For such a survey, see Henry William Spiegel, *The Growth of Economic Thought* (Durham: Duke University Press, 1971), pp. 1–6. At the same time, we shall note in due course, facts of Scripture play a crucial role in the economic program and theory of the Mishnah, e.g., the Sabbath, slavery, the sabbatical and jubilee years, the protection of the weak, and the dignity of labor.

4. Joseph A. Schumpeter, *History of Economic Analysis* (New York: Oxford University Press, 1954), p. 54.

5. But the Talmuds refocus matters in their topical programs, laying far greater stress on the study and application of the civil code, the fourth of the six divisions of the Mishnah, omitting all reference to the code of purities, and in other ways reframing the composition through choices within and among the given repertoire of topics.

6. Of these four parts, the Talmud of the Land of Israel, or Yerushalmi, attends to three and the Talmud of Babylonia, or Bavli, to three, both of them omitting Purities. Two further divisions

of the document as a whole deal with everyday affairs, one, Damages, concerning civil law and government, the other, Women, taking up issues of family, home, and personal status. That, sum and substance, is the program of the Mishnah. Both Talmuds take a keen interest in these divisions.

7. I had reached that reading of the logic of the Mishnah in various volumes of my *History of the Mishnaic Law* in complete ignorance of the wonderful work of G. E. R. Loyd, *Polarity and Analogy: Two Types of Argumentation in Early Greek Thought* (Cambridge: Cambridge University Press, 1966). I came upon the work only through my interest in modes of thought in the Judaism of the dual Torah, which I called "the logics," and in comparing those logics with others. Lloyd stresses the interest, in Greek thought, in relationships of "same," "like," "other," "different," "contrary," and "contradictory," and, in my work on the Mishnah, I was able to show, stage by stage, how reflection on these relationships could have generated laws built from Scripture to the statement now contained within the Mishnah, e.g., in Zabim and in Niddah. I might note that the frequently cited judgment of Saul Lieberman that the rabbinic literature contains no evidence of knowledge of Greco-Roman philosophy may be correct as to the utilization of key words or phrases but is false as to the utilization of received and established modes of thought. Full bibliography and discussion of that issue will be found in the forthcoming study of philosophy and the rabbis by Robert Berchman, and I need not pursue it here.

8. The Tosefta, ca. A.D. 300, a collection of complementary materials for the Mishnah, does not sustainedly reveal equivalent traits.

9. The relevance of grammar and syntax to the argument that the Mishnah forms a closed system is simple. If there are traces of diverse theories of formulation and redaction of materials in our division, which would reflect the individual preferences and styles of diverse circles over two hundred years, we cannot point to them. The unified and cogent formal character of the Mishnah testifies in particular to the program and plan of its ultimate tradent-redactors. We learn in the Mishnah about the intention of that last generation of mishnaic authorities, who gave us the document as we have it. It is their way of saying things which we know for certain. The language of the Mishnah and its grammatically formalized rhetoric create a world of discourse quite separate from the concrete realities of a given time, place, or society. The exceedingly limited repertoire of grammatical patterns in which all things on all matters are said gives symbolic expression to the notion that beneath the accidents of life are a few, comprehensive relationships: unchanging and enduring patterns lie deep in the inner structure of reality and impose structure upon the accidents of the world.

10. That observation forms the counterpart of my stress, in chapter 1, on the Jews not forming a single economy, continuous in a linear development from beginning to end. We cannot study as a single unitary and harmonious entity "Jewish law" any more than we can "Jewish economic history," though that has not prevented nearly everybody who works on the subject from doing just that. Certain practices to be sure characterized all. But these too do not validate the premise that such a thing as "Jewish law" operated, even in the points in common, pretty much everywhere. The fact that Jews ordinarily observed certain taboos, e.g., concerning the Sabbath day and forbidden foods, hardly changes the picture. On the basis of the prohibition of pork and the observance of a common calendar one can hardly describe a common law of Jewry, hence "Jewish law." Such evidence as we have of diverse Jews' laws points in the opposite direction. What these sets of laws shared in common in part derives from the Scripture all revered. What turns up in a number of contexts in further measure proves so general or so fragmentary as to yield no trace of a single, systematic and comprehensive law common among Jews. An example of the latter— something too general to make much difference—is the marriage contract. It is a fact that marriage contracts occur in the Jewish community records of Elephantine, in the fragments found from the time of Bar Kokhba, and in the setting of mishnaic law. But in detail the contracts that have been found scarcely intersect. The Mishnah's rules governing the scribal preparation of such contracts hardly dictated to the authorities of fifth century B.C. Elephantine or second century A.D. Palestine how to do their work. When, therefore, we wish to investigate the history of Jewish law, in point of fact we must follow the course of distinct bodies of sources. Each of these several

systems of law applying to diverse Jewish groups or communities emerges from its distinct historical setting, addresses its own social entity, and tells us, usually only in bits and pieces of detailed information, about itself alone.

11. Let us rapidly review the various types of evidence for the antiquity of numerous facts utilized by the Mishnah's framers in the construction of their system. Some legal facts in the Mishnah, as in other law codes of its place and age, derive from remote antiquity. Categories of law and investment, for instance, prove continuous with Akkadian and even Sumerian ones. It has been shown that the linguistic and legal basis of Mishnah's rules goes back to Assyrian law. Other important continuities in the common law of the ancient Near East have emerged in a broad diversity of research, on Elephantine law for instance. The issue therefore cannot focus upon whether or not the Mishnah in diverse details draws upon established rules of jurisprudence. It assuredly does. Yet another mode of demonstrating that facts in the Mishnah's system derive from a period substantially prior to that in which the Mishnah reached closure carries us to the data provided by documents redacted long before the Mishnah. For one example, details of rules in the law codes found in the library of the Essene community of Qumran intersect with details of rules in the Mishnah. More interesting still, accounts of aspects of Israelite life take for granted that issues lively in the Mishnah came under debate long before the closure of the Mishnah. The Gospels' accounts of Jesus' encounter with the Pharisees, among others, encompass rules of law, or topics dealt with, important to the Mishnah. It is, for instance, not merely the datum that a writ of divorce severs the tie between wife and husband. The matter of grounds for divorce proves important to sages whose names occur in the Mishnah, and one position of one of these sages turns out to accord with the position on the same matter imputed to Jesus. It follows that not only isolated facts but critical matters of jurisprudential philosophy came to the surface long before the closure of the Mishnah.

12. Indeed, proof of the claim that there was not merely law characteristic of a given group, but *the* law, shared by "all Israel," should derive solely from the Scripture common to all Israel everywhere. The theory of a single, continuous law rests upon the simple fact that all Israel by definition acknowledged the authority of Scripture, its law and theology. It must follow that, in diverse ways and within discrete exegetical processes, every group now known to us drew its basic legal propositions from Scripture and therefore contributes evidence on the unilinear formation of a single law, based upon a single source, common to all Israel, that is, *the* law, or Law. In examining the notion of the law, as distinct from the theory, argued here, of diverse systems of law, we turn to the critical issue. It concerns not whether a given rule derives from exegesis of Scripture. That issue, by itself, provides trivial and not probative insight. Rather we want to know how the several systems now known to us define their respective relationships to Scripture. That is to say, we ask about the nature of scriptural authority, the use of Scripture's facts in a code, or system, of law. The answer to the question settles an important issue. If two (or more) systems of law governing groups of Israelites turn out to respond to, to draw upon, Scripture's rules in much the same way, then these discrete systems merge at their roots, in a generative and definitive aspect of their structure. In consequence, we may conclude that the two (or more) systems do form part of a single common law, once more, the law. But if two or more systems of law approach Scripture each in its own way and for its own purposes, then we have to analyze each system on its own terms and not as part of, and contributory to, the law.

13. Most of the Mishnah conforms to a single program of formulation, and that set of rules on formulation derives from encompassing decisions concerning redaction. But what about the history of the law and its formation into the system we now have? As a matter of fact, details of the system of the Mishnah's law emerge within the final document as attributions that withstand a simple test of verification to figures who flourished at the turn of the first century A.D., though details, commonly routine facts of a common law, may originate as much as two thousand years earlier than that. From that point onward, there is in the Mishnah a process of tradition. The law of the Mishnah takes shape in a twofold process. Once a theme is introduced early in the history of law, it will be taken up and refined later on. Also, in the second and third stages in the formation of the Mishnah, after the destruction of the Temple in A.D. 70 and then after the defeat of Bar

Kokhba in A.D. 135, many new themes with their problems will emerge. These, however, are without precedent in the antecedent thematic heritage. The common foundations for the whole always are Scripture. The law of the Mishnah is like a completed construction of scaffolding. The foundation is a single plane, the Scriptures. The top platform also is a single plane, the Mishnah itself. But the infrastructure is differentiated. Underneath one part of the upper platform will be several lower platforms, so that the supporting poles and pillars reach down to intervening platforms; only the bottom platform rests upon pillars set in the foundation. Yet another part of the upper platform rests upon pillars and poles stretching straight down to the foundation, without intervening platforms at all. So viewed from above, the uppermost platform of the scaffolding forms a single, uniform, and even plane. That is the Mishnah as we have it, six divisions, sixty-three tractates, 531 chapters. But viewed from the side, that is, from the perspective of analysis, there is much differentiation, so that, from one side, the upper platform rises from a second, intermediate one, and, in places, from even a third, lowest one. And yet some of the pillars reach directly down to the bedrock foundations. What is new in the period beyond the wars is that part of the ultimate plane—the Mishnah as a whole—which in fact rests upon the foundations not of antecedent thought but Scripture alone. What is basic in the period before 70 A.D. is the formation of that part of the Mishnah which sustains yet a second and even a third layer of platform construction. What emerged between the two wars, of course, will both form a plane with what comes before, that platform at the second level, and yet will also lay foundations for a level above itself. But this intermediate platform also will come to an end, yielding that space filled only by the pillars stretching from Scripture on upward to the ultimate plane of the Mishnah's completed and whole system.

14. In the model of the Mishnah I should furthermore claim that many, though not necessarily all, of the canonical documents of formative Judaism may constitute, each on its own, statements at the end of a sustained process of rigorous thought and logical inquiry, applied logic and practical reason. The only way to read a reasoned and systematic statement of a system is defined by the rules of general intelligibility, the laws of reasoned and syllogistic discourse about rules and principles. The way to read a traditional and sedimentary document by contrast lies through the ad hoc and episodic display of instances and examples, layers of meaning and eccentricities of confluence, intersection, and congruence. That is why I maintain that tradition and system cannot share a single crown and that, as the formative documents of Judaism demonstrate, Judaism constitutes *not* a traditional but a *systemic* religious statement, with a hermeneutics of order, proportion, and, above all, reasoned context, to tell us how to read each document. We cannot read these writings in accord with two incompatible hermeneutical programs, and, for reasons amply stated, I argue in favor of the philosophical and systemic, rather than the agglutinative and traditional, hermeneutics.

15. See Barry Gordon, "Biblical and Early Judeo-Christian Thought: Genesis to Augustine," in S. Todd Lowry, ed., *Pre-Classical Economic Thought: From the Greeks to the Scottish Enlightenment* (Boston, Dordrecht, Lancaster: Kluwer Academic Publishers, 1987), pp. 43–67, and the commentary by Roman A. Ohrenstein, "Some Socioeconomic Aspects of Judaic Thought," ibid., pp. 68–76.

Note also the following items, among many:

R. Barraclough, *Economic Structures in the Bible* (Canberra: Zadok Centre, 1980).

Roland de Vaux, *Ancient Israel* (London: Darton, Longman, and Todd, 1978).

Barry Gordon, *Economic Analysis before Adam Smith: Hesiod to Lessius* (London: Macmillan, 1975).

———, "Lending at Interest: Some Jewish, Greek, and Christian Approaches, 800 B.C.–A.D. 100," *History of Political Economy* 14 (1982): 406–26.

Frederick C. Grant, *The Economic Background of the Gospels* 1926; reprint, New York: Russell and Russell, 1973.

B. J. Meislin and M. L. Cohen, "Backgrounds of the Biblical Law against Usury," *Comparative Studies in Society and History* (1963–64): 6.

Ben Nelson, *The Idea of Usury* (Chicago and London: University of Chicago Press, 1969).

E. Neufeld, "Socio-Economic Background of Yobel and Shemitta," *Rivista degli studi orientali* 33 (1958): 53–124.

Robert North, *Sociology of the Biblical Jubilee* (Rome: Pontifical Biblical Institute, 1954).

Roman A. Ohrenstein, "Economic Analysis in Talmudic Literature: Some Ancient Studies of Value," *American Journal of Economics and Sociology* 39 (1980): 22.

———, "Economic Aspects of Organized Religion in Perspective: The Early Phase," *The Nassau Review*, 1970, 27–43.

———, "Economic Thought in Talmudic Literature in the Light of Modern Economics," *American Journal of Economics and Sociology* 27 (1968): 185–96.

———, "Economic Self-Interest and Social Progress in Talmudic Literature," *American Journal of Economics and Sociology* 29 (1970): 59–70.

———, "Some Studies of Value in Talmudic Literature in the Light of Modern Economics," *The Nassau Review*, 1981, no. 4:48–70.

Morris, Silver, *Prophets and Markets: The Political Economy of Ancient Israel* (Boston: Kluwer-Nijhoff, 1983).

J. Viner, "The Economic Doctrines of the Christian Fathers," *History of Political Economy* 10 (1978): 9–45.

16. Georgescu-Roegen, *Analytical Economics,* cited in M. I. Finley, *The Ancient Economy* (Berkeley and Los Angeles: University of California Press, 1985), p. 19.

17. The same may be said of the politics of a religious system, which, like any politics and therefore also statement of political theory, will encompass the institutionalization of power in the context of social action

18. That is not to suggest that all Judaisms encompass economics, or that all documents of the Judaism of the dual Torah deem important the consideration of policy in regard to allocation of scarce resources or securing the increase and preservation of wealth. Quite to the contrary, we know about Judaisms that utterly ignore economics as a matter of theory and have little to say about material matters even in the context of ethics. Nor do all documents of the Judaism under study here interpret wealth in concrete terms at all.

19. That is where I part company with those who deem all forms of society "subject to objective analysis into a finite number of immutable elements." When talking about the same thing, people in different contexts can mean different things.

20. As we shall observe presently, the household in the system of the Mishnah constituted not only the basic unit of production or economic activity, but also the fundamental building block of society, conceived as formed of villages, themselves made up of households. "Israel" then consisted of villages comprising households. In the derivative writings of the Judaism of the dual Torah, by contrast, "Israel" was the extended family of Abraham, Isaac, and Jacob, and the division by households, that is, rational economic units, was replaced by the (mythical) division by tribes, that is, the sons of Jacob.

21. I follow E. C. Marchant, trans., *Xenophon: Memorabilia and Oeconomicus* (London: William Heinemann, and New York: G. P. Putnam's Sons, 1923). For a judgment upon Xenophon, note John Fred Bell, *A History of Economic Thought* (New York: Ronald Press, 1967), p. 25, n. 15: "Economics students will find his essay . . . a very original work." Finley found less merit in the same work, and the great economists Schumpeter and Polanyi saw still less.

22. *Cyropaedia* 8.2–5, quoted by M. I. Finley, "Aristotle and Economic Analysis," in M. I. Finley, ed., *Studies in Ancient Society* (London and Boston: Routledge and Kegan Paul, 1974), p. 27.

23. Finley, "Aristotle and Economic Analysis," p. 41.

24. Ibid., p. 18.
25. Ibid., p. 19.
26. Ibid., p. 19.
27. Ibid., pp. 19ff.

28. Ibid., p. 22.
29. Ibid., pp. 22–23.
30. Ibid., p. 22.

31. I should encourage others to do so; it seems to me the way forward for any study of Jews' economies and the theory of economics characteristic of Judaisms in various times and places as well as Jews' economic behavior in relationship to theories of economics generated or fostered by their Judaisms. I cannot imagine a more correct mode of framing the question.

CHAPTER THREE

1. "Aristotle Discovers the Economy," in Karl Polanyi, Conrad M. Arensberg, and Harry W. Pearson, eds., *Trade and Market in the Early Empires: Economies in History and Theory* (Glencoe: The Free Press, 1957), p. 79.

2. See in this connection my *Judaism: The Evidence of the Mishnah* (Chicago: University of Chicago Press, 1981), pp. 230–286.

3. Joseph A. Schumpeter, *History of Economic Analysis* (New York: Oxford University Press, 1954), p. 54.

4. I consulted a variety of works on the subject of not only the theory of economics, but also the economic history of antiquity. I need hardly call attention to all of them. These seemed to me of fundamental importance:

Carlo M. Cipolla, ed., *The Economic Decline of Empires* (London: Methuen, 1970).

Richard Duncan-Jones, *The Economy of the Roman Empire* (London: Cambridge University Press, 1974).

Tenney Frank, *Aspects of Social Behavior in Ancient Rome* (1932; reprint, New York: Cooper Square Publishers, 1969).

Sally C. Humphreys, *Anthropology and the Greeks* (London: Routledge & Kegan Paul, 1978).

———, "History, Economics, and Anthropology: The Work of Karl Polanyi," *History & Theory* 8 (1969): 165–212.

———, "Economy and Society in Classical Athens," *Annali della Normale Superiore di Pisa* 39 (1970): 1–26.

A. H. M. Jones, *Ancient Economic History* (London: H. K. Lewis, 1948). This important programmatic statement requires rereading every few years, since it shows how a first-rate mind can set forth a problem and then go about solving it.

Odd Langholm, *The Aristotelian Analysis of Usury* (Bergen: Universitetsforlaget, 1984).

S. Todd Lowry, ed., *Pre-Classical Economic Thought: From the Greeks to the Scottish Enlightenment* (Boston, Dordrecht, Lancaster: Kluwer Academic Publishers, 1987). See his "The Greek Heritage in Economic Thought," pp. 7–30, and its excellent bibliography.

A. Leo Oppenheim, *Ancient Mesopotamia: Portrait of a Dead Civilization* (Chicago: University of Chicago Press, 1964), certainly one of the most intelligent books ever written, and an inspiration for a whole generation.

Karl Polanyi, *The Livelihood of Man,* ed. Harry W. Pearson (New York: Academic Press, 1977), in particular pp. 145–276.

———, Conrad M. Arensberg, and Harry W. Pearson, eds., *Trade and Market in the Early Empires: Economies in History and Theory* (Glencoe, 1957: Free Press). In that book I found of special interest the essays by A. L. Oppenheim, "A Bird's Eye View of Mesopotamian Economic History," pp. 27–37, and Karl Polanyi, "Aristotle Discovers the Economy," pp. 64–96.

M. I. Rostovtzeff, *Social and Economic History of the Hellenistic World* (Oxford, 1941).

A. A. Trever, *A History of Greek Economic Thought* (1916; reprint, Philadelphia: Porcupine Press, 1978).

Max Weber, *The Agrarian Sociology of Ancient Civilizations,* trans. by R. I. Frank (London: NLB, 1976). Translated from Max Weber, "Agrarverhältnisse im Altertum," in *Handwörterbuch der Staatswissenschaften,* 1909. The pages on ancient Israel, pp. 134–46, cover only the preexilic period.

———, *General Economic History* (Glencoe, 1950: Free Press).

For further bibliography, see especially see the excellent and compendious bibliography in Morris Silver, *Economic Structures of the Ancient Near East* (London and Sydney: Croom Helm,

1985). That seems to me the best starting point for further research on the economic history of the Greco-Roman and Near Eastern worlds in antiquity.

5. Edwin Cannan, *Origins of Economic Theory* (London: P. S. King & Son, 1929), p. 3.

6. Robert Lekachman, *History of Economic Ideas* (New York: Harper, 1959), p. 3.

7. Ibid., p. 3.

8. Polanyi, "Aristotle Discovers the Economy," p. 79.

9. Ibid., p. 80.   11. Ibid.

10. Ibid.   12. Ibid., p. 88.

13. Ibid., p. 90. I also consulted Polanyi, *The Livelihood of Man;* see in particular pp. 145–276.

14. As indicated in chapter 1, I have tried to avoid those components of Polanyi's interpretation that have come under interesting criticism. My appeal to the authority of Polanyi in this chapter concerns his analysis and interpretation of Greek economic theory, not his picture of the economics of remote antiquity.

I find especially suggestive the comments of Sally Humphreys: "Thus, what disturbed the philosophers of the fourth century was not, as Polanyi thought, an increase in profit-making on price differentials, but the disembedding or structural differentiation of the economy, leading to the application of 'economic' criteria and standards of behavior in a wide range of situations recognized as economic above all by the fact that money was involved; the old civic virtues of generosity and self-sufficiency were being replaced by the market attitudes of the traders" (p. 211). See Sally C. Humphreys, "History, Economics, and Anthropology: The Work of Karl Polanyi," *History & Theory* 1969., 8 (1969): 165–212. Note also Otto Erb, *Wirtschaft und Gesellschaft im Denken der hellenischen Antike* (Berlin, 1939), cited by her. Humphreys asks an interesting question: "Would a decrease in the importance of market institutions in a society which had reached this level of differentiation produce a revival of the attitudes whose loss Aristotle and Polanyi deplored? In the Roman Empire the state increasingly had to take over the functions of the market system in order to ensure an adequate supply and distribution of food to the city population. This change was accompanied by an increase in private redistribution. The process of bureaucratization of the economy and the rise under the influence of Christianity of new attitudes to economic matters has never really been studied" (p. 211). We return to this question in the concluding chapter.

15. In addition to the works in the history of economic thought that are cited in the notes below, I also consulted the following:

John Fred Bell, *A History of Economic Thought* (New York: Ronald Press, 1967), pp. 13–32.

Mark Blaug, *Economic Theory in Retrospect* (Cambridge: Cambridge University Press, 1978).

William F., Campbell, "The Free Market for Goods and the Free Market for Ideas in the Platonic Dialogues," *History of Political Economy* 17 (1985): 187–97.

Edwin Cannan, *A Review of Economic Theory* (London: P. S. King and Son, 1929), pp. 1–4.

Henri Denis, *Histoire de la pensée économique* (Paris: Presses Universitaires de France, 1966), pp. 7–57.

Barry Gordon, "Aristotle and Hesiod: The Economic Problem in Greek Thought," *Review of Social Economy* 21 (1963): 147–56.

———, "Biblical and Early Judeo-Christian Thought: Genesis to Augustine," in S. Todd Lowry, ed., *Pre-Classical Economic Thought: From the Greeks to the Scottish Enlightenment* (Boston, Dordrecht, Lancaster: Kluwer Academic Publishers, 1987), pp. 43–67. This essay on rational action in regard to scarcity seems to me little more than a paraphrase of ancient writings, with no important analytical side at all. What we have here is not economics but sayings on themes in some way deemed relevant to economics. I find no attention to how people understood the economy to work or even to the conception, in ancient times, of an economy. All of the issues important to Finley and Schumpeter, on which I have concentrated in this chapter, are neglected. What I find is neither "economic analysis" nor any other kind of analysis. This is the sort of writing that gives economic history a bad name for merely collecting and arranging. But Ohrenstein, cited below, is worse.

————, *Economic Analysis before Adam Smith: Hesiod to Lessius* (New York: Barnes and Noble, 1975).

Alexander Gray, *The Development of Economic Doctrine: An Introductory Survey* (London: Longmans Green and Co., 1931).

Sally C. Humphreys, "Economy and Society in Classical Athens," *Annali della Normale Superiore di Pisa* 39 (1970): 1–26.

————, "History, Economics, and Anthropology: The Work of Karl Polanyi," *History and Theory* 8 (1969): 165–212.

M. L. W. Laistner, ed., *Greek Economics* (New York: Dutton, 1923).

. Robert Lekachman, *A History of Economic Ideas* (New York: 1959: Harper, 1959). This book is delightful reading.

S. Todd Lowry, ed., *Pre-Classical Economic Thought: From the Greeks to the Scottish Enlightenment* (Boston, Dordrecht, Lancaster: Kluwer Academic Publishers, 1987), pp. 7–76.

R. McKeon, *Introduction to Aristotle* (Chicago: University of Chicago Press, 1973).

A. E. Monroe, *Early Economic Thought* (Cambridge: Harvard University Press, 1924).

Roman A. Ohrenstein, "Commentary: Some Socioeconomic Aspects of Judaic Thought," in S. Todd Lowry, ed., *Pre-Classical Economic Thought: From the Greeks to the Scottish Enlightenment* (Boston, Dordrecht, Lancaster: Kluwer Academic Publishers, 1987), pp. 68–76. This article is entirely uninformed on its subject, as the bibliography by itself proves. I am puzzled by the inclusion of these ramblings in what otherwise appears to me a very competent collection of essays under Lowry's editorship.

————, "Economic Thought in Talmudic Literature in the Light of Modern Economics," *American Journal of Economics and Sociology* 27 (1968): 185–96.

————, "Economic Self-Interest and Social Progress in Talmudic Literature," *American Journal of Economics and Sociology* 29 (1979): 59–70.

————, "Economic Analysis in Talmudic Literature: Some Ancient Studies of Value," *American Journal of Economics and Sociology* 39 (1980): 22.

————, "Some Studies of Value in Talmudic Literature in the Light of Modern Economics," *The Nassau Review*, 1981, no. 4:48–70.

O. Popescu, "On the Historiography of Economic Thought: A Bibliography," *Journal of World History*, 1964, no. 8:1ff.

Kurt Singer, "*Oikonomia:* An Inquiry into the Beginnings of Economic Thought and Language," *Kyklos* 11 (1958): 29–54.

C. J. Soudek, "Aristotle's Theory of Exchange," *Proceedings of the American Philosophical Society*, 1952, no. 5:96ff.

Joseph J. Spendler, "Aristotle on Economic Imputation and Related Matters," *Southern Economics Journal* 1955, 21.

Jules Toutain, *The Economic Life of the Ancient World* (New York: Knopf, 1930).

Max Weber, *Economy and Society: An Outline of Interpretive Sociology*, ed. Guenther Roth and Claus Wittich (Berkeley: University of California Press, 1978).

The bibliography in Lowry, pp. 27–30, seems to me particularly informative. I found very interesting the contrary position to that of Lowry, outlined by William F. Campbell in Lowry, pp. 31–42.

16. William I. Davisson and James E. Harper, *European Economic History* 1, *The Ancient World* (New York: Appleton-Century-Crofts, 1972), p. 126.

17. Henry William Spiegel, *The Growth of Economic Thought* (Durham: Duke University Press, 1971), p. 13.

18. Ibid., p. 15.

19. Joseph A. Schumpeter, *History of Economic Analysis* (New York, 1954: Oxford University Press, 1954), p. 53. But we should not ignore Polanyi's quite contrary view. "He will be seen as attacking the problem of man's livelihood with a radicalism of which no later writer on the subject was capable—none has ever penetrated deeper into the material organization of man's life. In effect, he posed, in all its breadth, the question of place occupied by the economy in

society." See his "Aristotle Discovers the Economy," p. 66. He was, Polanyi says, "trying to master theoretically the elements of a new complex social phenomenon in statu nascendi" (p. 67). The debate on the value of Aristotle's economics carries us far from the purpose at hand, which is only to outline the ideas of economic theory in circulation in antiquity so as to place, within that outline, economic ideas found in the Mishnah.

20. Davisson and Harper, p. 122. But that is the very point that Polanyi finds important.

21. See M. I. Finley, "Aristotle and Economic Analysis," p. 27. I found Finley's article unusually perspicacious and helpful, even by Finley's own very high standard. In the field of classics, populated as it is with brilliance, he is the single most interesting mind I have encountered in this study, and he competes with the inestimable Karl Polanyi and Joseph Schumpeter, a triumvirate with no counterpart in any field I have ever explored.

22. Schumpeter, p. 53.

23. Lewis H. Haney, *History of Economic Thought: A Critical Account of the Origin and Development of the Economic Theories of the Leading Thinkers in the Leading Nations* (New York: Macmillan, 1920), pp. 51–81. Inheritance: pp. 54–55.

24. Lekachman, p. 6.   27. Ibid., p. 56.
25. Schumpeter, p. 55.   28. Haney, p. 58.
26. Ibid., p. 56.

29. Schumpeter, p. 55; Finley, "Aristotle and Economic Analysis," p. 27.

30. Ibid., p. 60.

31. Finley, "Aristotle and Economic Analysis, p. 30.

32. Ibid.   34. Spiegel, p. 25.
33. Ibid., p. 40.   35. Ibid., p. 26.

36. Finley, "Aristotle and Economic Analysis," p. 41.

37. Ibid., citing *Politics* 1257a24–30.

38. Ibid., p. 44.

39. M. I. Finley, *The Ancient Economy*, p. 23. But others differ, for their own reasons, from Finley's judgment. The issue is not one on which I can enter an opinion.

40. S. Todd Lowry, ed., *Pre-Classical Economic Thought: From the Greeks to the Scottish Enlightenment* (Boston, Dordrecht, Lancaster: Kluwer Academic Publishers, 1987), p. 11.

41. Finley, "Aristotle and Economic Analysis," p. 49.

42. Ibid.

43. Ibid., p. 50. I cannot find an elaboration of this exceedingly interesting idea elsewhere in Finley's corpus, but I also do not claim to be an expert on that corpus. We shall want to know who is in, and who is outside of, the economics of the Mishnah. I am inclined to find a considerable correspondence between Finley's observation on Greek economics and what we shall presently observe concerning Judaism's economics.

44. Finley makes this point in *The Ancient Economy* as well.

45. Spiegel, p. 28.

46. Ibid., p. 28. I hold no brief for the definition of "private property" here or elsewhere.

47. Schumpeter, p. 57.

48. Ibid., p. 58.

49. Ibid., p. 60.

50. Ibid., p. 61.

51. Schumpeter, pp. 61, 62. This is a difficult matter, and Schumpeter has had his critics. It is not an issue to which I can make a contribution.

52. Ibid., p. 62.   58. Ibid. Contrast Spiegel's account,
53. Spiegel, p. 27.   cited above, n. 17.
54. Schumpeter, pp. 62–63.   59. Lekachman, p. 15.
55. Davisson and Harper, p. 128.   60. Haney, p. 74.
56. Cited in ibid., p. 132.   61. Schumpeter, pp. 66ff.
57. Schumpeter, p. 65.   62. Haney, p. 76.

63. Ibid.
64. Schumpeter, p. 69.
65. Ibid., p. 71.
66. Spiegel, p. 35.
67. Ibid., pp. 37–39.
68. Compare ibid., pp. 42–43.

69. Ibid., p. 44.
70. Ibid.
71. Ibid., p. 45.
72. Schumpeter, p. 71.
73. Cited in ibid.
74. Ibid., p. 72.

75. Finley, *Ancient Economy,* pp. 26–27, citing Georgescu-Roegen, *Analytical Economics,* p. 111.

76. Finley, p. 26.

77. I consulted, for instance, the following:

A. M. Andreades, *A History of Greek Public Finance,* vol. 1 (Cambridge: Cambridge University Press, 1933).

T. F. Carney, *The Economies of Antiquity: Controls, Gifts, and Trade* (Lawrence: Coronado Press, 1973).

P. R. Coleman-Norton, F. C. Bourne, and J. V. A. Fine, eds., *Studies in Roman Economic and Social History in Honor of Allan Chester Johnson* (Princeton, 1951: Princeton University Press).

Moses I. Finley, *Studies in Land and Credit in Ancient Athens, 500–200* B.C. *The Horos-Inscriptions* (New Brunswick: Rutgers University Press, 1951).

————, *Studies in Roman Property* (Cambridge: Cambridge University Press, 1976).

Tenney Frank, *An Economic History of Rome* (Baltimore: Johns Hopkins Press, 1920), a particularly representative item, e.g., "agriculture . . . the early trade . . . the rise of the peasantry . . . new lands for old . . . ," and so on, with no encompassing chapter that explains the economy and how it worked.

Paul Guiraud, *Études économiques sur l'antiquité* (Paris, 1905; reprint, New York: Burt Franklin, 1970), e.g., evolution of work, capital in Athens, population, etc.

R. J. Hopper, *Trade and Industry in Classical Greece* (London: Thames & Hudson, 1979).

A. H. M. Jones, *The Roman Economy. Studies in Ancient Economic and Administrative History* ed. P. A. Brunt (Oxford: Basil Blackwell, 1974), e.g., "over-taxation and the deline of the Roman Empire," inflation, census records, church finance, the cloth industry.

Jean-Philippe Lévy, *L'économie antique* (Paris: Presses universaires de France, 1964). In English: *The Economic Life of the Ancient World* (Chicago and London: University of Chicago Press, 1967). Lévy does not seem to have addressed the challenge of Polanyi and his colleagues at all (!).

H. Michell, *The Economics of Ancient Greece* (Cambridge: W. Heffer & Sons Ltd, 1957).

Jules Toutain, *The Economic Life of the Ancient World* (New York: Alfred A. Knopf, 1930).

78. Polanyi, Arensberg, and Pearson, p. xvii.

79. T. F. Carney, *Economies of Antiquity,* p. 17.

80. Carney, p. 33. Prior quotations: pp. 19–32 passim.

81. Finley, *Ancient Economy,* p. 27.

82. That is despite Finley's inviting suggestion, not developed so far as I can see, of a reason for the failure of the development of economics as an advanced philosophical subject, even by Aristotle. In responding to Schumpeter's judgment of the intellectual limitations of Greek economics, Finley proposes that the more active economic classes were not citizens, and Greek economics was an aspect of the political economy of the *polis* (I should call it the intersection of *polis* and *oikos*), in which metics did not figure. That is an engaging idea, but while Finley says he develops it in the concluding chapter of his *Economics,* I find it difficult to locate the passages to which he refers us. That is why, despite my admiration for his writing, in this matter there seems to me to be somewhat less than meets the eye.

83. Barry Gordon, "Biblical and Early Judeo-Christian Thought," in S. Todd Lowry, ed., *Pre-Classical Economic Thught: From the Greeks to the Scottish Enlightenment* (Boston, Dordrecht, Lancaster: Kluwer Academic Publishers, 1987), pp. 65–67, provides some bibliographical references on the matter. He refers to the following items:

R. Barraclough, *Economic Structure in the Bible* (Canberra, 1980).

Roland de Vaux, *Ancient Israel* (London: Darton, Longman, and Todd, 1978).

Frederick C. Grant, *The Economic Background of the Gospels* (1926; reprint, New York: Russell and Russell, 1973).

Ben Nelson, *The Idea of Usury* (Chicago: University of Chicago Press, 1969).

Robert North, *Sociology of the Biblical Jubilee* (Rome: Pontifical Biblical Institute, 1954).

The literature on this subject may be followed in the bibliographies of these works; it is enormous, and from the viewpoint of assembling and describing facts it seems to me compendious. It has no bearing whatever on our problem.

84. Haney, p. 37.

85. Whether or not there were in later recensions of the Judaism of the dual Torah economic theories of systems is a question demanding study in its own terms, document by document. My general impression is that there was an "enchantment" current in the world, encompassing the economy, such that if people only studied Torah, they would find their material needs met as well. That fantasy took the place of sustained interest in material transactions, so that the later Judaic systems no longer took much of an interest in household, market, wealth, in making the systemic statements. The authors of the Mishnah remembered an Israel that comprised a nation, a state, a society, and an economy and thought deeply about the requirements of such a palpable social world. The later authors, continuing the exegesis of the Mishnah in the two Talmuds, and undertaking the exegesis of Scripture in the Mishnah compilations, by contrast, could not imagine a world in which "Israel" constituted an autonomous social entity, in full charge of its own affairs and fate, and hence moved systemic discourse away from economics and, as a matter of fact, from politics as well. That seems to me a hypothesis worth exploring.

86. Edwin Cannan, *Origins of Economic Theory* (London: P. S. King & Son, 1929), p. 11.

CHAPTER FOUR

1. "Aristotle Discovers the Economy," in Karl Polanyi, Conrad M. Arensberg, and Harry W. Pearson, eds., *Trade and Market in the Early Empires: Economies in History and Theory* (Glencoe: The Free Press, 1957), p. 79.

2. Any conception that the Mishnah has (merely) restated the distributive economic theory of Leviticus without adapting that theory to its own concerns collides with the simple fact that the economics of Leviticus does not invoke, as its principal building block and unit of production, the household, while the economics of the Mishnah is inconceivable without that same irreducible economic entity.

3. The household is a theoretical construct, not a concrete entity, in mishnaic discourse. The laws of the Mishnah recognize full well that people lived cheek by jowl in houses set into courtyards in the village, and when it wishes to refer to places of residence, it does not speak of households and householders, but rather, residents of a courtyard, e.g., throughout tractate Erubin. That makes all the more interesting the usage of "householder," surveyed presently.

4. See Ramsay MacMullen, *Roman Social Relations* (New Haven: Yale University Press, 1966), on wealth and the landowner, pp. 5ff. Absentee land ownership is not within the purview of this discussion, and I find it difficult to see how the Mishnah takes account of enormous wealth in the form of absentee holdings. Quite to the contrary, if a piece of land is held, as to usufruct, for three years, without the intervention of a putative owner, the squatter acquires ownership; that is precisely the opposite of a law meant to accommodate the absentee landowner.

It will be helpful to define here two words important in this chapter, "usufruct" and "usucaption." The former refers to the right to utilize the produce of property without owning the property, e.g., a husband has the right to usufruct of property owned by his wife and may dispose at will of the produce of the wife's property. The latter refers to acquiring ownership of a property through unimpeded utilization of that property over a defined span of time, e.g., three years. Usucaption can involve not only the ownership of a property but also the ownership of a certain customary right, e.g., location of an oven or a dovecot, right of access to a property, right of use of water, and so on. If the original, and putative, owner knew that the person utilizing the property or the right or benefit that belonged to him was doing so and failed to object, the property or property right (e.g., right of access) falls into the domain of the second party. In American history "squatter's rights" forms a roughly comparable conception.

5. Robert Lekachman, *History of Economic Ideas* (New York: Harper, 1959), p. 3.

6. The same is true of the social foundation for the metaphysics of the Mishnah. For discussion of the role of the householder in the critical matter of classification, and the central place of the will or intention of the householder in the working of the system of the Mishnah, see Howard Eilberg-Schwartz, *The Human Will in Judaism: The Mishnah's Philosophy of Intention* (Atlanta: Scholars Press for Brown Judaic Studies, 1986), in particular, pp. 145–80. Eilberg-Schwartz quite properly treats the householder, the one assumed to own beasts that have been set aside by the owner for a particular sacrifice, as the central figure in the issues at hand.

7. I paraphrase Claude Mossé, *The Ancient World at Work,* trans. from the French by Janet Lloyd, (New York: W. W. Norton & Co., 1969), p. 49.

8. By contrast, the household formed for purposes of sharing a lamb sacrificed for the Passover offering by definition cannot include a gentile, and a convert must be circumcised before he can partake of the meat of the shared beast. Here "household" stands for cultic family, not economic unit of production. It is a social category lacking economic dimensions; hence "householder" never occurs in the context of the Passover sacrifice and who shares in it. We find instead an odd usage, *haburah,* or circle of participants. Once more the precision of word choice in the pages of the document points to the systematic conventions that governed the formulation of the document.

9. See Chayim Yehoshua Kasovsky, *Thesaurus Michnae,* vol. 1, *A–G* (Jerusalem, 1956), pp. 400–401, s.v. *baal.* There are further usages, e.g., the plural, *to, with, and,* and so on. The statements given here suffice to make the point. My argument does not rest on the frequency or distribution of word usages. But the householder, as a matter of fact, is so specific and technical a category that he appears only in passages to which ownership of a domain, that is, a unit of production, is at issue. All of the division of Purities, for one important example, manages to deal with individual Jews ("Israelites") without once invoking the figure of the householder in particular. The precision in terminology of the Mishnah, the selection of particular categories or classifications for particular purposes, is impressive.

10. Compare M. I. Finley, *The Ancient Economy,* (Berkeley and Los Angeles: University of California Press, 1985), p. 123. I mean to emphasize that in the pages of the Mishnah we cannot distinguish town from country.

11. I cannot point to a passage in which it is assumed that a woman is head of a household. But women can own land and engage in the economic activities of a household, so I imagine that, in theory, the system could accommodate a woman householder. In practice, however, a living woman is always taken to relate to a man, first her father, then her husband, and, when he is deceased, to her male sons or stepsons, who support her as a widow. It is further taken for granted that when a woman is divorced or widowed, she will remarry within a brief spell, so that the marriage settlement is meant to tide her over until she does so. Or she reverts to her "father's house," which means that she rejoins the household of her father, if he is alive, or of her brothers, if he is dead.

Nor can I point to a single passage that suggests gentiles cannot hold land and conduct establishments, but the Mishnah legislates for "Israel." The fact that gentiles hold land does not form a systemic fact but an inert one, and when the Mishnah speaks of "householder," so far as I can see, it always takes for granted it addresses an Israelite one.

12. Finley, *Ancient Economy,* p. 95.

13. The implications of such a perception for "all Israel," the modes of conceiving the nation as a whole in its land—these questions will win our attention in the next part of my studies on the political economy of Judaism. They are not important here.

14. That formulation should not obscure the point that the Judaism of the dual Torah that inherited the Mishnah and restated its system in other terms entirely had no economics other than

that of the Mishnah, and accorded to economics a substantially diminished role by comparison to the system of the Mishnah. My claim is based on the fact, which I shall demonstrate, that its social categories bore no relationship to the unit(s) and means of production, in the way in which those of the Mishnah's system did. They found definition in other categories and classifications entirely.

15. I use the word "capitalists" to mean those who invest wealth in ongoing money-making ventures; I do not mean to innovate in any way.

16. The system of the Mishnah can imagine an unattached woman constituting a household on her own, but she is so rare and exceptional as to fall quite outside the imagination of the system builders. That is why I shall take for granted that the mishnaic system speaks only of males when it talks about the householder, just as, when it addresses certain functions assumed to be carried out only by women, such as cooking, it will always use the feminine form.

17. I follow Donald R. Bender, "A Refinement of the Concept of Household: Families, Co-residence, and Domestic Functions," *American Anthropologist* 69 (1967): 493–504. Bender summarizes his thesis as follows: "Families (as specific types of kinship structures), co-residence, and domestic functions are three distinct kinds of social phenomena." Families are not to be identified with households. They are to be distinguished from households, "the former having as their referent kinship, the latter having as their referent presumably propinquity or locality. In fact, this distinction left the job only half done, since the concept of the household, as formulated, included two distinct kinds of social phenomena: co-residential groups and domestic functions. While all three very frequently correspond, they also can and do vary independently." MacMullen's identification of the landholding with the family (*Roman Social Relations,* p. 27) as "the hard shell around the peasant community" is an error. I find this account impressionistic and conceptually rather thin. It is not clear that he read any anthropological writing on the definition of the household.

18. Bender, p. 492: "The thesis to be presented here presupposes the complete conceptual divorce of the household from the family."

19. Ibid., p. 493.

20. In seeing the household as an economic unit pure and simple, I speak only of the Mishnah's household and in no way address the complex data and definitions surveyed by Bender.

21. The equivalent is to equate the white Southern slaveholder, in command of a large plantation, with "the South," even though the vast majority of residents of the South before the Civil War were not slaveholders or held fewer than four slaves. Why "the South" should have found its definition in the way it did, therefore, forms a counterpart question to why control of the means of production, owning and farming land in particular, should for the Judaism of the Mishnah have formed the center of the political economy.

22. Finley, *Ancient Economy,* p. 50.   24. Ibid.

23. Ibid.

CHAPTER FIVE

1. Finley, citing *Politics* 1257a, 24–30.

2. William I. Davisson and James E. Harper, *European Economic History* 1, *The Ancient World* (New York: Appleton-Century-Crofts, 1972), p. 115.

3. Ramsay MacMullen, *Roman Social Relations* (New Haven: Yale University Press, 1966), p. 54.

4. Davisson and Harper, p. 123.

5. Sally C. Humphreys, "History, Economics, and Anthropology: The Work of Karl Polanyi," *History & Theory* 8 (1969): 205.

6. Davisson and Harper, p. 123.

7. Ibid.

8. The pertinence of "profit motive" for antiquity is not beyond question. It means not merely the desire to acquire wealth, but the propensity to make profits for the sake of profits, for the sake

of making more profits: accumulation for its own sake. Such a conception, it seems to me, lies entirely outside of the frame of reference of the Mishnah. Indeed, I cannot point to a single passage in rabbinic literature of late antiquity in which anyone even imagines the condition of accumulation for its own sake.

9. Karl Polanyi, *The Livelihood of Man,* ed. Harry W. Pearson (New York: Academic Press, 1977), p. 69.

10. Davisson and Harper, p. 115. I use their language.

11. Ibid., p. 123.

12. I cannot explain what is meant by "value," e.g., the value of the worker's work, which clearly is taken into account, as against the "true value" inherent in an object up for sale in the marketplace.

13. Joseph A. Schumpeter, *History of Economic Analysis* (New York: Oxford University Press, 1954), p. 61.

14. Polanyi, *Livelihood,* p. 80.

15. Lewis H. Haney, *History of Economic Thought: A Critical Account of the Origin and Development of the Economic Theories of the Leading Thinkers in the Leading Nations* (New York: Macmillan, 1920), p. 60.

16. Schumpeter, p. 61.

17. The Mishnah never represents householders as lending money to one another. It knows about factors who make a market in commodities and who provide capital to the householder, e.g., in the form of animals to be tended, raised, and then sold, with both parties sharing in the profits. The Mishnah's interest in factoring contracts is to assure that the farmer not work for nothing.

CHAPTER SIX

1. Cited by William I. Davisson and James E. Harper, *European Economic History,* vol. 1, *The Ancient World* (New York: Appleton-Century-Crofts, 1972), p. 132.

2. M. I. Finley, *The Ancient Economy* (Berkeley and Los Angeles: University of California Press, 1985), pp. 35–36.

3. Wealth in the system of the Mishnah also involves capital in the form of beasts, but this is not taken into account here. When beasts really do come under intense scrutiny, it has to do with the cult and its requirement. To the cult beasts are capital in a way in which, to the householder, they are not.

4. Finley, *Ancient Economy,* p. 56.

5. That judgment forms part of a larger theological premise of the system, which is that God is the ultimate householder and landowner of the land of Israel, with householders only joint tenants, with God, in possession of their properties. Since all wealth was real and not movable, and since God owned everything and shared ownership with the householder, the conception of true wealth fit well into the theological datum of the system.

6. The most current statement on the subject of usury is Paul E. Gottfried, "The Western Case against Usury," *Thought* 60 (1985): 89–98. See also Benjamin Nelson, *The Idea of Usury: From Tribal Brotherhood to Universal Brotherhood* (Chicago: University of Chicago Press, 1969).

7. But Ex. 22:4, which says that one must make restitution for "the excellence" of field or vineyard [JPS: "he must make restitution for the impairment of that field or vineyard"] is understood to require payment of real property of the top grade in restitution for torts of the specified classification. The details of the Mishnah's system derive from a variety of sources, as I stressed in chapter 2. But the utilization of details drawn from Scripture and the importance accorded to one scriptural fact or detail but not another one express what is particular to the system of the authors of the Mishnah.

8. Penalties for sins, by contrast, are not subjected to sanctions of fines exacted in real estate. Real estate transactions are exchanges of wealth, and sins, such as are subjected to flogging, have nothing to do with wealth.

9. I shall repeat this point to underline its systemic centrality, even though the pertinence of

the strict and narrow definition of landed wealth, meaning real estate in the land of Israel in particular, will make sense only in chapter 7.

10. The "Israel" of the Mishnah refers to both the entire people and also the individual, and it is on that account that ownership of property in Palestine by a Jew, that is, land in the land of Israel by an Israelite, can by individual and personal, not only collective or symbolic of the collectivity. That is the theological basis for private property within the system of the Mishnah, so it would seem to me. But the problem of wealth, as I have framed it, does not require us to explain how an individual, on his (or her) own account, can own anything at all. It is clearly not on the sufferance of community ("all Israel"), even less so of government, temple, or priesthood. The right to personal, private, individual ownership is treated as inherent and intrinsic, and that seems to me joined to the definition of the individual as "Israel," as much as "all Israel" is "Israel." I should see this topic as deserving attention on its own.

11. For the reason specified in the preceding note. But, as I said, I do not wish to elaborate on this point now, because I think it forms part of the Mishnah's anthropology, with which I do not deal in this book. But this notion of private property in the Mishnah requires qualification. Since God owned the land and was deemed partner to all landowners, the conception of the absolute right of private ownership, with which we are familiar, is not the same as was operative here. Now private property formed a conditional and a stipulative domain.

12. Compare Davisson and Harper, p. 124.

13. But the Mishnah is remarkably vague about who takes responsibility for supporting rights of ownership, guarantees transfer of title, enforces sanctions, and takes charge of the rights of private property. I cannot point in Mishnah-tractate Sanhedrin, for example, to a single passage that places the Jewish government imagined in that tractate in charge of the everyday economy and market. The tractates that do deal with lost and stolen property, deeds and real estate, and other aspects of civil law and government do not allude to the sanctions and who enforces them, only to decisions and how they are to be reached. The silence of the Mishnah's writers on concrete law enforcement, as distinct from their enormous obsession with penalties for sin, e.g., in Mishnah-tractate Sanhedrin chapters 7 through 11, strongly suggests a problem in the conceptualization of the state. But we may postpone solution of that problem until work on the political part of the political economy of Judaism.

14. Ramsay MacMullen, *Roman Social Relations* (New Haven: Yale University Press, 1966), p. 48.

15. Joseph A. Schumpeter, *History of Economic Analysis* (New York: Oxford University Press, 1954), pp. 62–63.

16. Finley, *Ancient Economy*, p. 41.

17. Ibid., p. 128.

18. The key is that the householder who held land (the Israelite who owned a piece of real property in the land of Israel) was like God, who owned the land of Israel. We shall return in chapter 7 to the working out of this conception.

19. In drawing the distinction between the small holder and the industrial estate, I follow Claude Mossé, *The Ancient World at Work*, trans. from the French by Janet Lloyd (New York: W. W. Norton, 1969), p. 62.

20. The meaning of "usury" in this system will emerge clearly in the cases we consider as "interest" pure and simple. Any payment for the use of money or "payment for waiting on repayment" is regarded as usurious. There is no distinction resting on the difference between excessive and acceptable rates of interest. "Usury" moreover may cover actions in compensation, e.g., provision of free rent, or even psychological compensation, e.g., special deference to the lender on the part of the borrower.

21. Schumpeter, p. 54.

22. By "usury" Scripture's authors meant whatever they meant; that is of no interest to us. I do not imagine that the framers of the Mishnah were philologians, knowledgeable in comparative Semitic philology, and I take as fact that, whatever they understood by a word, they imputed also to Scripture's authors. Hence the true or historical meaning of *neshekh* and *ribit* as the priestly

writers of the fifth century used the words bears no particular relevance to our problem. For all we know, the authors of the Mishnah really did receive "traditions" from the ancient priesthood, seven hundred years earlier, about the meaning of these and other words. It would not affect in any measure at all the simple fact that our authors made *their* choices for *their* purposes, imputing to words meanings they deemed those meanings to have, in the context they defined, for the sense and system they proposed to impute and compose.

23. See my *History of the Mishnaic Law of Holy Things,* (Leiden, 1979: E. J. Brill). vol. 4, *Arakhin. Temurah* (Leiden: E. J. Brill, 1979), pp. 77–78.

24. Theoretically, then, his income must derive from the service that he performs, which adds value to the products he handles; so Professor Genovese (personal letter).

25. I have not dwelt upon the conservative character of Aristotle's thought, his incapacity to come to grips with a market economics and his introduction of the considerations of "natural and unnatural" activity and transactions. For him the market is an intrusive factor, to be kept in check. Any representation of Aristotle's as a market economics would be as much a distortion as identifying the Mishnah's as a market economics. Quite to the contrary, both economic theories, the one stated in general terms, the other spelled out only in its details, share the trait of somehow holding together two contradictory theories of economics. But each party has chosen to preserve the received distributive economics, that of status and intervention of nonmarket forces into the market's working, and both look backward to thousands of years of distributive economics. In Aristotle's case, economic historians concur, market economics was a new development. But in the instance of the Mishnah, that was not the case. Indeed, that temple that formed the centerpiece of the Mishnah's distributive economics was then not standing, and the priesthood that was to make the system work had no real tasks or authority. The appeal to archaic times (in the Mishnah's case, the days of Moses at Sinai) formed part of the cultural baggage of the Second Sophistic, in which the Mishnah, temporally at least, finds its place, but that matter is to be investigated in a discussion of the Second Sophistic, not of the matter of economics.

CHAPTER SEVEN

1. William I. Davisson and James E. Harper, *European Economic History,* vol. 1, *The Ancient World* (New York: Appleton-Century-Crofts, 1972), p. 123.

2. For an account of the archaizing tendency of the Second Sophistic in general, that is to say, the age of philosophy in which the Mishnah's authors did their work, see E. L. Bowie, "Greeks and their Past in the Second Sophistic," in M. I. Finley, ed., *Studies in Ancient Society* (London and Boston: Routledge & Kegan Paul, 1974), pp. 166–209. Bowie shows that "the archaism of language and style known as Atticism is only part of a wider tendency, a tendency that prevails in literature not only in style but also in choice of theme and treatment, and that equally affects other areas of cultural activity."

3. Davisson and Harper, p. 125.

4. Whether or not other economic theories express broader systemic values or are simply disembedded from systems and structures is not at issue in this account. It seems to me clear that all expositions of Aristotle's economics find it possible to show the coherence of his economics with his larger systemic, philosophical concerns. But why Aristotelian economics read in light of Scripture, much like the economics of the Judaism of the Mishnah, formed out of the marriage of Aristotle and Scripture, should have served Latin Christianity so long (and so well) as it did, I do not know.

5. How about "and the fulness thereof, the world and they that dwell therein"? The same reasoning leads to the view that God owns all the produce of the world and that everyone is God's slave. But in the system as it unfolded, Israel is described as God's slaves, and the system is consistent in its reading of both the bondage of Israel to God and the status of the land, that is, the land of Israel in particular, as God's particular land.

6. As we shall see, it is not only at the exact moment, but, as a matter of fact, in response to the householder's own decision and intention that God takes an interest in the crop. Before the

householder exercises his ownership of the land through disposing of the crop, God does not exercise his ownership, except passively, by dictating the conduct of the means of production. What this means is that, within the anthropology of the Mishnaic system, God responds to man's emotions, attitudes, and intentions, and so reveals what I believe we may call anthropopathism. The conception of God as emotionally consubstantial with man therefore is embedded, even, in the economics, as we shall presently see. In this connection, Abraham J. Heschel, *The Prophets* (Philadelphia: Jewish Publication Society of America, 1962) explores the anthropological theology of prophetic writings along the same lines. But I know no study of the emotional correspondences between God and man other than my *Incarnation of God: The Character of Divinity in Formative Judaism* (Philadelphia: Fortress Press, 1988), in which the matter plays a central role.

7. Louis E. Newman, *The Sanctity of the Seventh Year: A Study of Mishnah-Tractate Shebiit* (Chico: Scholars Press for Brown Judaic Studies, 1983), p. 19.

8. Ibid.

9. Martin S. Jaffee, *Mishnah's Theology of Tithing: A Study of Tractate Maaserot* (Chico: Scholars Press for Brown Judaic Studies, 1981), p. 1.

10. Ibid. 13. Ibid.

11. Ibid. 14. Ibid., p. 4.

12. Ibid., p. 2.

15. Ibid., p. 5.

16. Davisson and Harper, p. 124.

17. Richard S. Sarason, *A History of the Mishnaic Law of Agriculture,* vol. 3, *A Study of Tractate Demai* (Leiden: E. J. Brill, 1979), p. 9.

18. Roger Brooks, *Support for the Poor in the Mishnaic Law of Agriculture: Tractate Peah* (Chico: Scholars Press for Brown Judaic Studies, 1983), p. 18.

19. Brooks, p. 18. 22. Ibid., p. 20.

20. Ibid. 23. Ibid., p. 49.

21. Ibid., pp. 18–19. 24. Ibid., p. 51.

25. See Margaret Wenig Rubenstein, "A Commentary on Mishnah-Tosefta Bikkurim, Chapters 1 and 2," *Approaches to Ancient Judaism* 3 (1981): 47–87.

26. Ibid., pp. 49–50.

27. Newman, p. 199.

28. Alan J. [Avery-]Peck, *The Priestly Gift in Mishnah: A Study of Tractate Terumot* (Chico: Scholars Press for Brown Judaic Studies, 1981), p. 3.

29. Ibid., p. 3.

30. Ibid., p. 21.

31. Since at stake here is hierarchization, I am justified in invoking the notion of caste, in line with Louis Dumont, *Homo Hierarchicus* (Chicago: University of Chicago Press, 1980). I refer to "scheduled" ones in particular, because there are other castes—groups of persons bearing the same indicative traits, e.g., women, slaves, minors—that are hierarchized in the Mishnah's vast hierarchization of all social reality, but that are not accorded a special share in, or claim upon, the distribution of scarce resources, as are the priests, Levites, and poor. The ones on the schedule within the larger hierarchical structure then fall into the classification I have invoked here.

32. The poor do not have to separate from food they receive as a scheduled caste the share that the priesthood would otherwise claim (M. Pe. 8:2–4). Since God cannot lay claim on the same share twice, produce designated as *peah* is exempt from separation of tithes (M. Pe. 1:6).

33. Brooks, p. 1.

34. Peter J. Haas, *A History of the Mishnaic Law of Agriculture: Tractate Maaser Sheni* (Chico: Scholars Press for Brown Judaic Studies, 1980), p. 1.

35. It should be clear that some cultic requirements have no bearing upon the market, e.g., the requirement to cover up the blood of a slaughtered beast (M. Hul. 6:1) has no bearing upon the suitability of the beast. Not cooking the beast in its mother's milk (M. Hul. 8:1) would have no bearing upon the suitability of the meat for sale in the Jews' market. So too not mixing dairy with meat products (M. Hul. 8:2) on the face of it does not intervene in the market, but only in

the practice of the home. Another instance of a cultic rule with no bearing upon the market is the requirement to let the dam go from the nest (Dt. 22: 6–7/M. Hul. 12:1–2), which seems to me to have a negligible affect upon the supply of fowl in the market.

36. Irving Mandelbaum, *A History of the Mishnaic Law of Agriculture: Kilayim, Translation and Exegesis* (Chico: Scholars Press for Brown Judaic Studies, 1982), p. ix.

37. Ibid., p. 1.   42. Ibid., p. 18.
38. Ibid., pp. 2–3.   43. Ibid., p. 117.
39. Newman, p. 15.   44. Ibid., pp. 139–40.
40. Ibid., pp. 115–16.   45. Ibid., pp. 28–29.
41. Ibid., p. 16.

46. Howard Scott Essner, "The Mishnah Tracate *Orlah:* Translation and Commentary," *Approaches to Ancient Judaism* 3 (1981): 105.

47. [Avery-]Peck, pp. 1ff.   49. Jaffee, p. 28.
48. Ibid.   50. Sarason, p. 4.

CHAPTER EIGHT

1. See Jacob Neusner, ed., *Soviet Views of Talmudic Judaism: Five Papers by Yu. A. Solodukho in English translation* (Leiden: E. J. Brill, 1973). The papers were translated from the Russian by Professor Sam Driver, Brown University, and then extensively edited by me.

2. Solodukho was born on June 20, 1877, in Oshmiany, Poland. In 1899 he completed his studies in Voloshin. In 1905 he passed the examination for the course of study in the Teachers' Institute of the Riga Educational Region, in the field of history. From 1900 to 1915 he worked on various Hebrew journals. From November 1, 1934, to August 15, 1950, he served as a Learned Collaborator of the Oriental Studies Institute of the Academy of Sciences of the U.S.S.R. in Leningrad. During that period, on June 15, 1938, he defended his dissertation, and the theses of the dissertation are the subject of this part of my discussion. He then received the degree of Candidate of Historical Studies. His work involved the sustained effort to read into talmudic literature Marxist perspectives on class struggle, the role of slavery and entrepreneurship, the development of the middle class, and the like. I was introduced to his work by the late Professor E. J. Bickerman, Columbia University, in 1969. I arranged to have five of his essays translated into English and published them with responses of my own in the book cited above. To my knowledge, that book has not received a single review or even a printed notice since it was published, except for one British reviewer who thought it was naughty to read the Communists.

3. The opening thesis of his "Slavery in the Hebrew Society of Iraq and Syria in the Second through Fifth Centuries A.D." The article was first printed in the *Academy of Sciences of the U.S.S.R. Institute of Oriental Studies Bulletin.* In my *Soviet Views,* the cited passage occurs on p. 1.

4. Originally: *Notes of the Oriental Institute* (Moscow) 14 (1957): 31–90. Driver's translation is in *Soviet Views,* pp. 10–66. I had to cut the paper, because of repetitions, but overall my colleague, Professor Driver, and I were able to make available in English Solodukho's ideas as well as the sources and argumentation he provided.

5. Solodukho, p. 11.   7. Ibid., p. 12.
6. Ibid.   8. Ibid., pp. 12–13.

9. And I do have the sense, as I stated in my edition of his papers, that much of his story is more or less made up. For example, he says, "Up to the period under discussion, [meaning the third century A.D.], the direct producers in the agrarian economy of Iraq were primarily free farmers, individually working plots of land which belonged either to them personally or to the village community. Beside small landholdings of the direct producers and the communal use of land was larger land ownership. Large landowners were not very numerous. They represented hereditary landed gentry of the ranking aristocracy, and leasers of state taxes" (pp. 17–18). Now if Solodukho refers to the period before ca. A.D. 200 as the time prior to the period under discussion, then it is the simple fact that we have not got a single source deriving from, or even merely

referring to, Jews and their society, that tells us that "the direct producers in the agrarian economy of Iraq were primarily free farmers." Not one source tells us the opposite either. Accordingly, one can say whatever one wants, there being no evidence of any kind. And so, I must say, for many of his statements.

10. The agricultural benefits, after all, could have been achieved in a more orderly way by leaving fields fallow in a series that would not disrupt normal production. Doing it all at once was hardly the best way. Promising that God would provide, while requiring the householder to empty his storage bins for scavengers, hardly gained for the priesthood the confidence of practical folk, I should imagine, absent Scripture itself.

11. Mark Blaug, *Economic Theory in Retrospect,* 3rd ed. (Cambridge: Cambridge University Press, 1978), p. 4.

12. Ibid.

13. Ibid., p. 6.

14. Professor Genovese (personal letter) comments, "The facts do matter. Solodukho went wrong precisely on the facts. He wrongly posited a hegemonic class of big landowners and slaveowners. Had he gotten his facts straight, he could have made a strong case for his general ideas on the centrality of class relations even in a peasant society."

APPENDIX ONE

1. I refer to my *The Making of the Mind of Judaism: The Formative Age* (Atlanta: Scholars Press for Brown Judaic Studies, 1987). That is the first of the components of this tripartite study; each part of course stands entirely on its own.

2. It seems to me that the obverse side of rational action with regard to scarcity is rational action with regard to wealth, its increase and preservation. But I do not mean to contribute to the theoretical definition of economics in so stating.

3. On the other hand, I cannot place the word economics in quotation marks, thus "their 'economics,'" so calling into question the conception that they had an economics at all. That is what is gained by reversing the order of the words of the definition, going from *economics is . . .* to *. . . is economics.*

APPENDIX TWO

1. No one familiar with the history of economic theory will imagine that the Judaic thinkers were alone in their incapacity to think theoretically about economics. In fact, we have to wait until the nineteenth century—and then to the end of that century—for the birth of economics as a theoretical science. But I shall offer a reason particular to the Judaic tradition for that prevailing fact.

2. In this connection see my analysis of the social, including the economic, history of Salo W. Baron and the assembly of this-and-that under the rubric "economics" characteristic of that work, in *History and Theory,* October, 1988.

Index of Biblical
and Other Texts

General Index

Abba Saul, commingling produce, 87
Agriculture: commingling produce, 87–88,
 123–24, 128; economics of 15–16, 18,
 26–28, 34, 43–44; factoring and futures,
 99–102, 108–11; forgotten sheaf, 119–
 20, 125; householder and role in market
 economics, 50–71; tithes and gifts to poor
 94, 114–35
Appointed times, 15–16, 18, 22
Aqiba: usucaption, 60; and wealth, 94
Arensberg, Conrad M., 46
Aristotle, 1, 4–8, 10, 14, 28, 50, 68, 140;
 commerce and trade, 74, 76, 78–80,
 82–83, 90; economics of, 33, 35–42, 44,
 49; and wealth, 93, 98, 100–102, 112
Augustine, 44
Avery-Peck, Alan J., 122–23

Barter, 79–87, 90–91, 93, 98–99, 101
Brooks, Roger, 119–20

Cannan, Edwin, 34, 36, 49
Carney, C.T.F., 46
Cato, 42–43
Christianity, view of wealth, 43–44, 49
Chrysostom, John, 44
Cicero, 27, 42
Cleanness and uncleanness 22–23
Clement of Alexandria, 43
Columella, Lucius Junius, Moderatus, 43
Commerce and trade, 1, 15, 23, 35–36; bar-
 ter, 79–87, 90–91, 93, 98–99, commin-
 gling produce, 87–88, 123–24, 128;
 distributive economics, 6–13, 26, 44–45,
 72–91; fraud, 78–79, 82–86; usury,
 39–40, 42, 93, 99–102, 106, 111

Damages, liability for, 15–16, 56–58,
 88–90
Davisson, William I., and James E. Harper,
 9–10, 73–74, 99, 114, 118
Democritus, 37
Distributive economics, 6–13, 26, 44–45,
 114–35; in commerce and trade, 72–91;
 and Marxism, 136

Eliezer, and wealth 93

Factoring and futures, 99–102, 108–11
Finley, M. I., 29–30, 39–40, 45, 47–49,
 68, 72, 93
Fraud, 78–79, 82–86

Gamaliel: factoring and futures, 110–11;
 usury, 112

Haney, Lewis H., 38, 83
Harper, James E., and William I. Davisson,
 9–10, 73–74, 99, 114, 118
Household management, 1, 4–6, 10, 14,
 26–29, 35, 37–39, 42–46; distributive
 economics, 114–35; role in market economics, 50–71

Ishmael, usucaption, 60–61

Jaffe, Martin S., 116–17, 121
Joshua, and wealth, 94
Judah: commerce and trade, 77; commingling
 produce, 87; damages, liability for, 89;
 distributive economics, 132–33; factoring
 and futures, 108–9; fraudulent dealings,
 83–84, 86; usucaption 60–62

DATE DUE

HIGHSMITH   #LO-45220